Is Your Balloon About to Pop?

Is Your Balloon About To Pop?

Owner's Manual for the Stressed Mind

Bob Kamath, M.D.

Is Your Balloon About to Pop?

Table of Contents

Part Three: Liberation from Stress

Author to Reader

Most depressed and anxious patients I treat have no clue why they have their dreadful symptoms. They only know that their personal physicians have found no physical basis for them. When told that their symptoms have been brought on by excessive stress combined with poor coping, almost all these patients are baffled. They are not aware of the role that highly stressful events and problems played in bringing on their illnesses, nor are they aware of the painful emotions they experienced in response to those events and problems. Many of them claim they have had no stress at all in their lives. When asked if they know what stress is, they think for a while, shake their heads and smile innocently. Those who admit to having had any stress invariably say, "I handled it just fine. I just didn't let it bother me. I was strong through it all."

To all my clients, stress is a great mystery. All profound mysteries have the simplest explanations. This book attempts to demystify stress and its related phenomena without resorting to psychiatric jargon. Instead of explaining stress symptoms using convoluted theories, it uses common sense and a simple model of the mind. The simplicity of language and repetition of concepts in the book are necessitated by the fact that most stressed people, regardless of their level of intelligence, education and professional success, are not informed of even the most basic issues related to stress. Furthermore, they all have deeply rooted erroneous beliefs about coping with and managing stress. Almost all these beliefs have to do with the efficacy of some type of physical activity, such as walking, jogging, exercising, weight lifting, taking hot tub baths, relaxation techniques, yoga, meditation and the like. These beliefs are not easy to replace with newer ones. Besides, people are continually bombarded with inaccurate and useless information by the uninformed media: "Eat a carrot a day!" "Raise dogs!" "Ride a bicycle!" "Sniff your spouse's armpit!" and the like.

Learning new knowledge requires repetitive reading and ongoing practical application. The learning process in the stressed-out people is often hampered by persistent stress symptoms, such as lack of interest, inability to concentrate, decreased ability to retain what is learned, forgetfulness, mental exhaustion, fear of reading something that might be too upsetting and many other factors. Sometimes, severely stressed-out people have attitudes such as closed-mindedness, pessimism, skepticism and cynicism, which are the very factors that led to their being stressed-out. All these factors may result in a decreased ability to learn and retain new information. A stressed-out person might need to read this book ten times before he can assimilate its essence and apply it practically.

Writing this book was necessitated by the recent trend of exclusive drug treatment of stress disorders, the dearth of experienced therapists and the absence of a tell-it-as-it-is manual that explains stress in simple terms. Properly read and understood, and diligently applied in practice by the stressed-out person, the information in this book can greatly minimize his suffering and the chances of his needing additional drug treatment. Just knowing what is happening to him might itself be a great relief. When all else fails, read the manual!

Bob Kamath, M.D.
March 21, 2007

*This book is dedicated to my clients who
taught me all that I know about stress*

Part One

The Nature of Stress

CHAPTER ONE

Stress in a Nutshell

This chapter gives a general outline of stress and various stress-related issues. In the subsequent chapters, each of these issues will be explained in greater detail, with examples. I recommend that readers, especially those with stress disorders such as depression and anxiety, review this chapter thoroughly several times and understand the model of the mind before proceeding to the next chapter.

1. Stress is contagious.

Yes, stress is contagious. There is much truth in the following story: An irate woman verbally abuses her timid husband, a schoolteacher. Humiliated, the teacher takes his anger out on his student by paddling him. Outraged over the unjust punishment, the student kicks his hapless dog. The resentful dog bites the lazily snoozing cat. The incensed cat works out its frustration by mauling an unlucky rat. Running scared for its life, the wounded rat topples an oil lamp, shattering it into a thousand pieces on the floor. The burning oil from the broken lamp sets the house on fire. Carried by the blowing wind the raging fire jumps from house to house and spreads rapidly across the doomed town. The whole town goes up in smoke—all because of the wrath of one woman.

Not only does stress adversely affect the health of people

suffering from it, but it also negatively affects everyone around them. A stressed-out boss can upset all his underlings and create an intolerably tense atmosphere at work. These upset workers might take out their anger, helplessness and frustration on their family members. Sometimes I see many workers from the same company, all seeking psychiatric help immediately after a new boss has come on board. Sometimes I see several siblings at the same time for the treatment of depression or anxiety; their histories reveal that, several decades earlier, they were all traumatized by an alcoholic father who routinely brutalized the whole family. Or a stressed father of a four-year-old boy suddenly wants to abandon his family; his history reveals that his parents split up when he was four years old. A grown man sexually abuses an innocent child; he reveals that he was sexually abused by an adult when he was a child. A woman gives up her child for adoption soon after giving birth, because her own mother gave her up for adoption soon after she was born. An African American man abandons his wife and his newborn baby, because that is what his father, grandfather and great-grandfather did to their families. Thus, the ripple effect of stressful events can be felt not only by the people in the immediate circle of those events, but also by several generations to come. *Arguably, stress has a far greater direct or indirect negative impact on humanity than any other single factor.*

2. Stress means getting upset about something.

Since stress means different things to different people, we need to get a firm handle on this slick term before we can make sense throughout the rest of this book. Effective communication of a concept requires that the particular terms used in the book mean the same to the reader as to the author.

Simply put, *stress means getting upset about something.* One's peace and tranquility of mind are gone.

A stressed person is an upset person. He experiences one or more painful emotions, such as fear, hurt, sadness, anger, guilt, etc. in his conscious mind, in response to whatever has upset him. He is fully aware of these emotions. Because of their effect on his brain chemicals, he might experience some transient stress symptoms: irritability, sleeplessness, headache, poor concentration and the like. Once he has coped with the situation that has upset him, the painful emotions will disappear, he will calm down and his stress symptoms will go away. For example, one might become upset over losing his job. He might feel sad, hurt, fearful, guilty, ashamed and angry. He might experience many stress symptoms, such as sleeplessness, anxiety, tension, headaches and the like. After a while, he accepts the reality that people find jobs and lose them, lose jobs and find new ones. He calms down, gets another job and moves on with his life. *The opposite of being stressed or upset is feeling calm.*

We can compare the conscious mind to a balloon: when the mind is "inflated" with painful emotions, one experiences stress symptoms. When these painful emotions disappear from the conscious mind/balloon, it "deflates," or shrinks, and the stress symptoms disappear (see picture 1).

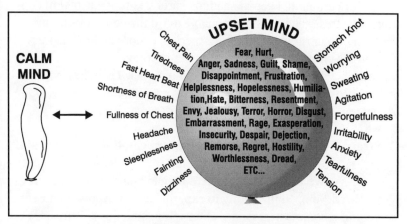

Picture 1: When painful emotions "inflate" the conscious mind, stress symptoms appear.

Rule #1: When painful emotions appear in the conscious mind/balloon, we experience stress symptoms. Conversely, whenever stress symptoms are present, the conscious mind/balloon is filled with painful emotions.

We can illustrate this point with following example: If there is sufficient smoke in the room, the fire alarm will go off. Conversely, if the fire alarm goes off, there must be significant amount of smoke in the room.

The conscious mind inflates and deflates with painful emotions day in and day out in response to numerous upsetting events and life problems. Even our dreams can upset us, inflating the sleeping mind with painful emotions and causing stress symptoms to appear. For example, if I dreamed of being chased by a ferocious bear I would be scared, my mind/balloon would inflate with fear and terror, and I would have several stress symptoms: fast heartbeat, shortness of breath, sweating, etc. Upon waking up, I would realize that it was only a bad dream. My fear would disappear, my balloon would deflate and I would calm down. The more upset we are, the more painful emotions we experience in the conscious mind; the more painful emotions we experience, the bigger the balloon becomes and the more we are troubled by stress symptoms.

Learning to keep the balloon shrunk is fundamental to coping with stress. Those who are unable to rid the conscious mind/ balloon of painful emotions will experience more and more stress symptoms until the *balloon pops* and they come down with a stress disorder, such as depression or anxiety disorder. Then they will need a shrink to do the shrinking for them. *Now you know why psychiatrists are called shrinks!*

3. Stress symptoms are caused by painful emotions in the brain.

As we evolved into modern human beings over millions of years, we developed the ability to experience and express hundreds of *painful emotions* in response to upsetting situations. Thirty-six of them are responsible for bringing on many stress symptoms and disorders, and we will deal with those in some detail:

Fear, hurt, anger, sadness, guilt, shame, disappointment, frustration, helplessness, hopelessness, humiliation, hate, bitterness, resentment, envy, jealousy, terror, horror, disgust, embarrassment, rage, exasperation, insecurity, despair, dejection, remorse, regret, worthlessness, hostility, vengefulness, dread, sorrow, sinfulness, despondency, uselessness and powerlessness.

The presence of these potentially toxic, painful emotions in the conscious mind and brain causes the brain chemicals to change, resulting in the appearance of *stress symptoms*. In other words, *pain in the brain* is the basis of stress symptoms. The brain is connected to the body organs via circulating hormones and a vast network of nerves. Changes in brain chemicals are felt as changes in the *functions* of the body organs, such as the heart, lungs, stomach and skin. Stress symptoms are the brain's way of warning us: "I am sensing many painful emotions in your mind. Get rid of them as soon as possible or do something to stop them from coming in." This is no different from a fire alarm going off when it detects more than the usual amount of smoke in the room.

The brain is *hardwired* to produce different groups of stress symptoms in response to different painful emotions. For example, *fear* and its cohorts in the brain produce a "fight or flight" response; *sadness* and related emotions produce stress symptoms related to "grief"; *anger* and allied emotions produce an "attack" type of stress response; and *guilt* and related emotions produce "guilty" behavioral responses. Readers interested in mastering the art of coping with stress must thoroughly learn about the nature of painful emotions, how they produce different stress symptoms and how to handle them. In other words, one must become emotionally savvy. In coping with stress, one's Emotional Quotient (EQ) is more important than one's Intelligence Quotient (IQ). We will study more about the nature of painful emotions in Chapter Four.

4. Stressors pump painful emotions into the conscious mind.

A. Sensory input. The conscious mind is constantly bombarded with information from the world around us. The five senses—seeing, hearing, touch, smell and taste—are conveyor belts that bring thousands of bits of information into the conscious mind/balloon on a daily basis. This continuous inflow of information is known as *sensory input*. The nature of most of the incoming information is *neutral*; that is, we feel neither good nor bad about it. For example, if you look at a chair, you feel neither *good* nor bad about the chair. Some of the incoming information is perceived by the mind as good, and we feel happy about it. For example, if you get a phone call from your boss telling you that he is pleased with your performance and is giving you a big raise, you will feel happy. Some other information is perceived by the mind as *bad* for us. For example, if you are told that your performance at work is not good and you could be fired from your job at any time, you will feel very upset. The upsetting situations are known as stressors.

B. There are two types of stressors:

1. Bad events—such as the death of a loved one, the breakup of a relationship, betrayal or infidelity, an accident, robbery, assault, rape, the loss of a job, etc.—are extremely upsetting. They are *one-shot* painful events. When bad events occur, we experience many painful emotions in our conscious minds all at once, such as fear, terror, hurt, anger, sadness, guilt, shame and disappointment. The mind/balloon inflates suddenly with these painful emotions, and we experience severe stress symptoms.

2. Bad problems of life—such as problems with one's job, money, health, relationships, etc.—are *ongoing* life problems. They upset us a little bit at a time, day after day, week after week and month after month. Often, we *feel trapped* in these bad problems. In this case, the mind/balloon inflates gradually, over a period of time, with painful emotions such as anger, fear, bitterness, resentment, insecurity, frustration or helplessness, and the stress symptoms are not as dramatic as when they are caused by a single bad event. If unsolved, most bad problems lead to the balloon popping because of the relentless buildup of painful emotions in the mind. When the balloon pops, one is brought down with a serious stress disorder, such as major depression or panic disorder.

C. The bicycle pump as a model for stressors. Since bad events and life problems *pump painful emotions* into the conscious mind/balloon, let us represent them as a simple bicycle pump. Bad events and bad life problems have something else in common with

the pump: they both suck! We will read more about stressors in
Chapter Five.

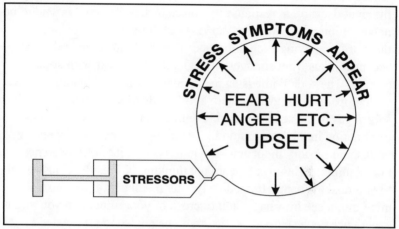

Picture 2: Stressors pump painful emotions into the mind.

5. The hidden mind is like a soda bottle with fizzy soda inside it.

How does the conscious mind decide what is bad for it? The
mind has a hidden compartment, like the basement of a house or the
hard drive of a computer, where it stores a large amount of information that is gathered over a lifetime. The information pertains to
whether an object or situation is good or bad for the mind: if it is bad,
how bad, as well as how to react to it. As the powerful hard drive
of a computer saves millions of bits of information in its numerous
folders and files, this hidden compartment of the mind holds its own
millions of bits of information. Every time the conscious mind receives some input from one or more of the five senses, it checks with
the hidden mind by asking, "What is this? Is it good or bad for me?
If it is bad, how do I react to it?" For example, if a stranger offered
you a cookie, your conscious mind would ask your hidden mind,
"Is this safe to eat?" Your hidden mind might say something such
as, "You don't know this person. The cookie he's offered could be
dangerous. Don't eat it." This type of interaction takes place between
the conscious mind and the hidden mind thousands of times a day. If
your hidden mind does not know whether something is good or bad

for you, your conscious mind will feel baffled or confused. A person whose hidden mind does not have the information needed to make the right decision in response to a piece of sensory input is said to be naïve, or innocent. We warn our *naïve* children about the dangers of the world by saying such things as, "Don't talk to strangers! Don't accept cookies from strangers! Don't get into the car with strangers!"

The soda bottle is an ideal model for the hidden mind. We can compare the hidden mind to a full bottle of soda. Just as the dissolved gas in the soda is invisible until the bottle is shaken, all the information in the hidden mind is *out of our immediate awareness* until some sensory input activates it and brings it to our awareness. For example, right now, you are not thinking of President Bush—until you read his name. Immediately after reading it, your conscious mind might see his image on the screen of your mind, and you might experience neutral, good or bad emotions related to him. After a while, his image will disappear from the screen and go back into the "Memory" folder of your hidden mind. We will read more about the hidden mind in Chapter Seven.

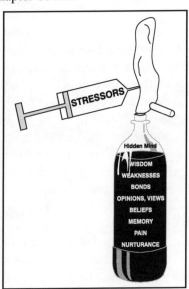

Picture 3: The hidden mind holds millions of bits of information in its folders.

6. Coping means shrinking the balloon.

Coping means getting rid of the toxic, painful emotions in the mind. This allows the brain chemicals to go back to their original position. Then the stress symptoms disappear. *In effect, coping with stress simply means being able to shrink the balloon by appropriate methods.* Coping requires us to become *aware* of the painful emotions in the conscious mind; get rid of them by *expressing* them; *cancel them out* by means of various mental skills; and skillfully turn off the pump by *solving the problems* that are hounding us. Then we calm down, and peace and tranquility return to the mind. It's as simple as that—except that stressed-out people are not able to do any of these things. That is why they need a shrink to do the shrinking for them. Unfortunately, most psychiatrists these days attempt to control the symptoms of depression and anxiety by coating the balloon with drugs, rather than by shrinking it or teaching people how to shrink it themselves. Therefore, this book will focus on guiding the reader to shrink his balloon. We will read more about how to shrink the balloon in Chapter Thirteen.

Let us represent coping by a tube coming out of the right side of the balloon (see picture 4). Now the model of the mind is complete.

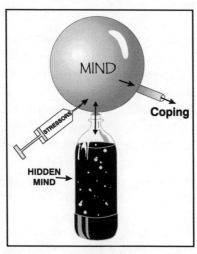

Picture 4: The model of the mind.

7. The model of the mind.

Let us briefly review the completed model of the mind. The bicycle pump in the picture above represents stressors. As soon as the conscious mind/balloon receives sensory input from the pump, it asks the hidden mind (soda bottle) about the nature of this input. When told, "This is bad," the conscious mind becomes upset. The balloon inflates with painful emotions, the brain chemicals change and stress symptoms appear. The side tube represents those actions that shrink the balloon. For example, if someone we love has died, the balloon will immediately inflate with painful emotions related to grief: sadness, hurt and sorrow. Inflation of the balloon will cause the appearance of severe stress symptoms: fullness in the chest, swelling of the face, intensely sad feelings. By grieving, crying, sobbing and expressing our emotions (using the side tube), we shrink the balloon and get rid of stress symptoms. Those who are able to keep the balloon shrunk all the time stay well.

The main idea of coping is that the *output of painful emotions should equal the input.* The reader must thoroughly understand this model of the mind and the interaction between its four components, to make sense of the various stress-related phenomena we will discuss in the chapters ahead.

8. Managing stress means leading a wisdom-based lifestyle.

Managing stress means living a lifestyle that minimizes the occurrence of bad events and problems. This boils down to making *wise choices* in all aspects of life. To accomplish this, we have to wisely manage our relationships, money, time, health, job and other aspects of daily life. The bottom line in stress management is that one should live a simple life, guided by wisdom. Whereas coping has to do with ridding the conscious mind of painful emotions *after* one has become upset, managing stress has to do with *preventing* upsetting events and problems from happening.

A wise person always *does the right thing.* For example, to avoid money problems, he lives within his means, saves money regularly, refrains from incurring nonessential debts, does not get into businesses about which he knows nothing, etc. To avoid health problems, he resists bad habits, gets adequate exercise, and takes good care of his body. To avoid conflicts with others, he holds back from imposing his views on people or taking advantage of their friendships; he engages others in adult to adult interactions, and so on. In effect, stress management means gaining a good deal of control over all aspects of one's life (the pump).

Stress management also requires that we avoid *making wrong choices* and *doing wrong things*. Both these mistakes are always based on deep-rooted personality weaknesses, such as greed, insecurity, possessiveness, arrogance, lust, hate and jealousy. Every serious life problem, whether it is connected to one's job, money, health or relationships, is fueled by a *personality weakness*. We will study how one could put leash on these weaknesses and more about stress management in Chapter Fourteen.

9. How stress leads to stress disorders.

To most depressed or anxious patients, why they suffer from these maladies is a great mystery. They go to their doctors with symptoms such as sleeplessness, anxiety, tension, crying spells, tiredness and poor concentration. After thoroughly examining and testing them, the doctors tell them that no medical reason can be found for their seemingly serious symptoms. To make sense of the symptoms, the doctors then say that the disorder is a result of a *chemical imbalance*. However, the truth is that the chemical imbalance is the end result of an extraordinary amount of stress combined with poor coping.

Reading this, almost all people in such a situation might wonder, "How could this be when I handled my stress so well by being strong?" Therein lies the problem. People who readily fall apart when upset never become sick with stress disorders. And curiously, by the time a person is down with a stress disorder, he has *blocked off* from his awareness almost all his painful emotions, as well as the memory of stressful events and the problems that caused them.

A. History of serious traumas. The symptoms of the

stressed-out person are just the tip of the iceberg (see picture 5). Every person suffering from stress disorder has been through many bad events and problems in his life, and he has experienced numerous painful, toxic emotions related to these problems. His balloon has inflated many times because of death of loved ones, abandonment, betrayal of trust, conflict, disappointment, assault, accident, physical, emotion and sexual abuse, breakups, serious illness and other tragedies. Bad memories of these events and problems, stored in his hidden mind, have become the submerged part of the iceberg.

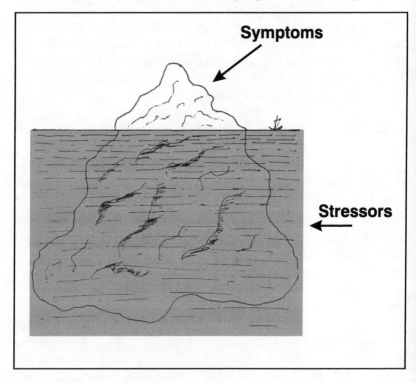

Picture 5: Stress symptoms are just the tip of the iceberg.

B. A stressed-out person has had an overdose of painful emotions. In response to these serious bad events and problems of life, the stressed-out person has repeatedly experienced large doses of toxic, painful emotions in his mind. We noted thirty-six of them above. The majority of stressed-out people admit to skilled therapists having experienced most, if not all, of these painful emotions in large doses, over several years prior to becoming sick.

C. Coping by burying. As painful emotions flood the conscious mind, the stressed person gets rid of them, shrinks his balloon and calms himself down by making *one simple mistake*: instead of shrinking his balloon by means of appropriate coping methods, he says to himself, "This is too upsetting for me. I will be strong. I will not think about it, I will not talk about it. I will just forget it." He simply puts the painful emotions out of his awareness by burying them in his hidden mind/soda bottle. In other words, he *bottles up* his emotions. The balloon shrinks, the brain chemicals go back to their normal state and the stress symptoms disappear. The prompt relief from stress symptoms gives the person reason to believe that he has handled his stress well, producing a false sense of security. Since this method of burying (hiding or bottling up) painful emotions in the hidden mind seems to work well, it becomes a habit. However, all the person is doing is transferring his painful emotions from the conscious mind/balloon to the hidden mind/soda bottle (see picture 6).

Picture 6: Burying causes the balloon to shrink, making a person feel calm.

D. The saturation point of the hidden mind. The problem is that the hidden mind *does not have a limitless capacity* to store painful emotions. As the person's hidden mind keeps filling up with painful emotions, he finds it harder and harder to calm himself down by burying them. When the hidden mind finally reaches its saturation point, he can no longer bury his painful emotions. Now, when painful emotions related to new bad events and problems appear in the conscious mind/balloon, they stay there. The re-inflated balloon responds by obeying Rule #1: When the balloon inflates, stress symptoms appear. We will read more about saturation point in Chapter Seven.

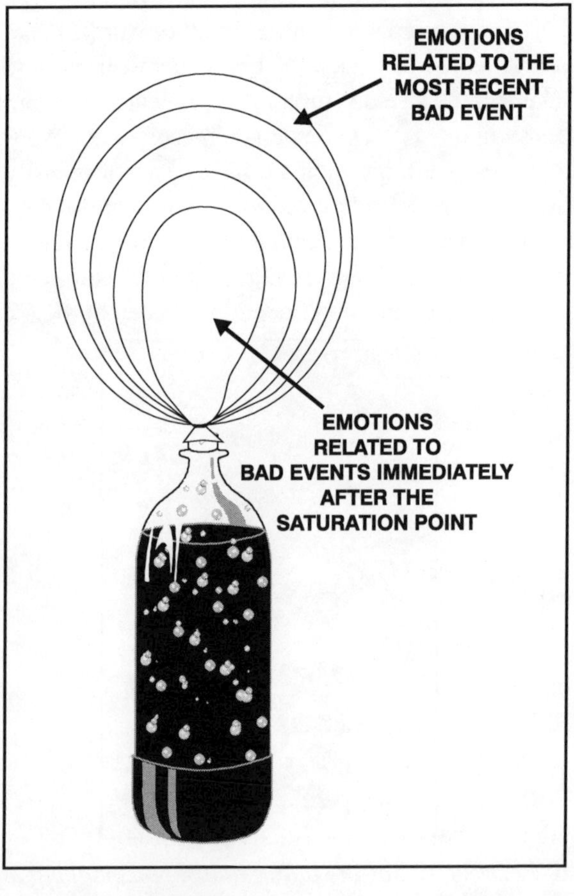

EMOTIONS RELATED TO THE MOST RECENT BAD EVENT

EMOTIONS RELATED TO BAD EVENTS IMMEDIATELY AFTER THE SATURATION POINT

Picture 7: After the saturation point the balloon starts to re-inflate.

As the balloon gets bigger and bigger, stress symptoms begin to reappear one by one, become persistent and get worse over time. As more painful emotions enter the balloon, it inflates even more and stress symptoms steadily worsen, such as poor concentration, anxiety, tension, depression, aches and pains, sleeplessness, irritability and impatience. If one asks this person, "How long have you had these symptoms?" he will say something like, "Oh, well, probably about three years." What this means is that his hidden mind reached its saturation point about three years earlier, and his balloon started re-inflating from then onwards. Unfortunately, most people do not seek psychiatric help until the balloon is about to pop, or until it has already popped.

E. Low stress tolerance syndrome. As stress symptoms reappear one by one, the person is at a loss as to why he has them. He also notices that when he is upset about something, he stays upset. No matter what he does, he cannot calm himself down. Why? Because he can no longer bury emotions in his hidden mind and shrink his balloon. This person is known as *stressed-out*. His symptoms have been warning signals sent by his brain chemicals to his conscious mind, saying, "Your soda bottle became saturated some time ago. Now your balloon is filling up with toxic, painful emotions. Get rid of them *properly* as soon as possible, damn it!" However, his focus now is on his increasingly uncomfortable stress symptoms, not his accumulating painful emotions. He's like a person who has not noticed the gradual build-up of smoke in the house, and whose main focus is on how to switch off the screaming fire alarm.

Some of these symptoms, such as chest pain, are very frightening. The person thinks they are caused by a real physical disorder, perhaps heart disease. Stress is the last thing on his mind, since he has thought all along that he was coping well with whatever was upsetting him. To get quick relief from his dreadful symptoms, he abuses alcohol or drugs or goes to see his doctor. His doctor diagnoses him as having a minor anxiety disorder or depressive disorder, and puts him on a tranquilizer or antidepressant medication. This takes care of his symptoms and gives him some temporary relief.

Over time, as more emotions accumulate in the conscious mind/balloon because of the inevitable stresses of daily life, the stress symptoms become worse. In addition, the painful emotions such as frustration and helplessness experienced in response to the unremitting symptoms themselves further inflate the balloon. *The severity of persistent symptoms depends upon the size of the balloon.* The bigger the balloon, the more stress symptoms there are. A person in this unfortunate predicament is said to be having *low stress tolerance syndrome* (see picture 8). Depending upon the size of one's balloon and the type of painful emotions in his balloon, he suffers from many stress symptoms: irritability, angry outbursts, sleeplessness, excessive sleeping, anxiety, tension, poor concentration, inability to shut the brain down, a hundred different thoughts and emotions swirling in the mind, near-panic attacks, depression and many more. Depending upon the predominance of symptoms, people at this stage of stress are often diagnosed with minor stress disorders such as generalized anxiety disorder (GAD), Dysthymic disorder or chronic depression, Cyclothymic disorder (minor mood swings), attention deficit disorder (ADD), Fibromyalgia and the like. Their balloon could pop at any time. To prevent this from happening, they avoid all sensory stimulation, including people, commotion, traveling to distant places, watching television or anything that might upset them. They become increasingly withdrawn from social activities. We will read more about low stress tolerance syndrome in Chapter Eight.

Is Your Balloon About to Pop?

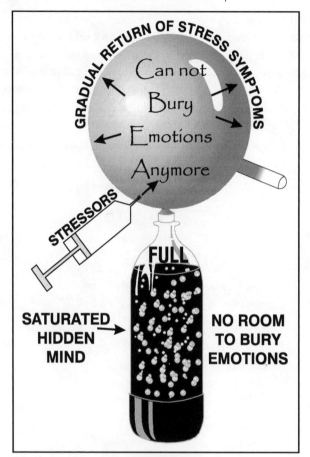

Picture 8: Low stress tolerance syndrome: the balloon is inflating again.

F. The breaking point of the balloon: the slow progression of symptoms finally results in stress disorder. While all this has been going on, the brain chemicals have kept changing in order to deal with the accumulating toxic, painful emotions in the brain or the conscious mind/balloon. Finally, goaded by a *precipitating* or triggering bad event—the straw that breaks the camel's back—the emotional pressure in the conscious mind/balloon reaches its *breaking point,* and the balloon pops. The changes in the brain chemicals have finally resulted in a *chemical imbalance*. At this critical moment, the mind continually feels, "I just can't take it any more!" The stress symptoms have finally *crystallized* into a relatively well-defined stress disorder, such as major depression, panic disorder, etc. (see picture 9). Unable to tolerate emotional pain, many people in this predicament experience suicidal ideas. We will read more about various stress disorders in Chapter Twelve.

Picture 9: The breaking point: a stress disorder is born.

G. The double whammy—a blast from the past. Some people's balloons pop suddenly and quite unexpectedly, and they are struck down with a major stress disorder like a bolt from the blue. In these people, a current painful event—say, the breakup of a relationship—brings into the conscious mind/balloon some painful emotions related to an old trauma buried deep in the hidden mind, such as being abandoned by one's mother or father in childhood. The fury of the painful emotions spewing from the hidden mind is so great that it pops the balloon (see picture 10). It is as if the soda bottle has been so vigorously shaken that fizz bursts into the balloon attached to the bottle's mouth. These people's soda bottles may not have been saturated at all, but they did hold, under pressure, painful memories of a very traumatic event in their past. Double whammy is a *blast from the past*. Sometimes, however, double whammy is milder in severity and causes only a few symptoms. We will read more about double whammy phenomenon in Chapter Nine.

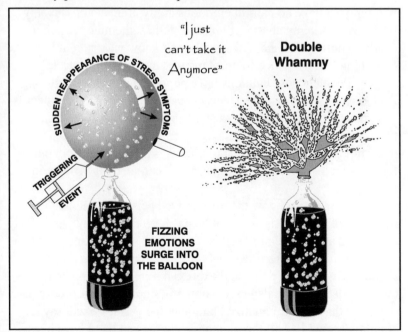

Picture 10: The double whammy: buried emotions fizz up and pop the balloon.

Bob Kamath, M.D.

H. Rule #2: The more severe the persistent stress symptoms, the less one is aware of the painful emotions in his mind and the stressors that caused them.

As the balloon begins to re-inflate, stress symptoms become worse, and a curious thing begins to happen: the stressed-out person becomes more and more focused on his symptoms—sleeplessness, anxiety, poor concentration, panic attacks, depression, mind racing—and less and less aware of his inner, painful emotions and the stressors that caused them. People in this condition often make statements such as, "I don't know why I feel so miserable," "I don't know why I cry all the time," "I can't sleep a wink, and I don't know why," or "I have panic attacks, and nothing has happened to bring them on." If you ask the stressed-out person directly, "Is something bothering you?" he will answer, "Nothing at all, except my panic attacks!" If you ask, "What painful emotions are you having in your mind?" he will reply, "I have no painful emotions in my mind at all. The only pain I have is in my chest." If you ask, "Did something happen recently to upset you?" he will say, "I don't know what it could be. The only thing that happened to upset me was my headache attack!"

People whose balloons have popped and who are suffering from serious stress disorders, such as panic disorder or major depression, have almost no awareness at all about their blocked off emotional pain or the stressors that caused it. Their total focus is now on the symptoms of the stress disorder. This is no different from one's focusing on the screaming fire alarm, rather than on the smoke in the room.

How do we know that the stressed person's mind/balloon is full of painful emotions, and that he has been through many seriously bad events and problems? Well, as soon as he starts talking with a professional who is *sensitive, empathic, non-critical and non-judgmental*, he will break down and express his emotions—much to his own surprise. He will also reveal numerous horrendous events and problems that have traumatized him over the years. He will say, "I didn't know I had all these emotions in me and that I have been affected by all these bad events and problems." Raising one's awareness of the blocked off painful emotions in his conscious mind/balloon is the first and the most important step in learning to cope with stress.

Since these people do not know why they have their seemingly serious stress symptoms, they begin to run to doctors in a futile attempt to find an answer. They are now on a *medical wild goose chase*, in a perpetual state of bewilderment. We will study this unfortunate phenomenon in greater detail in Chapter Eleven.

10. A case study in shrinking the balloon.

An eighteen-year-old woman, a university student, was brought to the emergency room of the local hospital by her friends because she had suddenly gone blind in both eyes. The woman made it clear that she was there only because her friends had forced her to come. She admitted to suffering from numerous other symptoms over the past several months: sadness, crying spells, headaches, sleeplessness, irritability and inability to concentrate. Obviously, her balloon had been inflating for a while. (Rule #1 above.)

When I saw her on the psychiatric ward, her face showed no emotion at all. When asked directly, she denied that she was upset about anything. (See Rule #2 above: No awareness of inner pain.) During the course of an empathic interview, she broke down and revealed that she had been extremely upset about her father, a retired policeman who lived about two hundred miles away and who had recently gone blind from diabetes. He was also seriously ill with heart disease, and he coughed all night long, almost choking on his own secretions. The woman worried a great deal over the fact that he was getting progressively sicker and his doctors were not doing anything to help him. When she had gone home during the Christmas holidays, six weeks earlier, she had found him in really bad shape. She was crushed when he told her that he could not see her, even when she stood six inches from his face. She had just made up with him after many years of estrangement, and was determined to make him proud of her. But alas, this was not to be.

Upon returning to school, the woman continued to experience painful emotions such as sadness, helplessness, hopelessness and frustration, because of this heartbreaking episode and the ongoing bad news about her father's health. Week after week, her balloon kept getting bigger and bigger. But, because she believed that grieving was a sign of weakness, she tried to put these emotions out of her awareness and pretended to be strong. She could not bury her emotions because her hidden mind/soda bottle was already saturated due to past issues. She worried constantly that her father might die at any time. To cope with her agony, she drank alcohol to excess.

In the course of our interview, the woman *became aware of* her sadness, helplessness, hopelessness and other painful emotions. She *expressed* them through crying, sobbing, sighing, moaning and groaning. Her emotions began to show on her face. As she continued to *grieve* and express her pain, her eyesight began to return. Her pupils, which had been as tiny as pinpoints, dilated suddenly, as if her brain chemicals had abruptly switched back to their original state. At this point, her eyesight improved dramatically.

As the woman continued to express her painful emotions, her balloon shrank and she felt a whole lot better. She developed the *insight* that her blindness was her way of countering, as well as expressing, her extreme feelings of helplessness. Since she could not do anything to help her father, she was "doing something" by going blind. She revealed that all her life she had been taught to believe that expressing painful emotions was a *sign of weakness*, so she held her emotions in. In the interview, I told her to keep expressing her emotions and not to deny them, and she was discharged immediately afterwards. When I saw her briefly three days later, she said that she felt even better, having convinced her mother to appoint new doctors to treat her father. This made her feel less helpless and more hopeful.

In this particular case, the patient was an open-minded person; her stress symptoms had been present for a relatively short time; she responded well to empathy; she was eager to learn new ways of coping; and she was willing to change. At this stage, I decided not to deal with the issues buried in her hidden mind (the reasons for her estrangement with her father and other buried issues), and focused only on the *current issues* that had caused her balloon to inflate. She could deal with the past issues later.

The majority of the patients I see do not fall in this category. By the time they show up in my office, they have been too sick for too long and are too closed-minded, negative and distrustful to reverse the chemical changes as dramatically as this woman could do. However, all is not lost for them. Human beings are endowed with a wonderful ability to change and adapt. No one is really beyond hope if he is willing to learn new ways to cope.

11. Five reasons why people become stressed-out.

The misery of stress and stress disorders, which millions of people in America suffer from, is preventable. It is based on the following five factors.

A. The lack of knowledge that the mind, brain and body are, in fact, one single unit, and that painful emotions affect our body organs, bringing on frightening physical symptoms and serious disorders. Ignorance of this single bit of information causes stressed-out people to ask such questions as, "How could my mind cause chest pain?" "How could stress cause my headache attacks?" "How could stress cause my heart to beat fast?" and to insist, "I am not imagining it! I am certain this is physical, not mental." They pursue repeated medical consultations with specialists to prove the point, and in the end, all they have to show for this *medical wild goose chase* is huge medical bills and three big Ds: disgust, disillusionment and demoralization.

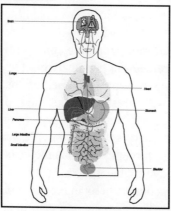

Picture 11: The mind-brain-body is one indivisible unit.

What we think and how we feel affects every single organ in the body. Painful emotions in the brain can cause frightening physical symptoms without anything being physically wrong. Because of the intimate and intricate connections between the mind, brain and body, prolonged stress can bring on physical disorders, such as irritable bowel syndrome, arthritis, Fibromyalgia, high blood pressure, heart disease, chronic fatigue syndrome, psoriasis and many more. People who are unwilling to accept this reality are doomed to be on a medical merry-go-round for the rest of their lives.

B. The erroneous focus on physical activity as a solution for stress. Every single stressed-out person, regardless of his level of education, intelligence, profession or social status, labors under the erroneous opinion that coping with and managing stress consist of doing something physical, such as jogging, exercising, taking hot tub baths or lifting weights. This focus on physical activities as a solution for stress symptoms is due to the fact that some of the most distressing stress symptoms are, indeed, physical, such as muscle tension and spasms, feelings of being "wound up," pain somewhere in the body, inability to relax, etc. However, this emphasis on *mindless* physical activity completely disregards the fact that stress is an emotional phenomenon. *Physical stress symptoms are caused by blocked off painful emotions in the mind.* Anyone interested in coping with stress must shift his focus from physical activity to learning to identify and deal with his blocked off painful emotions.

C. The use of inappropriate coping methods to calm down. Almost all stressed-out people harbor the erroneous belief that it is a *sign of weakness* to express their emotions, so they try to "be strong" when faced with stressful events and problems. When they are upset about something, they hide, bury or bottle up their painful emotions to calm themselves down. ("I don't want to think or talk about it. I just want to forget it!") When they can no longer hide their painful emotions, they indulge in denial ("I'm not upset. I have no problems."). They become experts in blocking their emotions off from their awareness. The unexpressed painful emotions get buried in the hidden mind and they disappear from their awareness.

Both these inappropriate ways of coping go utterly against nature. Their roots go back five thousand years, to when primitive man was being transformed into civilized man, and civilized society curbed the free expression of emotions as a way of taming primitive behavior. People who want to cope with stress must give up their hang-ups about expressing emotions, and reject burying and denial as coping methods.

D. The habit of indulging in distractions to cope with pain promotes burying.
    1. The most common distractions are *pleasurable activities* that millions of people indulge in: drinking alcohol to excess, abusing dangerous street drugs, smoking cigarettes, overeating, having promiscuous sex, gambling and overspending. These activities become bad habits that can lead to serious health, financial, family and legal problems. They block off painful emotions and promote the burying of those painful emotions in the hidden mind. The hidden mind of just about every alcoholic and drug addict is saturated and his balloon is full.
    2. When recreational activities, such as vacationing, hiking, trekking, skiing, cruising and the like, are used to escape from having to deal with emotional pain, they also facilitate the burying process. These *avoidance activities* are, basically, an inappropriate response to stress.

E. The preference for the short-term benefit of drug treatment to the long-term benefit of learning better coping methods. More and more people are resorting to *exclusive drug treatment* of their stress disorders due to the erroneous belief that their disorders are just the result of a chemical imbalance. They do not realize that unless they learn better coping methods, their stress disorders will keep getting worse over the years. Drugs merely coat the surface of the mind/balloon and temporarily reduce the tension inside it; they don't shrink the balloon. *In fact, psychiatric drugs facilitate the burying process no different than alcohol and street drugs do.* As more emotions build up in the balloon, it pops again, and now one has a "breakthrough" episode of his stress disorder. He will then need two, three or even four drugs to coat the balloon and to control his stress symptoms. Most doctors prescribing antidepressant medication base their decision on a list of symptoms provided them by drug companies rather than on adequate understanding of the stage of stress the patient is at. Nowadays, doctors prescribe medications even to people who are merely grieving over the death of loved ones. In fact, the inappropriate and reckless use of antidepressant drugs by uninformed doctors is now so widespread that many patients are "immune" to drugs by the time they see a competent psychiatrist. Instead of learning to cope with stress, these patients are perpetually in search of new drugs to control their stress disorders. We will study more about this unfortunate and increasingly common problem in the next chapter.

12. Summary: The five stages of stress.

Now that the reader has a fair idea of what stress is here is a glimpse of the stages of stress or emotional health that people experience. We will study these stages in greater detail as we go along. At any given time, everyone in the world is in one of the following five stages of stress (see picture 12).

Stage One: Stage of robust health. The person in this stage is in good emotional and physical health. He has no maladies. He enjoys life to the fullest. He is a wise person who always *does the right thing*. He is a highly aware person. He is good at getting rid of painful emotions from his mind and solving his life-problems. He has found *balance* in everything he does in life. His balloon is always shrunk. His soda bottle does not have many buried emotions. He does not abuse alcohol, drugs or indulge in other pleasurable things to cope with his everyday stress. Let me tell you, anymore it is harder and harder to find such people!

Stage Two: Stage of distress. In this stage, an emotionally well-adjusted person is temporarily upset due to a particular event or problem. He is now called a stressed person. He has many stress symptoms. However, he is *fully aware* of why he is upset. If you ask him, he will readily tell you something like "I am upset because I lost my job," or "My mother died," or some such thing. He does not have any hang-ups about expressing emotions. His balloon is full of emotions, but his soda bottle does not have any painful emotions related to the current upsetting event. He can calm himself down relatively quickly by ridding his mind of painful emotions and solving the problem. If his current life situation is a little too overwhelming, he might benefit from one or two visits with a trained counselor. For example, a middle-aged man is unable to grieve over his mother's death because he has harbored some anger towards her. Once he talks out his anger, he grieves over the loss and can go back to being his normal self. *It is best to avoid medication treatment at this stage.*

Stage Three: Stage of low stress tolerance. In this stage, the person is said to be stressed-out. His soda bottle is saturated, and he can no longer cope by burying his emotions. His balloon is inflated to varying degrees. He is unable to calm himself down. He is irritable, impatient, snappy and crabby. He is *not aware* of why he has these symptoms. His total focus is on his symptoms. If he sees a doctor, he will be diagnosed as having one or more minor stress disorders. At this stage, he may be helped by therapy alone in the hands of a very competent therapist if his stress symptoms are not too severe. However, most people seeking medical help at this stage end up taking one or more psychotropic medications. Most people at this stage respond well to medications. However, sooner or later they reach the breaking point and come down with a major stress disorder, unless they learn to shrink their balloon.

Stage Four: Stage of stress disorder. The balloon has finally reached its breaking point either due to gradual inflating of the balloon or double whammy. Because of a precipitating event, it has popped. Chemical changes in the brain have resulted in a *chemical imbalance*, and the diverse stress symptoms have crystallized into a relatively well-defined *stress disorder*, such as major depression or panic disorder. At this critical moment, the patient continually feels, "I just can't take it any more!" Counseling at this stage is generally useless, as the patient's suffering is so great that he has no awareness of his blocked off painful emotions. All he is looking for is quick relief from his numerous symptoms. Such patients need one or more drugs to control their symptoms. Even after they are treated with drugs, many of them just go back to the low stress tolerance stage (stage three). This explains why 30-50% of patients do not become completely symptom-free even with aggressive medication treatment.

Stage Five: Stage of despair. At this stage, the person has been through many successive breaking points resulting in *multiple* stress disorders: depression, panic disorder, psychotic disorder, high blood pressure, Fibromyalgia, irritable bowel syndrome, etc. He has probably been *traumatized* by the treatment process as well, and so he does not trust either therapists or doctors. He is fearful of drugs, or he is on multiple drugs for his multiple stress disorders. He has no clue, no trust, no hope and no desire even to try to get help. He has frequent suicidal thoughts. He considers himself totally and permanently disabled. He is constantly trying to get on some type of disability program. None of his healers seems to have a clue as to how he reached this stage of devastation.

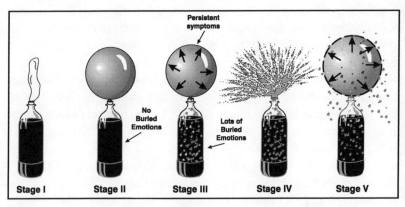

Picture 12: Five stages of stress: from robust health to despair.

In the next chapter, we will study why drugs have become so important in the treatment of stress disorders.

CHAPTER TWO

Enter the Drugs

1. The ascendancy of drugs is due to the inadequacy of counseling.

A. Why do drugs now reign supreme? Several factors have contributed to the ascendancy of drug treatment in psychiatry. First of all, drugs control stress symptoms promptly; nothing else even comes close. Second, most stressed-out people are so focused on their stress symptoms that they have little awareness, incentive, energy or tolerance left to get in touch with their inner pain and release it. Ideally, they will become more ready for insight once their symptoms are well controlled with drugs. However, once they feel better, most patients are not motivated to deal with the issues that preceded their disorders. Third, psychotherapy, commonly known as counseling, requires a high level of expertise, and such expert psychotherapists are few and far between. Even with a trained psychotherapist, the results of psychotherapy are, generally speaking, inconsistent, and they show themselves gradually, if at all; and besides, psychotherapy is expensive, time-consuming and painful. Fourth, most health insurance companies do not pay adequately for psychotherapy. Finally, drugs can be prescribed, however badly, by even the most inexperienced and uninformed doctor, as long as he has a pen in his hand and a prescription pad on his desk. These doctors have been thoroughly indoctrinated by drug companies into believing that treating a serious psychiatric disorder is a simple matter of giving the patient a pill a

Bob Kamath, M.D.

day.

B. Freud and psychoanalysis. Over thousands of years, man has attempted to understand the mysteries of the mind. Until the discovery of psychotropic ("mind-altering") drugs, approximately fifty years ago, our understanding of the origin of "neurotic disorders," as stress disorders were then called, was based on convoluted theories proposed by several psychoanalysts, chief among whom was Sigmund Freud. In the early part of the twentieth century, Freud theorized that stress ("neurotic") symptoms were a result of deep-rooted conflicts between different components of the mind. He talked about such complex, inscrutable ideas as conflicts between the id and the superego; the Oedipus complex; oral, anal and sexual drives; and other similarly mind-boggling stuff. To an average doctor, these psychological theories were extremely difficult, if not too bizarre, to understand, and even harder to apply in the evaluation and treatment of stressed patients.

C. Sex, sex and more sex! Doctors, including myself, often tried to apply these complicated theories in their busy psychiatric practice without much success, or with hilarious results. During the early years of my practice, in the early nineteen-seventies, I lost count of the patients who told me, "Yes, I saw many psychiatrists. All they talked about was sex! What the hell has sex to do with my depression?" A woman who had heard about psychiatrists' misguided obsession with sex reluctantly came to see me after she was coaxed to do so by her supportive relatives. After getting to know me well, she confessed, "It took me a lot of courage to see you, Doc. When I told my friends how scared I was of all the sex talk psychiatrists indulge in, they told me, 'No matter what he asks you to do, just don't remove your clothes!'" Of course, psychiatrists largely stopped talking about sex in the last two decades of the twentieth century, with the rapid escalation of the use of "mind-altering" drugs. Now, all they talk about is drugs, drugs and more drugs.

D. Novices made a mess of psychoanalytic theories. A popular offshoot of psychoanalysis was the dubious explanation that depression is anger turned inwards. A lot of therapists labor under this and other patently senseless ideas about why people become stressed. A middle-aged woman, depressed over the loss of her sister, reported that a therapist she saw wasted two valuable sessions arguing with her about why she sat on one chair during her first session and another during her second session. Her explanation—that she could not sit on the same chair again because there was a stack of books on it—did not satisfy the therapist. He insisted there must have been some mysterious, unconscious reason. The woman's problem was solved in one educational session with me, in which she learned that her depression was due to *incomplete grief.* Her guilt over not being there for her sister before she died had interfered with the grief process. Once she got over her guilt, she completed the grieving process and moved on with her life. Such bizarre incidents, not uncommon during therapy with novice therapists, have given many patients a sense of dread and imparted an aura of mystery and disgust to the whole process of psychological therapy.

E. Therapists often push patients over the edge. Nowadays, however, the most serious problem with counseling is the sudden precipitation of a serious stress disorder resulting from indiscriminate probing by the therapist immediately after therapy had begun. In effect, the therapist brings buried emotions up from the patient's soda bottle into his already fully inflated balloon, causing it to pop. In such cases, patients often become suicidal and end up on the psychiatric ward. This is the peril of being in therapy with an inexperienced therapist who does not have a clear picture of which *stage of stress* the patient is in, or of the phenomenon of the *double whammy.* This "therapy-induced double whammy syndrome" has never received the attention it deserves from anyone in either the mental health field or the health insurance industry. I have lost count of the patients who have been traumatized by such indiscriminate probing in psychotherapy.

F. The unconscious is the gift of psychoanalysis. Psychoanalysis gave us a foot in the door in terms of our understanding of the mind, but it did not answer most of our questions. Because of its obscurantism, widespread misapplication, high cost, poor results and many other problems, psychoanalysis has now practically fallen by the wayside as a therapy tool. Now, most psychiatrists in practice are drug-treatment-oriented, since this is simply a matter of making a list of the symptoms the patient complains of and prescribing drugs to control them. These psychiatrists do not apply psychoanalytic techniques, simply because it would require too much time and mental effort to figure out the troubled minds of their patients. However, the most fundamental tenet of psychoanalysis—the existence of the *unconscious or hidden mind*, commonly referred to as the subconscious—is not only still valid, but also crucial to an understanding of the phenomenon of stress and its related issues.

2. Drugs have shifted the focus from the mind to the brain.

A. A chemical imbalance was suspected in stressed-out patients. Over the past fifty years, the development of several anti-anxiety, antidepressant and antipsychotic medications gave the medical community the much-needed evidence for believing that there is a physical/chemical basis for mental disorders. The basic theory is that as a result of stress, something goes wrong at the junction of the nerve endings (synapses) in the brain. This disrupts the re-absorption of certain brain chemicals, known as neurotransmitters—serotonin, norepinephrine and dopamine—back into the nerve endings. As a result, something goes wrong in the transmission of electrical waves in the brain. This, in turn, leads to the appearance of stress symptoms. The antidepressant drugs give a nice chemical coating to the damaged nerve endings, improve the re-uptake of brain chemicals, re-establish the electrical wave system and make the stress symptoms go away.

B. Stress disorders were medicalized. To doctors, who are invariably more comfortable with the body than with the mind, the simple phrase "chemical imbalance" came in handy to explain to their patients the nature of depression and other stress disorders. Gradually, the gross term "chemical imbalance" came to replace the somewhat murky term "mental conflict" as the cause of many mental disorders, and thus the process of the medicalization of mental disorders began to crystallize. The trend towards *medicalization* got a big boost in the late nineteen-eighties, because of a whole new group of antidepressant drugs that came into the market. These drugs, known as serotonin-specific re-uptake inhibitors (SSRI), became popular because of the ease of administration (a pill a day) and their alleged lack of side-effects. Every one of us is familiar with these drugs: Prozac, Zoloft, Paxil, Luvox, Celexa and Lexapro. The pendulum has thus swung from one extreme ("It's all in your head") to the other ("It's all in your brain"). To a great extent, medicalization overcame the stigma of mental disorder, and millions of stressed-out patients began to accept drug treatment for their stress disorders. Again, it was easier for people to get help when they thought they had a physical condition rather than a mental one, and drug treatment became the proof of this concept.

C. Message to patients: A pill a day can keep your stress away. Nowadays, the message given to patients—promoted by drug companies and delivered by doctors—is loud and clear: "A pill a day can correct your chemical imbalance and cure your depressive and anxiety disorders. This problem is no less physical than diabetes." Because of the prompt alleviation of symptoms available through drugs, most stressed people do not feel the need to acknowledge or address the bad events and problems that brought on their maladies or to learn new coping and stress-managing skills. This suits the medical profession just fine, since the insurance industry refuses to pay adequately for either education or counseling to go along with drug therapy.

3. The medicalization of stress disorders has unintended consequences.

A. Drugs give a false sense of security. Once a patient feels better with drugs, he believes that as long as he keeps taking the drugs, he will be all right. The problem is, life keeps bringing in more painful emotions, and the balloon has no space for them. All the drugs do is give a nice chemical coating to the inflated balloon, strengthen it and slightly reduce the tension inside it—*but they do* *not shrink the balloon.* To shrink the balloon, one must get rid of his painful emotions, and keep doing it forever. Furthermore, when stress symptoms are eliminated through drugs, the unexpressed emotions get buried in the hidden mind (if there is still any space left in it), just as they do when people cope by abusing alcohol or street drugs.

B. Breakthrough episodes and immunity to drugs are common. When a patient exclusively relies on drug treatment for his stress symptoms, painful emotions keep accumulating in the conscious mind/balloon as more bad events and problems occur. The balloon continues to inflate, the stress symptoms become worse, and the beneficial effects of the drugs are cancelled out by the accumulating toxic, painful emotions in the brain. This is no different from a repetitive injury to a joint that results from the faulty use of a limb: while the patient's pain is masked by anti-inflammatory drugs, he continues to abuse the joint, which cancels out the benefits of the drugs. In the case of stress, the accumulating *emotional pressure* ultimately breaks through the drug-coated balloon, resulting in a *breakthrough episode* of the stress disorders. A patient will often say, "It looks like I've become immune to this drug." Now the doctor gives the patient's balloon a second drug coating to strengthen it, either by increasing the dosage of the same drug or by adding another drug. This latter procedure is called *drug augmentation.* Every one or two years, the doctor adds a new drug to control worsening symptoms. Finally, when drugs can no longer keep the balloon from popping, the patient is declared to be *treatment resistant* or a *refractory* case. The patient is now totally immune to drugs.

C. Multiple drug use for the treatment of stress disorders is now glorified. "Polypharmacy," a practice, abhorred by doctors until recently, of prescribing numerous medications to control a wide range of stress symptoms, is now glorified by drug companies and promoted by leading drug-oriented psychiatrists, who get huge payoffs from the drug companies to spread the message of chemical imbalance. Millions of people who are currently receiving drug therapy for a chemical imbalance may become immune to treatment in the near future. Of course, by that time there will be newer drugs on the market to tackle this serious complication of exclusive drug treatment. Nevertheless, no one can deny that here we are on a rather slippery road.

D. More stress disorders appear over time. As time passes, most exclusively drug-treated patients who refuse to learn better coping skills steadily come down with additional stress disorders. Their balloons suffer second, third, fourth or fifth *breaking point*s, resulting in four or even five stress disorders. These include multiple emotional disorders, such as depression, anxiety, and psychotic disorders occurring concurrently; irritable bowel syndrome; high blood pressure, Fibromyalgia; chronic fatigue syndrome; heart disease and metabolic diseases from overeating or drugs; and skin diseases such as psoriasis and dermatitis. Now these patients end up taking ten to fifteen different drugs to control their symptoms. I frequently see this phenomenon in people who apply for Social Security Disability benefits.

E. Consequences of the trivialization of treatment.
        1. Medication phobia is common. Nowadays, just about every doctor, regardless of his specialty, prescribes "nerve medications" to whoever asks for them, more often than not without taking a detailed medical and psychiatric history. I know doctors who prescribe antidepressant medications to patients without even seeing them. There are also doctors who prescribe medications without a follow-up office visit for proper monitoring. Many of my patients tell me, "My doctor saw me for five minutes. He put me on an antidepressant medication and gave me a five-week supply of samples and a year's supply of prescriptions without telling me what to expect. When I took the first dose, I became very sick."
        Most doctors I know prescribe huge starting doses of antidepressant medications, which, in patients prone to anxiety, can result in severe anxiety symptoms. Many such patients suffer panic attacks because of the side-effects of the drugs. They run to the emergency room, believing that they have had an allergic reaction to the drug. Most of these people subsequently develop severe *medication pho-*

bia. They fear antidepressant medications so much that just thinking about taking them can bring on a panic attack. Right now, over twenty-five percent of the new patients who come to see me suffer from severe medication phobia, which causes a serious problem in finding the right treatment for them. When I tell them that it is not the drugs they should be afraid of, but the doctors prescribing them, it makes little impact on their befuddled minds. These are my toughest customers.

2. The development of suicidal ideas in a patient after starting drug therapy reflects poor management. Immediately after beginning a large dose of antidepressant medication, many people's anxiety symptoms become intolerable and they develop suicidal ideas. Often, they have not been briefed about the possible side-effects, nor have they been prescribed anti-anxiety medications to ease the initial anxiety. If the patient's balloon is already full, the stress of anxiety symptoms can simply pop it, resulting in suicidal ideas, suicidal attempt or completed suicide. In my thirty-six years in this business, not one of my patients has ever complained of suicidal ideas owing to antidepressant medications I have prescribed. This is because I always start medications in extremely small doses, increase them in very small doses and thoroughly educate the patients about what to expect. In addition, I give my patients free access to me twenty-four/seven. If the anxiety becomes intolerable, I prescribe an anti-anxiety medication on a temporary basis. In the controversy of "drug-induced suicidal ideas" drugs have been unfairly blamed for the mistakes doctors have made.

3. We are on the verge of becoming a bipolar nation! Over the past ten years, drug companies have come up with five very expensive drugs, known as "atypical antipsychotic drugs," for the treatment of psychotic and bipolar disorders. The drug companies have done such a great job of wining and dining doctors while "educating" them about their wonderful drugs that now millions of people are casually diagnosed as suffering from bipolar disorder. Patients suffering from even minor mood instability, "mind racing," poor concentration and the like, which are all very common in the second and third stages of stress, are being misdiagnosed as bipolar. Troubled children acting out their anger are also misdiagnosed as bipolar. Almost all these patients are now prescribed potentially toxic drugs that could have serious long-term health risks. Thanks to the drug companies, we are on the verge of becoming a bipolar nation!

4. Antidepressant drug treatment can trigger manic episodes in some people. Doctors frequently prescribe antidepressant medications without checking the patient's history for mood swings or a family history for bipolar disorder. As a result, many patients develop true manic syndrome following antidepressant therapy. Manic syndrome is a potentially serious disorder with many possible financial, legal and family consequences. There seems to be little awareness in the medical profession about this potentially serious problem. Some drug-treated depressed patients who have reverted back to the third stage of stress are often labeled as having rapid-cycling type of bipolar disorder.

4. We need a new paradigm and a more balanced approach for the treatment of stress disorders.

If this trend continues, such phrases as "self-awareness," "introspection," "soul-searching," "insight," "the search for inner truth" and other good stuff will soon disappear from our vocabulary. We will lose our ability to calm ourselves down using our own inner mental and spiritual resources. We are on the fast track to becoming a drug-dependent, pill-popping, blame-something-else-for-our-problems society. If the half-truth that chemical imbalance causes mental disorders were able to liberate us from the stigma associated with such disorders, then the whole truth that proper coping with and management of stress could reverse the progression of a chemical imbalance (or at least halt its progress) should set us free, not only from the stigma but also from the stress disorders themselves.

The truth that the medical profession must now face is that exclusive drug treatment of stress disorders has declared self-awareness to be irrelevant. This is more dangerous than the stigma surrounding the disorders. The first great mistake the medical profession made was to endorse physical activity for the control of stress symptoms, instead of recommending *introspection.* The second great mistake was to recommend exclusive drug treatment for stress disorders. Our misplaced enthusiasm for drug therapy has blinded us to the grave dangers ahead of us. We are all having a great party on a luxury cruiser named Drug Lady, sailing along on the Niagara River, completely oblivious to the Great Niagara Falls just around the next bend in the river.

In this book, I attempt to bring the pendulum back to the center. In the treatment of stress disorders we need to find a balance between, at the one extreme, the exclusive use of drugs, and, at the other extreme, ineffective psychological counseling unsupported by any medication and education. A well-balanced combination of meaningful education, commonsense counseling and judicious drug therapy is essential to helping stressed-out people overcome their disorders and preventing future episodes. The time is ripe for a paradigm shift in the mental health field.

1. The term "mental disorder" should be replaced by "stress disorder," as stress is the main contributing factor in these disorders. This change in terminology should alert patients to the need to learn better stress-coping and stress-managing skills.

2. Education must be made an integral part of the treatment of all stress disorders. Often, education alone is enough to help people deal with their stress-related issues, especially in the early stages. Given simple explanation, proper insight and simple coping tools, most people in the early stages of stress are able to help themselves. Over twenty-five percent of the stressed-out patients I now see need only one session to get well. The case of the "blind" woman in Chapter One is an example.

3. Non-psychiatric doctors who routinely prescribe psychiatric medications based on symptoms alone must learn something about the mind, stress and stress-related issues. How ethically appropriate is it for them to prescribe psychiatric medications without even a rudimentary knowledge of the underlying issues contributing to the patients' disorders? How ethical would it be for a psychiatrist or neurologist to routinely prescribe cardiac medications to heart patients, hormones to women and antibiotics to patients with high fever, just because he has the license to write prescriptions?

4. Drug companies must put out the whole truth about stress disorders and the dangers posed by the long-term use of

psychiatric medications, instead of feeding the public the song-and-dance routine of "chemical imbalance" in television and newspaper advertisements. These companies are contributing greatly to the pernicious idea that drugs are the answer to all our miseries in life.

5. The health insurance industry must wake up and start collecting data on the wastage of medical resources incurred through the medical wild goose chase, commonly seen in uninformed, stressed-out people. Health insurers must at least pay for reading materials and educational seminars on coping with and managing stress. It is in their own best interest to educate their subscribers on stress-related matters.

6. School systems should introduce courses on how to cope with and manage stress in daily life. This could decrease the incidence of alcohol and drug abuse, currently so prevalent among students. Children educated about stress can grow up into adults who are better able to cope with life's inevitable stressful events and problems.

7. Therapists must take a fresh look at their treatment modalities, and give up jaded and outdated therapy techniques. Instead of baffling patients with psychological mumbo-jumbo, they should focus on educating their patients about stress; give them insight into the role painful emotions play in the origin of stress symptoms; provide them with simple tools to rid the mind of painful emotions; and heal them through meaningful interaction.

8. Psychiatrists must wake up to the fact that their profession has rapidly degenerated into an exclusively drug-oriented profession, thoroughly corrupted by the payola as well as the wining and dining by drug companies. Some of us seem to have lost our ethical mooring in the quagmire of money-making schemes. Greed has disconnected our minds from our inner wisdom. We need to bring psychiatry back on the ethical track. We must develop a broader, more balanced approach to the treatment of patients suffering from stress disorders, rather than merely masking their stress symptoms by drugging them up. We have to take back from the drug companies the responsibility of educating patients, as well as doctors, about stress disorders.

9. We need a simple, *dynamic theory* to explain the

functions and the dysfunctions of the mind, as well as to replace out-dated, jaded psychoanalytic theories. The new theory must be simple enough for even marginally educated people to understand and apply in their lives.

10. To accomplish these goals, we need a clear *model of the mind* that explains stress-related phenomena. The model should be simple enough for doctors to apply in practice and for patients to apply in everyday life. For example, when upset about something, the patient should be able to say, "My balloon is getting big!" When an upset person feels the need to calm himself, he should say, "I need to talk. I want to shrink my balloon a little!" When one is reliving an old trauma, he should be able to say, "The situation I am in is shaking up my soda bottle (bringing up emotions from my earlier trauma)." The treating doctor should be able to say to the patient, "Let me give your balloon a drug coating now. You can shrink the balloon after you feel better." A therapist should be able to say, "I know you have a lot of fizz (emotions related to old issues) in your soda bottle. We don't want to shake that bottle up just now. For now let's focus on shrinking your balloon." The balloon-soda bottle model enables patients to focus on their inner painful emotions instead of focusing on their stress symptoms. As we will read in Chapter Thirteen, this is the first step on the path to healing.

5. Almost anyone can beat stress by learning a few simple coping mechanisms.

   A. Remember, drug treatment deals only with symptoms. Uncontrolled stress ultimately leads to a chemical imbalance in the brain. No doubt, medications temporarily push our brain chemicals back to their normal state to some extent, resulting in the disappear-ance or decrease in the severity of stress symptoms. However, this only treats the symptoms in order to alleviate the misery they cause. It does not address the root cause of stress disorders: the build-up of toxic, painful emotions in the brain. Nor does it slow down or stop the progress of stress disorders. It is like the lowering of the blood sugar level of a diabetic patient with drugs alone—without educat-ing him about the cause and course of diabetes, without counseling him about diet and exercise and without motivating him to lead a healthier lifestyle. To fight the elephant of stress, drug treatment must be supplemented by education and counseling. The counseling can be some type of self-help or sessions with a trained therapist.

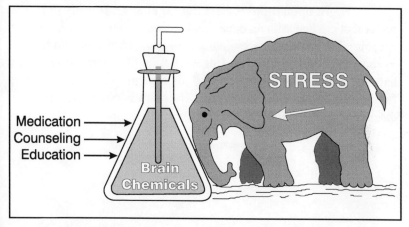

Picture 13: Drugs, education and counseling fight stress together.

B. You need to make a decision. Stress can be controlled, tamed and used to our advantage. By learning to cope with stress, we can enjoy life more fully and prevent the future occurrence of stress disorders. Even if one has come down with a stress disorder, once the symptoms are controlled with medications, he must make a decision: "Do I accept the idea that my disorder is a permanent chemical imbalance for which I will need drugs and more drugs forever? Or can I keep my brain chemicals in balance by learning to cope with stress better and by managing my life better?"

C. People with advanced stress disorders are often unable or unwilling to change. People who have suffered from one or more serious stress disorders for many years might need to take multiple medications for the rest of their lives. Most of these people are unable or unwilling to learn new coping skills, as their faulty coping methods have grown deep roots and are difficult to overcome. Such people's awareness about their inner life is poor. They are no different from morbidly obese diabetics who depend on large doses of insulin to control their sugar levels, refusing to exercise, lose weight and diet. As the years pass, they develop more serious complications and need more insulin and other drugs to keep them alive.

D. An open mind is essential for change. It is my firm belief that anyone with an open mind, adequate intelligence, the capacity for self-awareness and the motivation to change can learn to cope with stress. In this way, he can gradually reverse, or at least halt, the progression of a chemical imbalance in the brain, preventing future episodes of stress disorders. Let us now begin our journey of discovery in the field of stress.

———◄●◆●►———

CHAPTER THREE

From the African Savanna to the American Prairie

What we have studied so far poses several questions: Why do painful emotions play such an important role in stress? How did we come to acquire all these painful emotions? What tools did Mother Nature give us to deal with them? How did we learn inappropriate coping methods? Why are people so afraid of admitting or showing their emotions to their fellow beings? Why do they feel guilty when they break down and cry, as if they have done something terribly wrong? Why do they believe that expressing painful emotions is a sign of weakness? Why do they deny their emotions when they are obviously upset? Why do they block these emotions and hide them, instead of talking about them? Why is there a great deal more stress today than there was just a hundred years ago? Why do people delude themselves by thinking they are coping with stress when they perform some physical activity?

To answer these questions and many other riddles, we need to search for our ancestor who lived in the African savanna over a million years ago. Well, you don't have to go to Africa to look for him. You can find him right here, where you live. Just look in the mirror and you will find him. Let us trace the steps that primitive man took from his early evolutionary days in the African savanna to his modern life on the American prairie.

1. In the African savanna, fear, though unpleasant, saved mankind.

A. As primitive man evolved from the apes over millions of years in the African savanna, his constant concern was for safety from predators. Whenever his mind sensed danger from these predators, he experienced fear. Fear instantly brought on chemical changes in his brain, resulting in a "fight or flight" response, which expressed itself in fast heartbeat, heavy breathing, tense muscles, increased blood supply to the limbs, a feeling of being wound up and many more dramatic symptoms, collectively known as stress symptoms. This *alarm system* developed to give primitive man a jump-start, so that he could fight back or run for his life. Thus, primitive man was hardwired to have "fight or flight" stress symptoms when fear appeared in his mind.

B. This self-preservation response disappeared when the danger went away. Let us compare primitive man's conscious mind to a balloon. Whenever fear appeared in the balloon, it inflated and the man experienced the "fight or flight" response. When the fear disappeared, the balloon deflated and the man calmed down. Modern man responds to fear in exactly the same way.

C. Primitive man saved the memories of his dangerous encounters in his hidden mind the way information is saved in a file in the hard drive of a computer. The purpose of this was to enable the man to benefit from his past experiences. Thus, a "Lessons Learned" file came into being. These lessons improved the man's hunting and self-preservation skills. As his thinking process became more complex, nature provided the hidden mind with folders to better organize and store information essential for survival. In the process of his evolution, primitive man learned more about his environment and the nature of the different objects he encountered, and he filed this information in a "Knowledge" file. His brain grew in size, and the capacity of his hidden mind also grew, to store his burgeoning knowledge. He collected a great deal of information, which gave him a clue as to what was good for him and what was bad in the harsh environment of Africa. As a result, nature installed the "Belief" folder in the hidden mind. It was this folder that told him such things as, "The lion is a very dangerous animal. Stay away from it."

2. Primitive man conquered fear by joining hands with others.

A. Primitive man discovered that when he was in a group, he feared less for his safety and could hunt more effectively. His instinct for survival and his new ability to reason led him to join hands with other humans, and they formed a primitive human society. Primitive man took his first step in gaining rudimentary wisdom when he reasoned that there was safety in numbers. *Indeed, when primitive man became social man, the formation of a primitive society to counter fear became his first appropriate coping mechanism.* Even today, we feel much safer in a group than when we are alone, say, in the downtown area of a big city at night. Generally speaking, people with poor support system do poorly in life. To store this understanding, nature installed a "Wisdom" folder in the hidden mind. This folder would later become very big as man became civilized and it incorporated many existing files and acquired newer ones over time. The modern man's Wisdom folder has the following seven files: Lessons learned; Knowledge; Reasoning; Judgment; Insight; Moral values and Noble virtues.

B. The constant close proximity to other humans resulted in shared experiences in hunting and gathering, conflict and peace, and sickness and health. From these shared experiences, people gradually developed emotional attachments, or *bonds*, with each other. These bonds were based on the happy memories of shared events associated with new emotions: love, happiness, joy, security, etc. Thus, a "Bonds" folder came into being in the hidden mind.

C. As man experienced the inevitable loss of companions with whom he had bonded, a few new emotions appeared in his mind: sadness, sorrow and hurt. These painful emotions in the conscious mind gave rise to "grief" symptoms, such as crying, sobbing, sighing, moaning and weeping. They did not include "fight or flight" symptoms unless the loss endangered the man's sense of security. Thus, "grief" became hardwired into primitive man's brain as a response to loss, just as "fight or flight" was the response to fear. *Grieving over a loss became the second appropriate coping mechanism that man discovered.*

D. As the newly socialized primitive man's ties with others in the society grew, a *support system* came into being, mediated by bonding and emotional exchange. For the primitive social man, his ties to his society became a symbol of safety, security and self-preservation. Not belonging to the society, or being rejected by it, meant facing danger all alone. Whenever primitive social man feared the loss of his ties with other members of society, he experienced fear and anticipatory grief. This fear of societal loss or rejection, too, became hardwired in the brain over hundreds of thousands of years of evolution. To this day, in certain Eastern and Middle Eastern cultures, societal ostracism plays such an important role that death is considered preferable. Children who bring a bad name to the family are often mercilessly murdered. It is said that in Voodoo, a ritual tradition of West African origin, death can occur from massive hemorrhage in the adrenal glands if the targeted victim is told that someone important in his community has rejected him, even when he is living in a distant land. Broken ties with significant members of one's support system due to death, breakup or abandonment often lead to suicide attempts, even in modern Western societies. Many men and women either kill themselves or commit murder/suicide when they are abandoned by their spouses. The lack of a support system makes a person highly vulnerable to stress, and this has become the scourge of modern Western society. Lonely men suffer from more stress-related disorders and die younger than married men. Some lonely men become psychopaths, serial killers or rapists, just as rogue primitive men did a million years ago.

3. Primitive social man added more emotions to his inventory.

A. As time passed, continued intimate contact between members of society led to the evolution of more painful emotions. When any member of the society hurt or threatened an individual physically or emotionally, the individual developed dislike, resentment, anger, rage, hate and vengeance toward him. When these painful emotions appeared in his conscious mind, the primitive man's balloon inflated and he experienced "attack" symptoms: irritability, hostility, snapping, yelling, shouting, cursing, spitting, physically attacking and killing the offending party. As these new emotions came to represent man's need to "get even" with those who hurt him, they became hardwired in his brain. Even in today's civilized society, we see this need for vengeance against those who have hurt us in the form of verbal or physical attacks, murder and lawsuits. Vengeance –"eye for an eye and tooth for a tooth"- is the theme of most stories we read and movies we see. The legal system all civilized societies have, which punishes those who break the law, is a highly refined system of vengeance. When man developed verbal skills he learned to express his displeasure and anger verbally instead of physically. When man became civilized, he resorted to legal remedy to satisfy his need for vengeance. However, as civilization became more polished, man learned to forgive those who offended him. Forgiveness became the ultimate virtue of mankind. *Resorting to law for justice or forgiving those who offended him became man's third appropriate coping mechanism.*

B. To enable primitive social man to experience, display and express his newfangled emotions to his fellow beings, numerous facial muscles evolved over hundreds of thousands of years. Simultaneously, primitive social man's brain enlarged to make room for his newly learned survival and social skills. The blood supply to the brain increased enormously to help him process his emotions, and the blood supply to the facial skin and muscles also increased, enabling him to express these emotions by facial gestures. The modern man is capable of expressing hundreds of emotions merely by means of subtle facial gestures.

C. When he was upset about something—say, the death of a fellow human—primitive man's conscious mind became flooded with sadness and hurt, his balloon inflated and an enormous amount of blood rushed suddenly to his face and head. He experienced swelling and redness of the face, bloodshot eyes, stuffy nose, throbbing of the head, engorgement of the neck veins, knitting of the eyebrows, pouting of the mouth and many other facial and bodily symptoms. When a lion charged him, his face showed emotions of fear and terror. When he felt angry at another member of his clan, his face betrayed this emotion. These facial changes, which were due to increased blood supply to the facial skin, muscles and head, communicated to others how a person truly felt when he was upset for any reason. We are all capable of experiencing all these symptoms in their full glory, if only we let ourselves. Modern man describes emotional faces with such phrases as "red with rage," "green with envy," "ashen with fright," "dark with despair," etc. We describe people who effectively hide their emotions as "pokerfaced," "bland-faced," "mask-faced," "blank-faced," "impassive," "inexpressive" and other pejorative terms. Stressed people who tightly hide their painful emotions are described by their doctors as having a bland or blunted affect.

4. Grieving shrank primitive man's balloon.

By crying, sobbing, sighing, weeping, bawling, squalling, moaning, groaning, grunting, screaming, yelling, breast-beating and other bodily gestures, primitive man expressed his grief; and thus, he reduced his emotional tension and the blood flow in his head. The copious flow of salty tears reduced the blood volume in his head, just as a water pill does in people with high blood pressure. When he developed the ability to talk, he learned to verbalize his emotions, and this was how he shrank his balloon and calmed himself down. This overtly dramatic display of emotions and their free expression following the loss of a loved one was socially acceptable and, in fact, socially sponsored. All members of the social group knew exactly what the person displaying his emotions in this way thought, and how he felt about his loss. Whereas forming a human society was primitive man's method of coping with the fear related to environmental dangers, grieving was his way of coping with the loss of loved ones. By grieving, he rid his mind of sadness, sorrow and hurt and shrank his balloon. In many relatively less advanced societies of the world today, this is still the way people grieve. But as we became "modern," grieving became more and more muted.

We are so thoroughly hardwired to grieve when we lose someone with whom we are bonded that those who are now unable or unwilling to grieve are condemned to suffer various stress disorders, such as severe headache attacks, psychosomatic pain disorders and major depression. Here we must recall the notable saying of Dr. Harry Maudsley (1835-1918): "The sorrow that has no vent in tears may make other organs weep." Painful emotions that are not released through grieving or verbal expression are gradually buried in the hidden mind, becoming the foundation of future stress disorders.

5. Early civilization tried to tame the primitive social man.

A. Primitive man was essentially a creature of unbridled impulses. His basic goal was to survive in the wilderness, and he indulged in stealing, beating, attacking, murder and any activity that furthered his safety and survival. Approximately ten thousand years ago, as the number of people in primitive human society increased, the more enlightened elders in the society decided to organize it in order to eliminate conflicts and chaos. Society organized itself into families, neighborhoods and communities. The first attempts at such organization appeared in Mesopotamia. To bring order and peace, people created a social hierarchy and formulated explicit rules of behavior, or codes of conduct. Thus the process of civilization was set in motion. A primitive system of law and justice, a police force and prisons came into being. People who misbehaved were branded *antisocial*, criminal or evil, and they were punished according to the established laws and justice system: they were banished from society, imprisoned or even executed. Hammurabi's code and the Ten Commandments are but two later examples of such rules, meant to regulate the behavior of the members of a society. The rule of law and moral codes to regulate behavior became the hallmark of all civilized societies.

Yet even today, we see people who do not obey societal laws, rules and restrictions. They commit crimes exactly as some primitive men did a million years ago. Over two million of these primitive-minded men and women are now in our prison system, and perhaps millions more are living amidst us, some wearing three-piece suits. They commit robbery, kidnapping, rape, murder and just about every despicable act that primitive man was capable of. Every year, our society comes up with new laws to try to curb one antisocial behavior or another. The hardwired traits that helped the primitive man to survive in the wilderness have remained in the modern man as seven *personality weaknesses:* selfishness; hatred; arrogance, possessiveness, greed, jealousy and insecurity. All antisocial behaviors we see in modern man are directed by one or more of these personality weaknesses. These weaknesses are also at the root of most stress-producing problems we face in life: job, family, health, relationship, etc.

B. Simultaneously, early civilizations formulated subtle, or implicit, rules, to regulate the way members in the community interacted with one another. These etiquettes, or cultural norms, dictated how people should talk, walk, dress, eat, burp, fart, sneeze, cough, sleep, defecate, urinate, groom themselves, behave and express their emotions in their interactions with others in the society. Members of society passed these rules on by word of mouth and to their children by example. These behavioral norms varied from culture to culture; *etiquettes*, or cultural norms, were specific to distinct geographical areas. Even today, cultural norms of behavior vary from culture to culture. That is why a person from one culture entering another might suffer "culture shock." Many of America's problems with other nations of the world are rooted in the monumental ignorance of the American leadership and military about cultural differences between the U. S. and other societies. A simple example of cultural difference is that, in Western culture, a guest who burps loudly in front of his hosts after dinner is considered uncouth, whereas in some Middle Eastern countries, a guest who *does not* burp loudly after dinner in front of his hosts is considered a boor. An American mother would be worried to death if her sixteen-year-old daughter did not show any interest in boys, while an Asian Indian mother would be worried to death if her sixteen-year-old daughter did show an interest in boys. These cultural differences are becoming increasingly blurred as the process of globalization speeds up.

C. The norms of etiquette were meant to maintain peace, order, tranquility and decorum within society. "Thou shall not lose control of your temper," "Thou shall not curse," "Thou shall not create a scene in public," "Thou shall not fall apart"—these were a few of the hundreds of implicit rules society gradually clamped on its members. (Political correctness, so much in vogue in modern society, is a relic of these prohibitions: "Thou shall not say things that hurt others.") In this way, civilized society gradually stigmatized the free expression of emotion. Those who readily and dramatically expressed their emotions, as primitive man did, were considered weak, out of control or uncivilized. They were ridiculed or rejected. Thus, while these rules helped control how people expressed their angry feelings, they also stigmatized the fundamental coping mechanism: grieving. In modern societies, people who express themselves dramatically are branded as histrionic or *hysterical*. They are often accused of indulging in attention-seeking behavior (ASB). Many such people, if they have a flair for dramatics, end up as movie stars. This method of expressing forbidden emotions by means of socially acceptable, or even socially glorified, behavior is known as sublimation. I would go so far as to say that the dramatic arts arose as a way to express secret emotions through a medium that is acceptable to society; in plain words, "play-acting" those forbidden emotions.

D. Those who did not obey the cultural norms and rules were not put in prisons, as antisocial people were, but were chided, subtly rejected or ridiculed. Such rejection or ridicule was bound to upset the offending member, causing his balloon to inflate and thus bringing on uncomfortable stress symptoms. As we have seen, primitive man was already hardwired to feel extremely upset when rejected by his fellow beings. To avoid being ostracized, he would toe the line. So he internalized the social rules; they became his own. This process of civilizing primitive man by curbing his emotional expression came with a hefty price tag: serious *emotional constipation*.

Bob Kamath, M.D.

6. To be socially accepted, man built a prison of the mind.

A. Just thinking about violating these rules made a person feel fearful. ("I might be ridiculed or rejected.") Thus, guilt ("this is the wrong thing to do") and shame ("people will think less of me") came into being. A whole new set of painful emotions evolved: the guilt complex. Newly civilized man learned to put a leash on his impulse to express himself, just so that he could feel a sense of belonging. When he violated the rules, he felt guilt and shame, and he made amends by apologizing, expressing remorse and regret, or asking forgiveness. When society learned to forgive a repentant person, it declared this forgiveness a virtue. *Verbally expressing remorse and regret; apologizing to and asking for forgiveness from the offended party; and making appropriate compensation became the fourth appropriate way of coping.*

B. The rules meant to curb violent and aggressive behavior were needed to bring peace and order in society. But those rules that prohibited the expression of grief went directly against nature, as man was already hardwired to grieve and shrink his balloon whenever he was upset about losing someone or something. Thus the baby was thus thrown out with the bathwater: the grieving process, the second fundamental coping mechanism, was seriously compromised. Modern man has continued this dangerous tradition. The mantra "control your emotions," passed on in some families from generation to generation, became part of our collective psyche and behavior. Nowadays, even the normal expression of grief has come to be branded as creating a scene. The overt display of sadness can be labeled as hysterical. Crying over something is called maudlin. Expressing displeasure about something is labeled whining or griping. Some years ago, a decent presidential candidate lost his bid for the presidency to a crook because he shed a tear in public over someone denigrating his beloved wife. During the early years of my psychiatric training, I saw many of my colleagues roll their eyes every time a patient became "hysterical."

The stigma attached to the expression of emotions has resulted in people's repressing their emotions, even when they are extremely upset. "I had to be strong for my children," "I did not want my dying husband to see me fall apart," "I just could not let myself look ridiculous in front of all those people at the funeral," "I could not let my children down by becoming a crybaby," "I did not want to make a mess of myself in front of everybody"—these are common statements I hear from people who have ended up with serious depression and pain disorders, weeks or months after some tragedy. No one wants to be branded a chronic complainer, whiner, sissy, softy, milque-toast and whatnot. Whenever I attend a funeral, I am struck by the jovial mood of the family of the deceased. No moist eyes here! The family explains away the jovial mood by saying they are celebrating the dead person's life. Many of the relatives are either drunk or drugged, and the remaining ones are busy being strong for the others, or "celebrating." Many people, numbed after bereavement by alcohol or drugs, can hardly recall the events around the funeral.

Today, all the stressed patients I see in my office express fear, guilt and shame for weeping in front of me. When they break down and cry, they invariably say, "I'm sorry, I can't help it! I feel ashamed of myself." Some say, "Normally, I am not a crybaby. I was determined not to do this! I feel so bad that I'm like this." They feel guilt and shame for displaying their emotions openly. To them, doing so has always been an unpardonable weakness or a punishable crime. When I offer them a tissue to wipe their tears, they reluctantly reach for it and say, "Oh, what a pity that I need this damned tissue!" In fact, some people later confess to me that they were fearful I might put them in a straitjacket and commit them to a state hospital if they fell apart in my office. That, they thought, was the punishment they would get for expressing themselves freely.

Intolerance of the display of painful emotions is still common in the medical profession. I often get frantic phone calls from my doctor colleagues, saying, "Bob, I need your urgent help. I have this nice lady in my office and I want you to see her right now. I asked her how she was doing, and she just fell apart!" All the patient had done was to unburden her sorrow on the shoulders of a father figure in the privacy of his office. Yet, instead of comforting her, the doctor called a psychiatrist. The patient now gets the message, "If you break down and cry like this, you must be nuts. You're out of control. You need a shrink."

When we go against the rule of nature, we become sick. Society's misguided decision to stifle people in order to refine them laid the foundation for stress disorders. When a society makes rules to solve one problem, it often creates another, and common sense goes out the window. (We saw many instances of this in the way America reacted to the 9/11 terror attack.) Society has stigmatized the expression of emotions, and at least some people take these rules very seriously.

The stigma attached to the overt expression of emotion was later extended to emotional disorders, as these were also seen as evidence of one's being weak and not in control of his emotions, impulses and behavior.

C. As the process of civilization progressed, and as a result of the increasingly complex interactions with his fellow beings, human beings added more emotions to their repertoire: helplessness, hopelessness, worthlessness, bitterness, jealousy, envy. These painful emotions, being later additions, did not inflate the balloon that much, but they did cause significant stress symptoms when they appeared along with other emotions, such as fear, anger or sadness. In fact, emotions became connected to one another like links in a chain, and the appearance of one would cause the appearance of others: hurt could be followed by sadness, anger, vengeance, disappointment, etc. As man became civilized, he was curbing the expression of emotions, on the one hand, while on the other hand he was adding new painful emotions to his inventory.

(In the first chapter, we read about thirty-six of the hundreds of painful emotions of which we are capable. We will study all the painful emotions in greater detail in the next chapter.)

7. Civilized man added more sense objects to his inventory.

While all this was going on, human society became more complex, and the needs and wants of civilized man expanded enormously. He acquired new objects to which he could attach himself and considered them important not only for his safety and survival, but also for his comfort: horses, farm animals, pets, vehicles, household items and gadgets, as well as honor, fame, praise, liberty, power, etc. His desire for and attachment to these physical and abstract sense objects led to the feeling of possessiveness. Possessiveness means *entanglement*, or the inability to let go. People would experience greater grief when they lost objects with which they had become entangled, and would feel inadequate or vulnerable if they didn't have them. This is no different from a modern child being conditioned to feel inferior for not wearing a brand-name T-shirt. In other words, as civilized people became more and more entangled with an increasing number of objects, their potential to experience grief increased greatly. The fast-paced life of modern man is basically geared toward making more money so that one can become entangled with more sense objects.

8. To prevent societal ridicule, man learned to bury his emotions.

A. While civilized society curbed the expression of emotion, it did not give people any new tool to shrink their balloons. All it said was, "Thou shall not fall apart!" But, following the rule of nature that had been hardwired into mankind over millions of years, the primitive mind within cried out, "When I am upset, please let me fall apart! Let me shrink my balloon! Let me create a scene! Let me shed my tears and get this damned emotional pain out of my system! Let me scream bloody murder! Let me experience the ecstasy of being myself for once!" Yet the stern-faced, civilized mind within, following the five-thousand-year-old internalized rule of society, replied, "No, you can't do that. Don't you have any shame? Keep your bloody mouth shut! Stop whining! Hold back your tears. Control yourself! Stop wallowing in self-pity! Be strong! Don't you see how upsetting it would be to the people around you if you fell apart? If you don't know what to do with your painful emotions, just hide them someplace." This perpetual conflict between the primitive and modern mind is not merely the mother of all our mental conflicts; it is an ongoing civil war in our minds.

Modern society actively encourages people to hide their

painful emotions by declaring that those who keep a stiff upper lip under fire are heroes and role models. In the armed forces, such encouragement is not only necessary, but essential. Unfortunately, though, many people who break down and show their "weakness" in normal social situations are looked down upon as whiners, crybabies and wimps.

B. When the civilized mind had the upper hand, a person said to himself, "All right, I will be strong. I won't think about it, I won't talk about it. I will just forget it." He buried his painful emotions in his hidden mind—where they did not belong. To accommodate the buried, painful emotions, nature installed a new folder in the hard drive: the "Pain" folder. After burying some painful emotion in this way, a person's balloon shrank and he felt somewhat better. An uneasy calm settled in his mind. Unfortunately, all he had done was to transfer his painful emotions from the conscious mind/balloon into the hidden mind/soda bottle. He had solved his pressing problem for the time being; little did he know that it would soon come back to haunt him. *Burying painful emotions in the hidden mind thus became the first socially acceptable and sponsored inappropriate way of coping with painful emotions.*

Even when society does not give a damn whether one falls apart or not, some families cannot break loose from the chains of these rules, as they have made them their own. I often see several members of the same family coping with stress in this manner. They have all grown up believing that showing one's emotion was a sign of weakness, and have all ended up with serious stress disorders. So when we say, "Depression runs in the family," it is difficult to tell whether it is the burying habit or genetics that have brought on someone's depression. I believe that in some families, the inappropriate coping methods may become encoded in their genes; in others, they are passed on to the children by word of mouth, or by example.

When children are traumatized by physical, sexual or emotional abuse, they resort to burying, as their brains are not equipped to process painful emotions in large quantities or to express them appropriately. Furthermore, they are forced to bury their emotions because of the fear of being punished by their abusers, or even by their parents, if they speak out. In fact, parents very often refuse to believe their children, in order to protect themselves from feeling bad about what has happened. In other words, the parents themselves are in a denial mode. This adds salt to the child's wound of abuse. Most seriously abused children become very sick by the time they are eighteen years of age, because the hidden mind reached its saturation point long before then. Many adults who were abused as children report no memories of their childhood abuse; their behavior and stress disorders are the only clues to their horrendous childhoods.

9. As protection against society's ridicule, man learned to deny.

When the hidden mind/soda bottle had no more space for painful emotions, the newly civilized man was once again at a loss about what to do with them. As his balloon began to re-inflate, he felt and looked more and more upset. Curiously, however, when asked if he was upset about something, he learned to say no in order to avoid being ridiculed. For him, nothing was worse than projecting the image of being a weakling. He constantly told himself to be strong. To hide his distress even more, he began to tell tall stories about how wonderful he felt. Even when he felt terrible about something, he tried to fool people by saying, "I feel wonderful. Things in my life couldn't be better!" Thus the tendency to deny emotions and problems became common in stressed-out people in civilized society. However, the denier was merely fooling himself. Denial did not get rid of painful emotions from his mind, his life problems or stress symptoms. *Over the centuries, denial became the second socially acceptable and sponsored inappropriate way of coping with painful emotions.*

In the modern world, however, when a person admits to feeling bad about something, he loses the respect of his peers. People admire the strong, silent type. An alcoholic's denial of his drinking problem is an example of someone's avoiding the ridicule of society. That is why Alcoholics Anonymous encourages people to come out of the closet and declare publicly, "I am an alcoholic!" Amazingly, this public exposure of the person's weakness liberates him from the burden of shame and elevates him in the eyes of the enlightened members of society. Here, society has given him permission to admit his weakness and cancel out his shame. Likewise, psychiatrists and therapists, representing the more enlightened segment of society, give their patients permission to break down and express their emotions without guilt and shame in the privacy of their offices. This permission is implicit in the *empathy* they show their patients. Empathy in the listener has the power to break down denial in the patient, because the patient instinctively identifies it as a clue that the therapist understands and accepts his inner pain, and consequently that he won't be judged, criticized, rejected and ridiculed. It is amazing how a touch of empathy can instantly break down even the deep-rooted, internalized prohibition against expressing emotion.

10. People learned to express themselves by means of bodily symptoms.

A. When civilized man could not shrink his balloon and the emotional pressure in the balloon became unbearable, lo and behold! Mother Nature came to the rescue once again. She said, "In your desire to be civilized, you have gone against my rule and stifled yourself. Nevertheless, I will give you an escape route. I will give you the ability to express your painful emotions by means of physical symptoms. Since your society has not attached any *stigma* to physical symptoms, you will not be subjected to ridicule. In fact, those civilized fools will give you lots of attention and sympathy when you complain of serious physical symptoms! How does that sound to you?" To the stressed-out person, any relief was better than the agony he felt with his full balloon.

B. Therefore, human beings developed physical symptoms that came to represent unexpressed painful emotions in their minds. A person's unexpressed hurt feelings showed up as pain somewhere in his body: headache, stomachache, backache, pain in the neck, pain in the ass, etc. Unexpressed disgust showed up as symptoms of nausea and vomiting. When one could not express jealousy, he suffered heartburn and stomach ulcers. One's body expressed by means of seemingly serious physical symptoms whatever painful emotions he could not express verbally: blindness, deafness, paralysis, dizziness, weakness, nausea, diarrhea, vomiting, seizures, numbness of the skin, blotches, hives, breathlessness. Society did not object to these physical symptoms at all. In fact, it did quite the opposite: it gave the sufferer a great deal of support, attention and sympathy. To this day, civilized society has no clue about this ruse of nature. Health insurance companies often refuse to pay for the treatment of emotional symptoms but will readily pay for physical symptoms. *Expressing painful emotions by means of dramatic physical symptoms became the third socially acceptable and sponsored inappropriate coping mechanism.*

Here are some classic examples of painful emotions that are expressed through physical symptoms.

1. A middle-aged lady, unable to tolerate her husband's verbal attacks any more, went temporarily deaf. By going deaf, she was saying, in effect, "I feel helpless to cope with my husband's verbal abuse." With one counseling session, in which she expressed her helplessness, hurt and anger, she regained her hearing.

2. An outraged wife, unable to lash out at her unfaithful husband, lost her speech. She wanted to give her wayward husband a good tongue-lashing but was afraid of losing him. After she expressed her anger in writing, her speech came back.

3. A middle-aged man developed paralysis of his right arm as a way to repress his irresistible desire to beat the crap out of his tyrannical boss, which he could not do for fear of losing his job and going to prison. Once the man verbally expressed his rage, his paralysis disappeared.

4. A pastor, hurt over being dismissed by his congregation, experienced an unbearable stabbing pain in his back. Once he expressed his disappointment, hurt and sense of betrayal, the back pain gradually went away.

5. A young man, heartbroken and sad over the breakup with his girlfriend, complained of unbearable chest pain. In counseling, he grieved over the loss, let go of her, and his chest pain went away.

6. A young lady, burning with envy over her

neighbor's huge swimming pool, complained of severe, constant heartburn. Once she got over her envy in therapy, her heartburn went away.

7. A passive-natured boss developed pain in the neck after he hired a lousy secretary who messed up everything in the office. After he took charge of the office situation, the pain in his neck improved.

8. A child, upset over being sexually abused by a babysitter, complained of pain in the genital area. Once the mother acknowledged the child's suffering and fired the babysitter, the genital pain went away.

9. A young fellow, saddened over his grandfather's death from emphysema, complained of difficulty breathing. After grieving over the loss of his beloved grandfather, he started breathing normally.

10. Another young man developed spells of shortness of breath when he was unable to deal with feelings of being stifled by his domineering father. After his father acknowledged these feelings and backed off, the shortness of breath disappeared.

This list is unending. Without prompt professional intervention, such symptoms can become chronic and disabling. Continued paralysis of an arm can lead to what is called disuse atrophy. Continued stress-related blindness can cause degenerative changes in the eye grounds, leading to permanent loss of sight. Many Cambodian women who went blind when they found themselves unable to witness atrocities committed by Communists against their children did not receive timely counseling; most of them became permanently blind from chronic disuse of the retina. The longer a physical stress symptom lasts, the harder it is to get rid of.

11. To alleviate his stress symptoms, man abused alcohol.

A. The relief from emotional pain brought by the appearance of physical symptoms did not last long. Now the person had to deal with his physical, emotional, mental and behavioral symptoms brought on by the fully inflated balloon. When these stress symptoms became worse and he could not explain why he had them, he feared he was physically sick or going crazy. With this added fear in his balloon, the stress symptoms became even worse: headaches, chest pain, anxiety, tension, panic attacks, sleeplessness, agitation, sadness, poor concentration, crying spells and dozens of other symptoms. Ignorant of how this had come to pass, man desperately went looking for a remedy that could turn the alarm system off. Then he discovered alcohol. *Alcohol abuse became the fourth socially sponsored inappropriate coping mechanism.*

B. The stressed-out civilized person began to drink alcohol to control his stress symptoms. Thus, for centuries, alcohol was the main, though inappropriate, method of controlling stress symptoms for millions of people. In some cultures, opium was the substance of choice. Alcohol, being a strong sedative and analgesic, gave man temporary relief from emotional pain as well as stress symptoms such as physical pain, tension, sleeplessness and anxiety. However, since it is addictive, his body developed tolerance to it, so he had to drink more to achieve the same results. Soon he began to drink around the clock and was frequently drunk. When drunk, he was able to express his suppressed and repressed emotions freely. Society just said, "He's a drunkard," and forgave him.

C. Under the influence of alcohol, man freely expressed his anger, rage and vengeance, and his immediate family members took the brunt of his brutality. Alcohol abuse gave rise to generations of seriously traumatized people, who also learned to cope with their stress symptoms by drinking. The damage caused by alcohol rippled through generations. Alcohol became the single most important destructive chemical substance in the history of civilization. Civilized society recognized that, in the long run, alcohol created more problems than it solved, so it stigmatized alcoholism as a way of discouraging drinking. Alcoholics who lost control of themselves were labeled as drunkards, and routinely jailed to dry out.

Today, millions of people drink alcohol to drown their sorrows. Drunk drivers kill or maim thousands of people every year. Very few of them go to prison, since society, seeing itself in these drunkards, secretly condones them. For all you know, many law-makers, lawyers and judges may be coping with their life problems by getting drunk. Alcohol is implicated in majority of accidents and crimes committed in this country today. In spite of the stigma and legal restrictions, millions of Americans abuse alcohol to cope with their stress symptoms. The long-term adverse consequences of alcohol and drug abuse, and their complications for family, marriage, children, society, personal finances, health care costs and the national economy, are mind-boggling. Over fifty percent of the stressed-out patients I see grew up in families with at least one alcoholic or drug-addicted parent. When these people became adults, the repeated trauma of watching the stupid antics, shameful shenanigans and violent behavior of their drunk or drugged parents finally caught up with them. I have treated countless people who, as children, slept in the cornfields at night to escape from their drunkard fathers, who chased them with loaded guns. Most adult children of alcoholics suffer from some type of physical or emotional stress disorder, simply because their hidden minds became saturated with painful emotions by the time they were thirty years of age. Alcohol and drug abuse has done incalculable damage to humanity.

12. Man indulged in pleasurable activities to cope with stress.

Over time, people discovered various other pleasurable activities to ease the pain of unremitting stress symptoms: street drugs, smoking, overeating, promiscuous sex and gambling. None of them helped for long. Because of the detrimental effect they had on civilized society, they were declared vices and banned or stigmatized. Even though pleasurable activities gave some temporary relief from the tyranny of stress symptoms, in the long run they facilitated burying, and created serious health, financial, legal and family problems. *Indulging in various pleasurable activities became civilized man's fifth inappropriate way of coping with his stress.*

13. To warehouse the insane, state hospitals were built.

As civilized society became busy with industrialization, in the nineteenth and twentieth centuries, more and more people became traumatized by the side-effects of industrialization: alcoholism, broken families, child abuse and neglect. The Civil War, First World War, Second World War, Korean War and Viet Nam War all contributed greatly to national trauma. Millions of stressed-out people became seriously ill with major mental illnesses. In the absence of effective drugs to give immediate relief from their symptoms, the illnesses rapidly went from bad to worse. To help these unfortunate souls, civilized society did what it could under the circumstances: it warehoused them in large state hospitals, built specifically for this purpose. By the mid-twentieth century, hundreds of thousands of "mentally ill" people were languishing and receiving "moral treatment" in state hospitals, which dotted the landscape. Millions more quietly created their own prisons in their homes and became recluses as a way to prevent their mind/balloons from popping.

14. The clueless modern man goes on a medical wild goose chase.

By the fourth quarter of the twentieth century, medical science boasted modern medical tests to detect many physical disorders. Sophisticated blood tests, X-rays, C/T and MRI scans, endoscopies and the like became available for the detection of serious health problems. When the unenlightened modern man became frightened by his seemingly serious physical symptoms, such as chest pain, stomach pain and dizziness, he went on a medical wild goose chase, looking for physical reasons for these symptoms. He went from specialist to specialist and from one major medical center to another. He had himself scanned, scoped and X-rayed until no tests were left to be done. In the end, he became disgusted, disillusioned and demoralized. His health care costs, as well as those of society as a whole, kept climbing every year. The medical wild goose chase became the symbol of the monumental ignorance of both the individual and the medical profession about the role painful emotions play in the origin of stress symptoms. *The medical wild goose chase became civilized man's sixth socially sponsored inappropriate way of coping with stress.*

15. To counter stress symptoms, physical activity was recommended.

When the physical symptoms of stress were mild and chronic, people came up with activities meant to counter these symptoms. The most common low-grade, chronic physical symptoms were muscle tension and spasms, neck and shoulder pain, the feeling of being wound up, tiredness and exhaustion. To "work out tension," people engaged in numerous physical activities, such as exercising, walking, jogging, weight lifting, swimming, relaxing, taking hot tub baths, pouring drops of oil over the head and a hundred other useless or exotic activities. These activities did not require any thinking, so they were not upsetting. On the contrary, they quietly facilitated the burying process.

As society became more sophisticated, we added skiing, hiking, trekking, ocean cruising, sky-diving, bungee jumping and other activities that give the practitioner a temporary high. Not only were these activities useless for getting rid of stress symptoms, but they actually facilitated the burying process by distracting the mind from dealing with its painful emotions. *Physical activities to counter the symptoms of stress became civilized man's seventh socially sponsored inappropriate way of coping with stress.*

16. The double jeopardy of modern man.

Today, civilized man finds himself in a serious double jeopardy. On the one hand, his entanglement with an increased number of sense objects (wealth, vehicles, houses, gadgets and a thousand more objects, without which he feels miserable) has increased the potential for him to experience painful emotions on the loss of these objects. On the other hand, his ability to express his painful emotions appropriately has steadily decreased because of the tendency to bury and deny them. The inevitable result is a surplus of painful emotions in the balloon, so that the balloon keeps inflating and popping. Millions of people are becoming sick every year, and drug companies are frantically looking for more sophisticated drugs to treat symptoms of stress disorders. Some technical companies are coming up with non-drug treatments for depression through such methods as electro-shock therapy, transcranial magnetic stimulation and vagus nerve stimulation. While everyone concerned—medical professionals, drug companies, hospitals, health insurance companies and technical companies—is raking in money by treating unfortunate souls, no one is asking the simple question, "What can we do to prevent all these people from getting sick?" You know the reason: there is no money in prevention.

17. Our response to this problem is the discovery of more and more new drugs and gadgets.

On the one hand, civilized society built thousands of prisons to house and feed the millions of primitive-minded, antisocial criminals who defied its rules, disturbed the peace and disrupted order. On the other hand, society built hundreds of hospitals and trained hundreds of thousands of doctors to treat millions of people who became sick because they obeyed its rules too scrupulously. Society's only solace is that both these problems have employed millions of people; stimulated scientific research; fueled the economy; enriched doctors, drug companies, hospitals and health insurance companies; and benefited investors and building contractors. This nexus has created the greatest health care-industrial complex mankind has ever known. It is at least as big as America's military-industrial complex, if not bigger. Whether this is a matter of pride or shame is for you do decide. One thing is certain: drug companies are frantically searching for new drugs to peddle to the public. Doctors are eagerly waiting with pen in hand to prescribe them, and more stressed-out people than ever are holding their mouths wide open, ready to pop them. Like all the inappropriate coping methods mentioned above, these psychiatric drugs facilitate the process of burying or blocking off of painful emotions. Bizarre as it might seem to the reader now, one day history will judge that the drug treatment of stress disorders did as much harm to humanity as alcohol did, if not more. *Taking psychotropic drugs for the control of stress symptoms has become civilized man's eighth inappropriate, though currently necessary, way of dealing with stress symptoms.*

––––––●◆●––––––

CHAPTER FOUR

Pain in the Brain

P ainful emotions in the brain are the foundation stones of stress. Learning to identify and deal with painful emotions is the key to coping with stress. Therefore, we must learn as much as possible about the nature of these emotions. Those who are savvy in handling their own painful emotions and in tune with those of others are said to have a high Emotional Quotient (EQ).

Reminder:
Rule #1: When the conscious mind/balloon is inflated with painful emotions, one experiences stress symptoms.
Rule #2: When the balloon is full, one's focus is on his stress symptoms, and his awareness of his inner painful emotions is very low or non-existent.

The first step toward learning to cope with stress, then, is to shift the focus from stress symptoms to the blocked, painful emotions in the conscious mind/balloon. This is known as *raising awareness* of one's inner emotions.

In the first chapter, we identified the thirty-six painful emotions human beings acquired on the way to becoming civilized. By the time patients see a psychiatrist, they admit to having experienced large doses of most of these emotions in one context or another. In small doses, these painful emotions act as growth stimulants. However, in large doses, they become toxic to the brain, which results in serious changes in the brain chemicals. Let us now study their nature in some depth.

1. The nature of painful emotions.

A. A single painful emotion can create a cascade of emotions. Painful emotions do not exist in isolation. All painful emotions are connected to each other like the links in a chain. Sometimes, when we experience just one painful emotion, a cascade of them follows. For example, if I feel hurt or humiliated by someone's nasty comment, soon I might begin to experience a torrent of other emotions: anger, resentment, rage, bitterness, hate and vengefulness. An uncalled-for angry outburst at a loved one might be followed by guilt, shame, embarrassment, remorse, regret and worthlessness. This chain reaction is common after one has discovered spousal infidelity or received a serious emotional or physical injury through the negligent or deliberate action of another person. Behind every injury-related lawsuit is a cascade of painful emotions, which give rise to a need to exact revenge or gain compensation. Do not believe any person who sues and says, "I'm not doing this to get revenge."

B. The severity of stress symptoms depends on two factors:

1. The severity of the painful emotions. If we are extremely frightened about something, we will have many more serious "fight or flight" symptoms than if we are only slightly scared. If we are slightly sad over a loss, we will suffer less grief than if we feel very sad.

2. The number of painful emotions. If we experience several powerful painful emotions, such as fear, hurt, anger, sadness, etc. all at once, as it happens in the cascading phenomenon noted above, we will have many more stress symptoms than we will if we experience only one of these emotions. For example, a woman will experience a greater number of severe stress symptoms after discovering her husband's unfaithfulness than she would if he forgot her birthday. It is obvious that when we experience many painful emotions with great severity, we have many severe stress symptoms.

C. One's emotional reaction to a stressor depends upon his perception of the situation. The number and intensity of painful emotions experienced in response to a stressor depends on one's own perception. We are all different from each other in our reactions to bad events and problems. This is because of our differing genes, our innate temperaments, our emotional sensitivities, our past good and bad experiences, our cultural influences and many other factors. All these factors ultimately crystallize in our minds as beliefs, opinions, views and ideas. On every topic, each of us has his own unique belief, opinion, view or idea. All of this affects the way we perceive a given event or situation. When a certain stock takes a dive, one person might go into shock, believing that he has lost a great deal of money, and another might become ecstatic, believing that he has an opportunity to buy more stocks. One person might see you as a great friend and another as a great fraud. One person might judge someone a terrorist and another might declare him a freedom fighter. Some people are pro-abortion and others are anti-abortion. Some are conservatives, others are liberals. One man's trash is another man's treasure. The point is, what is bad for the goose might not be bad for the gander. Changing one's perception from negative to positive—seeing something good in what appears to be bad—is one of the most important coping strategies. For example, you have a choice of perceiving your critical, controlling, difficult boss as evil or simply as scared and deeply insecure.

D. It is inappropriate to "rate" stress responses. We have seen that what upsets one person very much might not upset another at all. In fact, what is outrageous to one can be hilarious to another. For that matter, what might upset someone today might not upset the same person a year from now, as his thinking and life situation could then be quite different. Therefore, it is inappropriate to generalize about stress responses and designate a particular "severity number" to a given stressful event (death of a spouse, 100; divorce, 98; etc.) The breakup of a relationship could devastate one person and re-lieve another. The discovery of a husband's infidelity could make one woman pass out in shock and cause another to comment wryly, "My husband is a wild man!" The death of a spouse could cause one person's balloon to pop and make another person's champagne bottle pop. Being fired from a job could drive someone nuts with distress and make someone else go bananas with delight. When it comes to people's reactions to bad situations, you never know what to expect.

2. Four complexes of painful emotions.

The thirty-six painful emotions noted in the first chapter belong to four different categories of primary emotions: the fear complex, sadness complex, anger complex and guilt complex. Each complex produces a fairly distinct set of stress symptoms. By knowing what stress symptoms he is suffering from, a person will know with a fair degree of accuracy which painful emotions he has in his conscious mind/balloon.

A. The fear complex

Fear and its related painful emotions are at the root of anxiety disorders, such as panic disorder and post-traumatic stress disorder, and psychotic disorders. These painful emotions produce a significant "fight or flight" response when they appear in the conscious mind/balloon. The "fight or flight" response can include emotional tension, anxiety, panic attacks, dizziness, trembling, shortness of breath, hot and cold waves over the body, poor concentration, worry, memory problems, inability to make decisions, sleeplessness, out-of-body experience, nausea, vomiting, diarrhea and muscle tension.

1. Fear is what we feel in response to something perceived as dangerous or offensive. Not only do we fear getting hurt; we also fear losing things that we are attached to emotionally, such as people, jobs, money, power, status, love, respect, etc. We can conquer fear through faith, courage, reassurance and prayer.

2. Terror is what we feel when we face a sudden serious, life-threatening event. Terror is an extreme form of fear. We can face it with fortitude. Terror often spawns heroes.

3. Horror is the shock we feel when we witness a

Bob Kamath, M.D.

frightening and dreadful event or situation. We can face it with outrage and determination to do something about it.

Picture 14: The fear complex and its related stress symptoms.

    4. Insecurity is what we feel when we are in a situation that makes us fear for our physical or emotional safety. The actions of others can also make us feel insecure. In the face of insecurity, listen to your instincts and do whatever you need to do in order to ensure your safety. If you feel insecure because of other people's success, improve your self-esteem.

    5. Envy is a feeling of discontent or resentment over the possessions or accomplishments of others. It is rooted in insecurity. Contentment with what one has dissipates envy.

    6. Jealousy is what we feel when we fear being pushed aside by others, or when we are made to feel insecure because of another person's accomplishments or possessions. It is a sign of extreme insecurity. People with good self-esteem do not feel jealous. Be content with your lot, and be happy for the success and wealth of others.

    7. Dread is what we feel when we are anticipating that something terrible is about to happen. Face it with courage. Ask yourself, "What is the worst that could happen?"

B. The sadness complex

Emotions in the sadness complex play an important role in mood disorders, such as major depression, bipolar disorder and pain disorders. Stress symptoms related to this group are crying, weeping, sobbing and sighing; feeling depressed, helpless, hopeless, worthless, useless, despondent, etc. Pain somewhere in the body for which doctors cannot find a physical cause is invariably due to unexpressed feelings of hurt.

1. Sadness means that one is feeling emotionally down or depressed. Sadness usually follows loss. Sadness is prominent in grief—when we lose someone or something we are extremely fond of. Grieving gets rid of sadness.

2. Hurt means that one's feelings are injured. It is a form of mental pain. Hurt often leads to anger. Solace and forgiveness are antidotes to hurt.

3. Sorrow is the lingering grief we feel when we have lost someone or something we are emotionally attached to. Express it, accept the loss and move on.

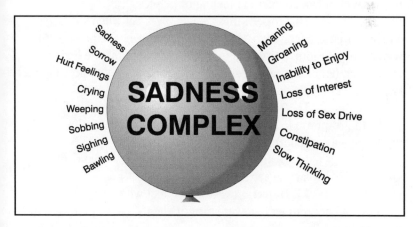

Picture 15: The sadness complex and its related stress symptoms.

4. Despondency is what we feel when we are deeply discouraged or when we experience hopelessness about a situation. Seek spiritual strength. Pray.

5. Uselessness is what we feel when others around us treat us as though what we think, feel and do does not matter at all. Recognize that there is no such thing as a useless person; it is only that your time has not yet come.

6. Powerlessness is what we feel when we have no means of fighting back against a situation we passionately believe to be wrong. Do all you can to empower yourself. Remember, every dog has its day!

7. Disappointment means that we feel let down by a turn of events or by people we trusted. You can overcome this by reducing expectations or demanding better performance.

8. Frustration is what we feel when we are not making headway with a goal despite our best efforts. Patience and persistence can help you deal with this emotion.

9. Helplessness is what we feel when we are completely at the mercy of a dangerous situation or person. A woman being raped at gunpoint is a classic example of helplessness. It is often followed by rage. Taking charge of the situation and doing something to deal with it can counter the feeling of helplessness.

10. Hopelessness is what we feel when we face a situation that is becoming steadily worse, and we have no hope of recovering our loss. For example, if one were told that he had terminal cancer, he might feel hopelessness. Faith and prayer often counter hopelessness.

11. Disgust is the loathing or the sickening feeling we feel in response to an offensive event or situation. Deal with it by walking away, or confront it head on.

12. Despair is what we feel when we have given up all hope. Find solace in action, faith and prayer.

13. Dejection is what we feel when we are disheartened by bad news or a downward turn of events. Don't give up hope. Keep trying.

14. Worthlessness is what we feel when our self-esteem has sunk to rock bottom. This usually follows a series of failures and losses. The feeling of worthlessness can be overcome by reminding yourself that we are all creations of God, and no one is truly worthless. Resolve to rebuild.

C. The anger complex

Some connection appears to exist between emotions in the anger complex and psychotic disorders such as paranoid schizophrenia, delusional disorder and manic psychosis. The painful emotions connected with anger all appeared in the course of the socializing process of primitive man. These emotions are at the root of most behavioral symptoms, such as irritability, snappishness, pacing the floor, wringing the hands, violence, vengefulness, angry outbursts, performing hostile acts, destroying property, committing murder, rape, vandalism and other hostile behaviors. Antisocial individuals are also filled with these symptoms. If you look back over their lives, you will find that they have built up a great deal of anger and rage over many years.

1. Anger means that one experiences sudden, extremely adverse, antagonistic emotions against someone or something. It is an extreme form of displeasure, and it usually follows hurt. Verbalization and forgiveness are antidotes to anger.

2. Hostility is the adverse feeling against those we dislike or hate. Continued hostility often leads to hostile actions. Hostility creates more hostility. Give it up, forgive and move on.

Picture 16: The anger complex and its related stress symptoms.

3. Vengefulness is what we feel when we want to get back at someone whom we perceive as having done us wrong. Leave it to the law or to God to punish those who have hurt you. Vengeful acts invariably land people in trouble of one kind or another.

4. Bitterness is an extremely distasteful feeling one has about a particular incident. It lingers in the mind for years. Counter it by forgiving and letting go. Move on.

5. Resentment is the simmering, low-grade anger one feels toward those he dislikes because of some hurt they have caused him in the past. Forgive, let go and move on.

6. Rage is a sudden and extreme form of anger, in which one is almost out of control. Control yourself before you hurt someone. Walk away. Resort to reasoning.

7. Exasperation is what we feel when we are irritated, annoyed or infuriated by a difficult situation or person. Do something to change the situation.

8. Hate is a powerful emotion of aversion or extreme dislike directed toward someone or something. Hate causes one to avoid the hated person and wish him ill. Hate often leads to violence, and violence leads to serious legal trouble. Hate hurts the person who harbors it for a long time, as it is an extremely toxic emotion. Hate can be overcome with forgiveness, love and spiritual awakening.

D. The guilt complex

The guilt complex, which lies behind every mental conflict, is the gift of civilization. Guilt arises over an action that is forbidden by society, or over an undone action that ought to be done. Some symptoms of the guilt complex are avoiding eye contact; avoiding personal contact; having shifty eyes; expressing remorse, regret and apology; and asking for forgiveness. Overindulgence of children is a sign of unconscious guilt in parents. Guilt-related emotions seem to be connected to severe forms of mood disorders, such as bipolar depression and major depression with psychotic features.

The complete absence of guilt-related emotions makes one an antisocial, criminal or evil person. When such people commit horrible acts against humanity, they suffer no guilt or remorse.

Picture 17: The guilt complex and its related stress symptoms.

1. Guilt is what one feels when he has done something that is not consistent with his own conscience, which is based on the values he has learned from parents, parental figures and society. Guilt makes us downgrade ourselves in our own eyes. People without any guilt become antisocial (primitive) in their behavior. Thieves, rapists, murderers, gangsters, etc. feel no guilt. Guilt is countered with compensation to those we have wronged or by begging for their forgiveness, expressing repentance and remorse, and offering sincere apology.

2. Shame is experienced when those around us whose opinion we value disapprove of our behavior. Shame means we feel downgraded in the eyes of others. (This emotion is fast disappearing in the United States!) Shame is overcome by public exposure and open confession. An alcoholic who feels ashamed can overcome his shame by publicly admitting he is an alcoholic. Immediately, his stock in society will rise.

3. Humiliation occurs when one feels belittled or humbled by another person, usually in the presence of others. Hurt, anger and rage often follow this emotion. Tolerate it with dignity, steadiness of mind and self-confidence.

4. Embarrassment is what we feel when we are

uncomfortable or disconcerted in a life situation, usually a situation that we created. Self-deprecation or humor can help.

5. Remorse is what we feel when we admit to having done something bad that was injurious to others. Apologize for your misdeed and move on.

6. Regret is what we feel when we realize that we have missed an opportunity or done something wrong. Forgive yourself, or ask for forgiveness, and do not make the same mistake again.

7. Sinfulness is what we feel when we have done something that we think is wrong, according to our religious beliefs. Renew your faith, repent, ask for God's forgiveness. Remember, "I say unto you, that likewise joy shall be in heaven over one sinner that repents, more than over ninety and nine just persons who need no repentance." (Luke 15.7)

3. Positive emotions can also cause symptoms of stress.

Joy, happiness, contentment, elation, euphoria, ecstasy and peacefulness are some positive emotions. It should be noted here that even pleasurable emotions cause brain chemicals to change, which results in the appearance of symptoms of stress. For example, when you meet or anticipate meeting someone you are in love with, you can experience flip-flopping of the heart, queasy feelings in the stomach, a quickened heartbeat, a warm feeling all over the body, fainting, swooning, shortness of breath and many other symptoms. Teenage girls jumping up and down and screaming hysterically at the sight or sound of their favorite entertainer are displaying behavioral symptoms of happy emotions. We see people doing this on TV shows such as The Price is Right. We sometimes describe people who demonstrate positive emotions as warm-hearted, and those without them as cold-hearted. In a serious stress disorder known as the manic episode, a person feels elated, ecstatic, euphoric, highly optimistic, grandiose and deliriously happy. Even though the onset of this disorder is triggered by stress, it is as if the conscious mind has suddenly been connected to a special "Joy" file in the hidden mind, and all the person's controls are gone. Unfortunately, buried emotions often disconnect manic people's conscious minds from the "Insight," "Judgment" and "Reasoning" files in the "Wisdom" folder, which results in bad decisions and actions. Almost all people who experience a manic episode fall into the abyss of severe depression once reality dawns on them. Because of this swing from the pole of one extreme mood to the pole of another, such people are referred to as bipolar.

CHAPTER FIVE

Stressors

This chapter deals with stressors: the bad events and life problems that upset us and cause painful emotions to appear in the conscious mind/balloon.

1. Stressors pump painful emotions into the mind.

Stressors are whatever upsets us, making painful emotions appear in the mind and causing the balloon to inflate. There are basically two stressors: bad events and bad problems. Life is full of them. If it's not one thing, it's another. In Chapter One, we chose a bicycle pump to represent life's bad events and problems. When we solve a life problem that has been hounding us, we are, in effect, turning the pump off.

It should be noted here, however, that regardless of how bad a stressor is, some good can come of it in the long run if one learns to deal with it. Wise people are able to make compost out of the garbage life gives them.

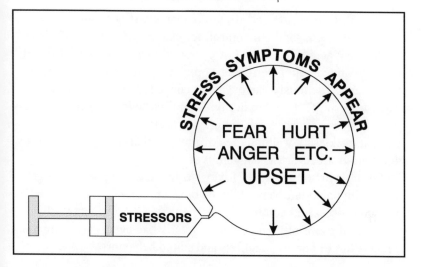

Picture 18: Stressors pump painful emotions into the mind.

2. A bad event is one in which we have lost someone or something.

A. Bad events are one-shot, extremely painful life events: the unexpected death of someone we love, the breakup of a relationship, the betrayal of trust, rape, assault, accident, divorce, loss of a job or money, being told of a terminal illness, and other tragedies. In all the above, we actually lose someone or something we were attached to, whether it is a person, a relationship, money, health, a job, or trust, security, love, respect, power or other sense objects. In bad events, the mind/balloon inflates suddenly and severely with painful emotions, resulting in a sudden increase in emotional tension and the appearance of severe stress symptoms. The proper responses to loss are accepting the loss, grieving over it and moving on with life.

It is worth noting, in passing, the reality that sooner or later we lose everyone we are attached to, through death, breakup or moving away. Life is nothing but a journey in which we lose everything and everyone. Those who learn to accept this reality cope well with the losses they face in daily life. Those who hang onto people and sense objects, unable to let go, suffer severe stress.

B. Bad events are often our own creations. Sometimes, bad events are beyond our control; for example, the death of a loved one in a car accident. Often, however, our own behaviors, based on our convoluted beliefs, erroneous opinions, distorted views and crazy ideas, lead to seriously bad events. A conceited man who drives his car while drunk ("I am not drunk; I can drive safely") is highly likely to be in a serious car wreck, injuring himself or others. A naïve lone woman, recklessly walking the downtown streets at night ("I don't think these streets are as dangerous at night as people claim!") will find trouble in no time at all. Likewise, the loss of a job ("I can get away with being late to work"), the breakup of a relationship ("I want to possess and control my girlfriend"), a car accident ("I like the thrill of speeding!") and other similarly bad events are often the direct result of our own reckless and stupid behaviors.

C. Some phenomena associated with bad events

1. Acute stress. The severe upset that is felt in response to a bad event is called acute stress. A woman who is assaulted or raped is likely to be in a state of acute stress. The balloon inflates suddenly, resulting in severe stress symptoms.

2. Emotional shock. In people who are vulnerable (whose soda bottles are saturated, and whose balloons are already full), certain bad events, such as a life-threatening accident or the sudden death of a beloved person, can cause an extreme type of stress reaction known as emotional shock. In emotional shock, the balloon is suddenly inflated and stretched to an extreme degree. Emotional shock can result in fainting, loss of control of the bladder or bowels, temporary paralysis, heart attack or stroke, curling up in the fetal position, becoming totally numb emotionally, an out-of-body experience or even death. Soldiers who come under tremendous bombardment in war cope with the terror like rabbits hunkering down in a hailstorm. Some of them go into what is called shell shock.

3. Emotional scars and baggage. Painful memories of a bad event or situation deposited in the mind's "Pain" folder can linger for a lifetime, leading to permanent changes in one's behavior. Betrayal by the spouse and consequent divorce can make such a traumatic impact on one's mind that he or she never marries again. Sexual abuse during childhood can cause a woman to dread having sex with her husband. The aftereffect of the traumatic breakup of a relationship in adolescence can forever mar one's future relationships with people of the opposite sex. We can see changed patterns of behavior after trauma at all levels of society. For example, the United States is a very different country today from what it was before September 11, 2001. Every one of us has emotional scars and baggage. They are the distinct warts, scars, lines and wrinkles on our personalities that make us what we truly are.

4. Acute stress often leads to chronic stress. Bad events often lead to bad problems. For example, the death of an elderly parent can lead to a chronic, acrimonious inheritance struggle amongst the surviving children. A bad car accident can lead to serious health, legal and financial problems. An ugly divorce can lead to a bitter and protracted custody battle over the children. The loss of a job can lead to financial and marital problems. A serious medical illness can lead to financial, marital and job problems. Most patients I see in my practice have histories of several bad events, complicated by one or more bad problems arising from them.

A case study. A thirty-five-year-old married man met with a major auto accident, resulting in serious injury to his leg. He had to undergo several surgeries on the leg, and was unable to work for over a year. The disability bruised his ego; the man felt guilty about not being able to work and provide for his family. Bills started piling up. His balloon inflated. He became irritable and hostile toward his wife. His insecurity showed up in his being suspicious of his wife, and he tried to control her movements. Because of their severe financial problems, the family had to move into his parents' house. Soon, friction arose between his wife and his mother. Now the wife began to feel upset, and their ten-year-old son began to have problems at home and at school. Such snowballing problems are common after most bad events.

3. Bad life problems cause chronic stress.

A. We feel trapped in bad problems. Bad life problems

are ongoing problems related to family, job, relationships, finances, health, neighborhood, church, etc. There are no easy solutions for bad life problems. These problems upset us a little bit at a time, day after day, week after week and month after month, and we often feel trapped in them. This type of stress is called chronic stress. Chronic stress guarantees that one will suffer from a stress disorder, as the bad problem (pump) keeps continuously filling the mind/balloon with painful emotions. Sooner or later, because of the relentless inflow of painful emotions, the balloon will pop, resulting in a stress disorder. Chronic marital conflict, a prolonged abusive relationship, ongoing sexual abuse, relentless emotional harassment at home or at work, unending money problems, chronic health problems, the incurable illness of a loved one (such as Alzheimer's disease) are some examples of chronic stress. People trapped in chronic life problems steadily come down with one stress disorder after another as they get older, from the accumulating painful emotions in their minds.

In chronic stress, we have not lost any sense objects as yet, but we are constantly afraid of losing them. For example, in marital problems, one is afraid of losing the love of the spouse; in money problems, one is afraid of losing his security; in a personal conflict with a friend, one is afraid of losing the friend's respect; in health problems, one is afraid of losing everything. This fear of losing someone or something to which we are attached is known as anticipatory grief. The proper response to bad life problems is to search relentlessly for a reasonably acceptable solution and then make the necessary sacrifices to achieve that goal.

B. Bad problems are bad for several reasons. No problem is truly unsolvable. Often, a life problem remains unsolved because we are not able or willing to make the necessary sacrifice of money, time, energy or relationship to solve it.

1. A bad life problem may be genuinely complicated, with no simple solution. Having to take care of a terminally ill or senile parent for years is an example of such a problem ("I just cannot admit my mom to a nursing home").

2. The person who has it is not aware that there is a problem ("We have a good marriage, even though we have not been

intimate in over three years"). This person is in denial.

     3. The person does not have the skill to solve it ("I don't know how to deal with my abusive boss").

     4. The person does not want to make the necessary sacrifice to solve it ("I cannot just walk away from my rightful inheritance"); or the person does not want to spend money on professionals who could solve it for him ("I can't spend that kind of money on lawyers"); or the person does not want to risk losing a relationship ("I just don't want to hurt his feelings").

     5. Lack of money prevents one from dealing with it (such as in the case of a health or legal problem).

     6. None of the available solutions is acceptable ("I'm damned if I do and damned if I don't").

     The vast majority of suicides in the U. S. are due to people's feeling trapped in a hopeless life situation—bad health, marital problems, family problems, financial problems, etc.—from which they find no escape. A dependent woman who feels trapped in a bad marriage to a brute she hates is one such example; a rich married man being blackmailed by his mistress is another.

     C. Bad life problems are often rooted in our own personality weaknesses. More often than not, bad problems are our own creations. Our deep-rooted personality weaknesses—greed, jealousy, hate, lust, insecurity, arrogance and possessiveness—and the patterns of behavior rooted in them are the cause of most of our bad problems. These traits were essential tools for survival for primitive man, in the dog-eat-dog environment of the African wilderness. However, civilized society considers these relics of our past to be evil traits. Invariably, behaviors rooted in these traits get people into one seriously stressful problem or another. For example, an insecure man might buy a big house and an expensive car to compensate for his insecurity, and consequently get into serious financial problems. A dependent and insecure woman might marry a rich alcoholic, and consequently suffer lifelong abuse at his hands. A greedy person, suspending his judgment, might get involved in a bad business venture conjured up by a con artist. Behind every life problem, whether in one's marriage,

Bob Kamath, M.D.

job, relationship, health or money, we can find the influence of one or more personality weaknesses.

People with strong spiritual values (and here I am not referring to religious fanatics) do not easily become trapped in bad life problems, because they keep their personality weaknesses under control by adopting a set of moral codes. Wisdom, not their personality weaknesses, guides their behavior.

4. Conflicts are potent sources of stress.

A. Interpersonal conflicts. Conflict with those around us is known as interpersonal conflict. The main reason for almost all interpersonal conflicts, whether between two people, two cultures, two religions or two nations, is that one side attempts to impose its will on the other. This is, by far, the most common of the conflicts that contribute to our daily stress. Conflict between parents and children, between the partners in a couple, between in-laws, friends, colleagues, employer and employee, etc. are in this category. Conflicts such as these result in anger, hate, fear, sadness, vengefulness and other powerful emotions. People with personality disorders experience more interpersonal conflicts than others do, because of their lack of "people skills."

B. Internal or mental conflicts. Conflict inside one's own mind, also known as mental conflict, results from the conscious mind's colliding with the hidden mind, resulting in such emotions as guilt, shame, self-directed anger, sadness and self-loathing. Invariably, the balloon inflates and severe stress symptoms appear. In mental conflicts, the conscious mind badly desires to do something that the hidden mind considers wrong. The personality weakness tells the conscious mind, "Go for it! You can get away with it." Wisdom says, "Don't do it, stupid! It is unethical and illegal." People with these kinds of conflicts often make such statements as, "I feel bad that I do such-and-such a thing, which I know I shouldn't do." After they have done it, they are full of remorse. We often erroneously refer to such people as split personalities, or Dr. Jekyll and Mr. Hyde. With mental conflicts, one feels like a yo-yo. People often express this dilemma by the overused phrases, "I feel confused" and "I have mixed feelings about it." We can easily identify people who have mental conflicts: their desires and actions are inconsistent with their core beliefs and moral values—and they constantly feel bad about it. A conflicted person is a person divided against himself.

A case study: A fifty-two-year-old woman lost her husband of thirty years, after a protracted illness. Their marriage had been more or less barren because of the husband's chronic sickness. The woman had been raised by strict parents, who planted strong moral values in her mind. After her husband's death, several younger men propositioned her. For once, she became aware that she had wasted most of her adult life, and she began to have highly enjoyable sexual relationships with these men, as though to compensate for lost time. However, after each encounter she felt guilty and sinful, and she often thought she was being a slut. In the course of one therapy session, she accepted the fact that she was entitled to some happiness in life. It was recommended that she pick only one of the men and have a steady relationship with him, to avoid feeling like a slut. She accepted this "take the middle course" advice, and resolved her mental conflict.

Another type of mental conflict is one in which a person does not do what he is supposed to do. In this case, the person's wisdom keeps reminding him that he is supposed to do the thing he is not doing, either because his conscious mind cannot do it or because it rebels against doing it. A penniless father who feels guilty for not paying child support is an example of this kind of conflict. Of course, deadbeat dads feel no guilt at all, as they are all primitive-minded people without any conscience.

5. "Good events" can also cause stress

When asked if they have any stress in their lives, many people say, "The only stress I have in my life now is good stress." Most people define good stress as a happy event or situation that puts some extra emotional, physical or financial burden on them: the birth of a baby, a promotion at work, passing an examination, a child's graduating from school, passing a medical examination with flying colors, etc. At first glance, these are wonderful things to happen to anyone. However, the birth of a baby can be stressful because of the additional expense, the loss of the wife's income, and the like. A promotion at work might mean more responsibility, more work, longer working hours and less time with the family. Passing an examination might mean one's having to search for a job and give up his dependence on his parents. A child's leaving home for college could cause the so-called empty nest syndrome in his parents, whose main focus in life thus far has been the child; now they must face issues between them that have never been addressed. A clean bill of health from a doctor could make one pass out in fear if he has been claiming ill health and collecting disability checks every month. So, to assess their real impact, we must look at the side effects that the so-called good stressors have on one's current life situation..

Sometimes, a happy event such as a second marriage can bring up buried emotions related to the previous marriage, causing serious stress. Childbirth can bring up buried issues related to one's own parents, again resulting in serious stress. We will study this phenomenon in a future chapter.

6. Success can be stressful.

Success in life brings fame and fortune. Success can go to one's head, causing the activation of various personality weaknesses in the hidden mind: greed, lust, haughtiness, jealousy, insecurity, possessiveness and hate. These deep-rooted primitive traits are so powerful that they invariably overrule a person's wisdom, so that he begins to act evil or stupid. One thing leads to another, and soon he is behind bars. CEOs of multi-billion-dollar companies who are now rotting in prison are classic examples of success gone awry.

Many people who secretly believe that they are unworthy become extremely stressed when they achieve success, and sabotage themselves by getting involved with drugs, alcohol, promiscuous sex, excessive spending and the like. We see examples of this among movie stars, politicians, athletes and entertainers. Michael Jackson and Elvis Presley are but two of thousands of talented and successful people we have heard about who lost their mental balance after achieving success. Such people can lose not only their heads, but also their fame and fortune; many have been disgraced beyond repair. The vast majority of lottery winners screw up their lives within one year after collecting their money. Some even become street people.

7. Women experience more stress than men do—because of men.

Women are six times more likely to suffer stress than men are. Why? Well, because of men. Starting in early childhood and lasting until late in life, women suffer sexual, emotional and physical abuse at the hands of the men they encounter: fathers, stepfathers, mothers' boyfriends, uncles, brothers-in-law, brothers, half-brothers, stepbrothers, teachers, coaches, trainers, boyfriends, ex-boyfriends, husbands, ex-husbands, doctors, pastors, preachers, therapists, stalkers, strangers, neighbors and pimps—you name it! As a man, this makes me want to hang my head in shame. Women fall prey to the lust, anger, rage and violence of men who are obviously functioning in the "primitive mind" mode. In the U.S., thousands of women are murdered in cold blood every year by men, usually boyfriends, ex-husbands or rapists, because they are seen as weak and easy targets and sex objects. We live in a male-dominated society, not much different in this way from the primitive societies of a million years ago. Most men have little awareness of their own contribution to this national tragedy and disgrace. The thousands of safe houses mushrooming around the nation stand as monuments to man's inhumanity to women.

Men are bad for women's mental and emotional health. Almost all women I see for stress disorders are experiencing marital strain. Conversely, women who have strong marriages develop immunity to stress. A loving husband's non-critical support, availability to listen, helpfulness in solving problems and his just being there when needed gives a woman immense immunity against stress. Some women whom I have seen for many years for the treatment of depression or anxiety suddenly become "cured" of their disorders immediately after their husbands die. This is the hard reality every man should know.

8. Abusive relationships are stressful, but extremely hard to break.

There are millions of women in the United States who are currently trapped in abusive relationships with primitive-minded men. They silently suffer routine physical, emotional and sexual abuse at the hands of brutes, whom these women identify as boy-friends, husbands, ex-husbands, uncles, stepfathers, fathers or pimps. Most abused women develop stress disorders sooner or later, even though they are willing partners in this tragedy. It must be under-stood that these abusive relationships are based on a complex system in which the women's socially sponsored weaknesses (insecurity, low self-esteem, helplessness, need for love, etc.) perfectly match their partners' primitive instincts (sexual, aggressive and territorial). These couples develop deep, sick bonds with each other, as they meet each others' deepest emotional needs to abuse and be abused. One should recognize the truth in the Eurhythmics song that says, "Somebody wants to abuse you, somebody wants to be abused!"

Most women in abusive relationships are intelligent, but their conscious minds are disconnected from their wisdom. They are so hungry for a little bit of love, attention or praise that they will tolerate any abuse to get it. We can see examples of abused women even amongst famous entertainers, such as Whitney Houston and Tina Turner, just to mention two. In fact, abused women are un-comfortable with men who treat them like ladies. Their toleration of abusive behavior is based on one or more of dozens of deep-rooted, faulty beliefs, some of which I list here: "I'm not worth crap," "I feel that I'm worth something when a man cares enough to slap me around," "I will suffer any abuse if I can get even a little bit of love and attention," "I am so insecure that I feel secure only when I'm with a brute," "When I let him abuse me, I have him hooked," "All men abuse their wives," "Men who don't know how to handle (beat up) women are not real men," and "I am nothing unless I have a man desiring me passionately." This list of sick beliefs is unending.

Sometimes, the abuse is mutual. This can result in serious injury to one or both parties. Such people have not outgrown the animal instinct to fight before they mate. This is a sick but pathologi-cally stable relationship. Of the hundreds of abusive relationships that I have dealt with, one stands out.

A case study: I was once asked to see a badly battered woman who had been hospitalized for serious facial and bodily wounds. She lay in bed, looking terribly ill, as though she had been punched, kicked and beaten severely. As I talked with her, I felt my balloon inflating with rage against the man who had perpetrated such brutality on this hapless woman. I fantasized about beating him up if I ever saw him, just to teach him what it felt like to be battered.

Just then, a burly man in a black leather jacket entered the room and introduced himself as her boyfriend. He was all tattoos, rings and other macho paraphernalia—a perfect example of primitive man living amidst us. He instinctively knew how I felt about the patient's pathetic appearance. Without asking him any questions, I said, "I think you people better split up before you murder her." At this, the man took off his jacket and started unbuttoning his shirt as though he were getting ready to fight with me. As I was preparing myself to be beaten to a pulp, he removed his shirt and politely showed me numerous bullet wounds, long, broad scars and burn marks all over his chest and back. Pointing at these with his hand, he said impassively, "Do you see these wounds? She did them to me!" Shocked, I turned my face to the woman in bed. What I saw shocked me even more. The battered woman was giggling and laughing uncontrollably under the blanket that she had by now pulled over her head! Such is the depth to which human depravity can descend. A week after she was discharged from the hospital, I saw them walking hand in hand at the local mall.

9. Stressors are essential for normal maturation.

Are stressors bad for our health? Well, in small to moderate doses, the painful emotions caused by stressors are useful for normal emotional growth and maturation, just as a small dose of fertilizer is essential for plants to grow to their full potential. In large doses, however, these emotions can become toxic and damage the normal growth and maturation of people, just as a large dose of fertilizer can ruin the health of a lush green indoor plant. This is especially true if these emotions are mishandled. A sixteen-year-old boy involved in a

Bob Kamath, M.D.

fender-bender can benefit from his scary experience and learn to be a better driver. On the other hand, a total wreck involving the loss of several lives can leave permanent emotional scars in the same sixteen-year-old, resulting in lifelong suffering, especially if he does not deal with the tragedy promptly and appropriately. Likewise, the fear of failing an examination can make us study harder and learn more; a healthy fear of the law is essential for one to become a law-abiding citizen; and a little bit of financial insecurity can make one work harder to succeed. In fact, a moderate amount of sustained stress often leads to creativity, and sometimes to genius.

Pampered children who have been protected from everyday life stressors are often ill-equipped to face life's problems. A tree that has been watered and fertilized regularly might look healthy, but might be unable to withstand even a mild thunderstorm because of its small, balled root system, which fails to anchor it firmly in the soil (see picture 19). Another tree, not so fussed over, might withstand even a great storm because of its extensive root system, necessitated by the self-motivated search for nourishment.

Picture 19: A pampered tree does not stand a chance in a storm

10. Who is more vulnerable to stress?

Here are a few reasons why some people experience more stress than others do:

1. The person's bicycle pump is working overtime. In other words, he has been hit by *too many bad events and problems* all at once, such as the death of a loved one, the loss of a job, and an accident. The person in this unfortunate predicament can fall apart under the weight of multiple stressors. His balloon can pop at any time, even if the hidden mind is not saturated.

2. People who are temperamentally *high-strung* or tense often overreact to bad events. They are like thin-skinned balloons, which inflate easily and pop easily. They cannot hold much pressure.

3. People who are *overly sensitive* to rejection, criticism and loss as a result of severe childhood trauma, such as abandonment or abuse, also overreact when they face loss or the threat of loss. They often develop negative attitudes and hang-ups, owing to their bad experiences. Their balloons were thick at one time, but have now become thin-skinned. A young man sensitized in childhood by parental divorce can be overly sensitive to a breakup with his girlfriend.

4. People who have *poor support systems*, or no relatives or friends to turn to, can feel totally lost in difficult times. They have no loved ones to see them through, no one to talk to, no one to help in times of trouble and sickness. No hands are wrapped around the balloon to protect it.

5. People who are *entangled*—excessively attached to and possessive of people, money, material things, etc.—suffer more severe stress when they lose these sense objects than do people who are less attached. Such people live constantly in fear of loss. Entangled people are not able to let go or walk away from the objects they are entangled with. They are trapped.

6. People whose actions are strongly under the influence of personality weaknesses in the hidden mind, such as greed, insecurity, selfishness, jealousy, arrogance, possessiveness and hatefulness, indulge in behaviors that lead to self-inflicted problems and

stress.

7. People who are *unaware* by nature cannot easily be transformed into people who are aware. An unaware person is unable to tune into the cues he receives from people around him or from within himself. So, when the axe falls, he is caught unawares. If he becomes more aware, he looks back at all those missed cues and says, "How could I have been so blind!" If one is smart, he learns fast from his past mistakes and becomes aware. Otherwise, he keeps making the same mistakes, and consequently becomes stressed out.

8. People who are unable to cancel out painful emotions from the conscious mind, because of a *lack of spiritual values* or wisdom (perhaps owing to a rebellious attitude against their parents while growing up), develop stress from continuing to live with those painful emotions. For example, a person who grew up without learning the virtue of forgiveness might be unable to forgive someone who has offended him. He continues to feel anger and hate inside his mind, to his own detriment.

9. People who are *naïve*, as a result of a lack of knowledge and experience, are often the victims of other people's greed and lust. Such people's "Knowledge" files have no information to protect them from being preyed upon by con artists.

10. People with *poor problem-solving skills* do not have the "How to Do" file in their hidden minds. They let their life problems brew for months and years, resulting in the mind/balloon's gradually inflating with painful emotions.

11. People who have *low self-esteem*, because of severe parental control, criticism and punishment, have the mantra, "I'm no good. I don't deserve anything. What difference does it make if I ruin my life?" Their lack of self-worth leads to self-destructive activities and often results in their buying big-ticket items to compensate for their low self-esteem.

12. People with *negative attitudes* and hang-ups have had many bad experiences in life, as a result of which they are pessimistic, negative, cynical and skeptical. Because of these attitudes, they become upset more easily than those who are more positive in outlook.

13. People with overfilled "Pain" folders have been

through many, many *traumatic life experiences*, and consequently have accumulated an enormous number of painful emotions. Their shock-absorbing systems are gone. After the "Pain" folder is filled up, the excess pain enters the balloon, causing stress symptoms. These painful emotions might also spew into the mind/balloon if they are triggered by a new traumatic event (double whammy).

14. People who have grown up *without adequate parental nurturance*—love, empathy, kindness, warmth and support—keep trying to get this support from others. They indulge in attention-seeking behavior (ASB); or their unmet need and craving for love, kindness, etc. can suddenly resurface in their mid-thirties or mid-forties, resulting in the "midlife crisis." This can lead to breakup and divorce.

15. Many people harbor blatantly stupid, *erroneous beliefs* about expressing emotion ("It's a sign of weakness," "I can't talk bad about my dead mom, because she's not here to defend herself," "I don't want to give my husband the satisfaction of seeing me cry"). Such people become stressed as a direct result of their own beliefs.

16. Anger and guilt can block grief. People who are harboring anger or guilt regarding a dead person *will not be able to complete the grieving process.* We will study this in some detail in the next chapter.

17. People who have an innate *inability to express emotion* are simply unable to get in touch with their inner pain and thus let it out. Most of these people were severely traumatized as children, and their only defense against the pain was to completely disconnect their minds from experiencing or expressing any painful emotion.

CHAPTER SIX

Bonds, Loss and Grief

I n the previous chapter, we saw how bad events result in loss, and bad problems result in fear of the loss of the sense objects that we are attached to. Every depressed and anxious patient has been through numerous losses and/or threatened losses, which he has not dealt with or handled properly. The reaction to loss is known as *grieving*. Learning how to deal appropriately with loss and the fear of loss is fundamental to coping with stress.

In the chapter dealing with human evolution, we read that grieving became hardwired into primitive social man as the second fundamental coping mechanism, and that the process of civilization curbed the free expression of emotion. Over the past five thousand years, man has acquired an increasing number of sense objects for his survival, security, comfort and happiness, and he has become increasingly *entangled* with these objects. We see examples of mindless entanglement all around us. For example, in order to be the first to buy the most recently released electronic toy, some people are willing to camp outside a department store in the bitter cold over a week before the sale begins. Another example of entanglement might be a snob who loses sleep because he doesn't own a 24,000-square-foot house, when a 2,400-square-foot house will do just as well.

Modern man faces the *double jeopardy* of more losses and less ability to grieve over them. Since we have developed into a highly industrialized society, people experience more painful emotions than ever before due to breakup, divorce, betrayal, abandonment, death, business failure and financial loss. It has become more urgent than ever that we learn to grieve over our losses. Let us now become familiar with some elements of grief.

1. Sense objects.

Sense objects are what we perceive by means of the five sense organs—the eye, ear, nose, tongue and skin. Some *tangible* sense objects are people (relatives and friends), money, house, car, property, pets and other things, which give us a sense of physical and emotional security. Some *intangible* sense objects are honor, fame, security, liberty, power, title, position, success, praise, respect, status, fame, love and other things, which boost our status in society. Our emotional attachments to these sense objects are known as bonds.

As we have evolved, we have come to identify these objects as essential for our survival, security, comfort, convenience and happiness. Nowadays, man keeps adding more objects to his inventory just for the pleasure of owning them, rather than for their practical value. Accumulating money has become an end in itself, rather than a means of survival and comfort.

2. Attachment can become entanglement.

By necessity, we are all emotionally attached to various sense objects to a greater or lesser degree. In general, our attachments to sense objects decrease as we become older and wiser. However, some people are excessively attached to sense objects and increasingly possessive of them. This is known as entanglement. We are said to be *entangled* with sense objects when 1) we hanker for them constantly; 2) we become possessive of them once we have them; 3) we have a hard time giving them up or walking away from them; 4) we feel miserable if we don't have them; and 5) we try to control them.

Entangled people take on other people's problems and become upset over them. They give unsolicited advice, interfere in others' affairs and try to impose their views on people. A mother who becomes entangled in her daughter's marital problems is an example. I have lost count of the people who indulge in stupid behaviors because of their entanglement with parents, in-laws, children, grandchildren or great-grandchildren. Entanglement disconnects people's minds from their reasoning, judgment and insight. We have all heard of people who are labeled co-dependent, overprotective, enablers, control freaks, manipulators and the like. Many of them harbor deep-rooted guilt about something they have done or not done in their relationships with the people they are entangled with. Such people are highly vulnerable to stress, because they constantly live in fear of losing those with whom they are entangled, and they are bound to be disappointed, hurt and shocked by the hostility, hate and rebellious behavior of these people. Here the reader might want to take note of the fact that all dependent relationships are hostile in nature.

A case study: A forty-five-year-old woman was extremely entangled with her twenty-two-year-old daughter. The woman carried deep-rooted guilt that, because of postpartum depression, she was "not there for her daughter" when she was born. Not only did she cater to her daughter excessively and spoil her, to compensate for her perceived lapse, but she also became extremely controlling. To disentangle herself from her control-freak mother, the daughter rebelled, misbehaved, and got into one serious auto accident after another. The mother's refusal and inability to let go of her daughter led to a serious bout of depression, which became worse over the years, requiring several drugs to control the symptoms.

Later we will read about how entanglement with money, power, fame, title, etc. disconnects one's mind from his wisdom (judgment, reasoning, insight, moral values and virtues), leading to stupid and evil behaviors. We see innumerable examples of this in people in leadership positions in public life. These people are all good candidates for stress disorders.

3. The nature of bonds, or attachments.

The "Bonds" folder in the hidden mind holds memories of our association with sense objects throughout our lives. There are two types of bonds.

A. Positive bonds. When the emotions related to our associations with sense objects are good (love, joy, happiness), we have positive bonds (+). The more positive bonds there are between two people, the closer they feel to each other. Positive bonds have a relatively short life, and they must be renewed constantly for one to remain bonded to the object in question. Positive bonds are created between people when they experience good times together. Young people of opposite sexes form positive bonds when they enjoy doing things together, such as eating, going to the movies, walking, sleeping, kissing and making love. Their desire to create more bonds between them leads to their getting married. A couple that does not constantly renew its positive bonds by continuing to do these things together grows apart, because the bonds holding them weaken and, after a while, die. Middle-aged couples who have grown apart are those who, for whatever reason, did not renew their bonds often enough.

B. Negative bonds. When the emotions related to our associations with sense objects are bad (anger, guilt, sadness), we have negative bonds (-). The more negative bonds there are between two people, the more they feel apart from each other. Negative bonds die very slowly. A person will remember an unkind word a lot longer than a kind word uttered a hundred times over. One negative bond can destroy many positive bonds. For example, one single act of unkindness on my part could destroy my long-standing positive relationship with a patient. Many couples are driven apart by negative bonds created by arguments, fights, bickering and feuding. Separation and divorce naturally follow. Sometimes this process can be one-sided, with one spouse completely clueless. I have seen countless men and women who were shocked to find out that their spouses wanted out of their marriage when they thought everything was hunky-dory.

A case study: A middle-aged man held two jobs. To make more money, he became involved in another side business and appointed his wife to run it. They found little time to be together, and what little time they had was marred by his complaining that she was ignorant of the business she was running for him. He was clueless as to what his wife thought and felt about their relationship, and so obsessed with making money that he lost all sense of his priorities. One fine morning, his wife told him that she was not in love with him any more and wanted out of the marriage. He was completely baffled and devastated by this declaration. Over the years, unbeknown to him, his wife had reduced her bonds with him to the point that he had become a mere acquaintance. Furthermore, she had accumulated many negative bonds, which effectively canceled out the few positive ones that remained between them. She had found another man to attach her bonds to—a man who paid more attention to her emotional and physical needs. By the time her husband realized his mistake, it was too late. I often tell my clients, "Every person has two jobs: his or her regular job, and his or her spouse."

The secret of any good relationship is to do and say things that you know make the other person happy (create positive bonds) and not to do or say things that you know make the other person unhappy (avoid creating negative bonds).

C. The six levels of bonding. Six levels of bonding are possible between any two people, and their level of bonding can be elevated or lowered. To elevate the level, the people must add positive bonds by doing enjoyable things together. To lower the level of bonding, they must reduce the frequency and intensity of their interaction. This might result in some grieving, but time will usually heal the loss, as positive bonds are short-lived in any case.

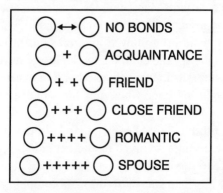

Picture 20: The six levels of bonding.

Level 1: Total strangers. There are no bonds between strangers. When you hear or read about the death of a person you do not know, you are not going to grieve. Bonds: zero.

Level 2: Acquaintances. These people know each other, but they have no close ties. Bonds: one +. If you lose this person, you might feel a little sadness.

Level 3: Friends. These people know each other well. They have been through many events together. They like to be with each other. Bonds: two +. If you lose this person, you will grieve quite a bit.

Level 4: Close friends. They have shared many pleasant and neutral events together. They like each other very much, are comfortable together and are willing to share their intimate feelings with each other. Bonds: three +. If you lose this person, you will grieve a great deal.

Level 5: Romantic friends. These people are in love. They think of each other almost all the time. When one thinks of the other, his heart might skip a beat, his stomach might feel a squeeze or he might sigh a lot. Bonds: four +. If you lose this person through death, breakup or moving to a different location, you can suffer severe grief.

Level 6: Spouses (or significant others). Their bonds are strengthened by their lifelong commitment to each other. They are very close, unless of course they have also created a lot of negative bonds. They share many happy memories. As children come along, the bonds are strengthened and multiplied. Bonds: five +. The loss of this person causes an extreme degree of stress to the survivor. (This type of relationship can occur between gays and lesbians also. The bonds between gays and lesbians are often stronger than in a heterosexual couple, and hence they can experience more grief upon the loss of the relationship.)

4. Grief means becoming upset over the loss of a sense object.

A. Understanding grief is fundamental to learning to cope. We must face the reality that we will lose everyone we are attached to through death, breakup or moving to a different location. Life is nothing but an exercise in facing one loss after another, and learning to overcome the fear of losing one thing or another. We are all on an escalator that slowly carries us through life. On this escalator of life, some people are ahead of us and others are behind us. When our time comes, we step off and take the final dive into the mysterious sea known as death.

We lose people we love when we experience a bad event such as death, divorce, breakup or accident. Our natural reaction is to grieve over the loss and move on. In grief, we pine for the object we have lost. The intensity of grief depends on the level of attachment to the lost person. People who are excessively attached to the person they have lost experience more grief than those who are less attached. People who are entangled with the lost person are often inconsolable.

A case study: A middle-aged woman was devastated by the suicide death of her only son, whom she had been extremely attached to. While raising him, she smothered him with excessive love and spoiled him rotten. Her grief over his loss was so great that, twenty years after his death, she was still grieving and visiting his grave on a daily basis. She just could not come to terms with his death.

The loss does not have to be complete for us to suffer grief. When we reduce the level of a relationship, we grieve. When we are demoted from a job, we grieve. When our car is dented and it no longer looks new, we grieve. In each of these cases, the level of bonding with a particular sense object is reduced.

In bad life problems, we have not lost any sense objects yet, but we are worried about losing them. We are said to be going through anticipatory grief.

It should be noted here that a spiritually enlightened person is not entangled with sense objects. He does not feel the need to grieve, because he has reduced his bonds or attachments with sense objects to such a low level that he does not experience pain when he loses them. This enlightened person has come to terms with the impermanence of life and all sense objects. He has disentangled himself from their clutches, while fully enjoying them within the framework of his wisdom.

B. The mechanism of grief. The realization of the loss of a person we love leads to the breaking down of bonds (pleasant memories) in the hidden mind/soda bottle. Memories of the lost person come up into the conscious mind/balloon from the hidden mind/soda bottle. When the conscious mind realizes that the person is lost for good, it becomes upset and experiences hurt, sorrow and sadness. The balloon inflates, chemical changes take place in the brain and we experience severe physical, emotional, mental and behavioral stress symptoms. Depending upon the level of bonding, we might experience chest pain, fullness in the chest, stomach pain, vomiting, intense sadness, etc. The conscious mind misses the lost person and wishes him back. When we release these emotions through acknowledging the loss, remembering past associations with the person, talking, crying, sobbing, sighing, bawling, moaning, groaning and other gestures, we are said to be grieving. The greater the level of bonding, the more one grieves over the loss. After we have released all the painful emotions from the conscious mind, the balloon shrinks, the brain chemicals go back to their earlier state and, gradually, we calm down. Pleasant memories of the lost person sans grief return to the hidden mind. Having completed the grieving and accepted the loss, we adjust to the new reality and move on. Then we try to build a new life by filling the void with other sense objects. The entire grieving process might last from six months to over several years. The main goal of grieving is to rid the mind of painful emotions and shrink the balloon.

C. Six types of grief reactions
    1. Uncomplicated grief. The case study described above is an example of uncomplicated grief: a mother grieving over the death of her teenaged son in an auto accident. In this type of grief, we experience painful emotions primarily belonging to the sadness complex: sadness, hurt, sorrow, despair, dejection, etc.

Bob Kamath, M.D.

2. Complicated grief. In this type of grief, one has lost a person with whom he had a love/hate relationship (both negative and positive bonds). The negative bonds were related to some very bad experiences, which resulted in anger, guilt, vengefulness, rage, shame, fear, etc. When painful emotions related to the fear, anger and guilt complexes appear in the grieving mind, they block the expression of grief-related emotions, so the balloon stays full and stress symptoms remain for a long time. After a while, the symptoms are buried in the soda bottle. By occupying space in the hidden mind/bottle, they set the stage for future depression; or they can resurface later, say, during the first anniversary of the death or following another death, precipitating a bout of depression (double whammy). The phenomenon of anger blocking the flow of grief and resulting in depression has often been misrepresented by the description, "Depression is anger turned inwards." This is total nonsense.

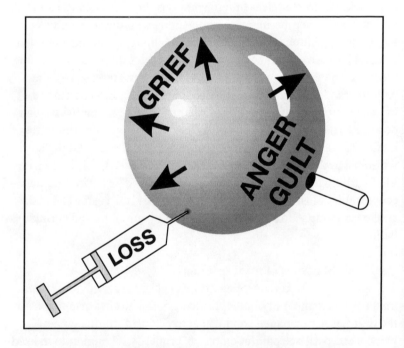

Picture 21: Anger and guilt can block the grief process.

A case study: A middle-aged man had a love/hate relationship with his rich mother, especially a few years before her death. He was angry at her for refusing to bail him out from his various business misadventures. When she died, he found out that she had willed her entire estate to her wise daughter. The son became extremely angry at both his mother and sister. At the funeral, he fumed rather than grieved. Soon, he was down with many stress symptoms, including irritability, angry outbursts, sadness and sleepiness. Gradually, he felt better, as the grief and anger became buried in his hidden mind. However, on the first anniversary of his mother's death, the grief and anger resurfaced and popped his balloon, resulting in a major depressive episode. Only after he got rid of his anger in therapy was he was able to complete the grieving process. He realized that, all in all, he had had a good mother, even though she had refused to cater to his unreasonable demands.

3. Grief related to betrayal or infidelity. In this case, one has not lost a person to death but has nevertheless lost trust in that person, and the relationship will never be the same. To the vast majority of betrayed spouses, the infidelity is even more painful than death. In a spouse's death, one grieves over the loss and moves on. In betrayal by a spouse, one must live with that person while harboring anger, rage, hate, resentment and other emotions in the anger complex, side by side with those in the sadness complex, with no end in sight. Since trust has gone out the window, whatever the betrayer says carries little weight. Many betrayed spouses break up with their spouse, grieve over the loss and move on with their lives. This is their way of solving the problem (turning the pump off). Others, weighed down by lifelong commitments related to money, house and children, stay on, becoming steadily sicker and sicker as their balloons inflate, month after month. Rebuilding such a relationship is mighty difficult.

In cases in which a man has betrayed a woman, I try to solace the betrayed spouse by explaining the evolutionary nature of the man's need to have sex with more people than one and the woman's need for security, love and appreciation. ("Men are after sex and women are after security.") In certain circumstances, the internalized societal prohibition ("thou shall not") breaks down, and people stray.

If the man or woman returns to his civilized self, offers a sincere apology, asks for forgiveness and promises never to stray again, he or she should be forgiven. Forgiveness is the ultimate virtue of the civilized person, and one can find the ability to forgive by resorting to one's spiritual roots. To continue hating the remorseful spouse is damaging to the person who harbors hate in his or her heart. It takes a great deal of spiritual strength to heal from these wounds, and often prolonged individual or marital therapy as well. The key to recovery is to link the mind up with the "Noble Virtues" file in its "Wisdom" folder.

When the betrayed spouse is a man, in addition to feeling angry, sad and hurt, he feels insecure in his masculinity. This leads to his reasserting his manhood by being overly aggressive or vengeful toward his wife. In such cases, repeated physical and/or verbal attacks are common. Men do not realize that by behaving in this manner, they are further alienating their spouses. Their anger has disconnected them from the "Reasoning" file in the hidden mind. If the betrayed man was traumatized when he was a boy by being abandoned by a significant person, his wife's betrayal can bring up the buried painful emotions with such fury that he will commit murder, suicide or both. Most homicide/suicides are committed by men who are unable to handle rejection and betrayal.

A case study: A thirty-year-old man became intensely agitated when his wife told him she wanted some space. Her behavior seemed more and more strange to him. Unable to figure out what was going on, he became anxious and depressed. He was admitted to a psychiatric hospital, where his history revealed that his mother had abandoned him when he was five years old. In the hospital, in the course of couples' therapy, the wife confessed to him that she was having an extramarital affair. Suddenly, it all made sense to the man. He said he felt better knowing the truth, and asked to be discharged from the hospital. The next morning, his wife called me to report that he had shot himself to death.

4. Anticipatory grief. This type of grief occurs when we are afraid of losing someone or something to which we are attached. When the object is a person, one anticipates losing the loved one through death, breakup or a move to a new location. If one has a terminally ill parent, spouse or child, and the dying person has been ill for a long time, one's grief can also be prolonged. The stress of watching someone die slowly, day after day, causes one's balloon to inflate gradually. This type of "slow-motion grief" can go on for months, or even years, and can be mistaken for depression. The problem with anticipatory grief is that the dying person is still alive, which makes it difficult to grieve for him. One keeps hoping that he will get better, and the hope interferes with the grieving. In this case, one suffers from many stress symptoms related to grief: crying, weepiness, sleeplessness, loss of appetite and the like.

A case study: A sixty-one-year-old woman complained of depression related to her eighty-year-old mother's terminal illness. The woman was an only child, and had been very close to her mother all her life, as she had lost her father at an early age. Two years before coming to see me, she had had a tiff with her mother, which upset the mother a great deal. For the first time in both their lives, some tension existed between them. Even though my patient felt that, in this conflict, she was right and her mother was wrong, she felt great guilt for hurting her mother so badly and more or less ruining their wonderful, long-standing relationship. This guilt seemed to have interfered with the anticipatory grief process, which had already been set in motion. The woman was at a loss as to what to do. I told her that she should set aside her self-righteousness, apologize to her mother and, without justifying her own behavior, sincerely ask for her forgiveness before she died. Otherwise, she might suffer even more guilt after her mother's death. Ridding her balloon of guilt would let the built-up grief-related emotions flow, and the balloon would shrink.

We see this type of complicated anticipatory grief reaction when one is fearful of losing something like his job, land or money.

5. Grieving over a breakup or divorce. One can have grief symptoms when a loved one becomes estranged and wishes to break up. In this scenario, in addition to experiencing anticipatory grief, there may also be hurt, anger, guilt and rage, which complicate the grief process. Divorce is extremely difficult for the rejected spouse to handle. On the one hand, he or she is angry and hateful at the spouse who wants the divorce. On the other hand, he

Bob Kamath, M.D.

or she wants the spouse to remain in the marriage. The abandoned spouse keeps pining for the spouse who has left the marriage. Denial ("He didn't mean what he said; I don't think he really wants to leave me") and hope ("I think she'll come around and we'll make it") interfere with the grieving process. Some rejected spouses rationalize by saying, "I think my spouse is depressed." The grieving process begins when the rejected spouse vents his or her anger, hate and guilt verbally; then he or she can renounce vengeance, accept the reality that the marriage is dead, and grieve over the loss of the spouse as well as the loss of the marriage. After grieving is over, the liberated spouse can move on with life.

A case study: A middle-aged man with a strong controlling streak (he must have been very insecure in his masculinity) was told by his wife of twenty years that she wanted out of the marriage. He was devastated by this news, and also became terribly angry at his wife. He felt humiliated that, in spite of his repeated pleading, she refused to remain in the marriage. He came to me to seek help to put the marriage back together. He spent two sessions berating his wife and telling me all kinds of horrible things about her. He even accused her of being a lesbian. He cooked up this lie to avoid facing his insecurity. I let him ventilate his anger freely, lest he explode and hurt his wife. It never once occurred to him to question why he would want to be married to such a horrible person. When at last I put this question to him, he was stumped. He dropped out of therapy, became floridly vengeful and began to leave harassing messages on his wife's answering machine, thus revealing his true nature. When the police did nothing to intervene, the wife contacted his boss and asked him if he wanted that kind of person working for him. The husband, employed at a leading soft-drink company, was promptly fired from his job. Unable to deal with this loss of face, he moved to a faraway state. The more appropriate thing for him to do would have been a little bit of soul-searching, grieving, learning some lessons from this experience, becoming a better person and rebuilding his life.

6. Loss in childhood can lead to overnight adult-hood. The sudden loss of a parent can result in the child's taking over the role of the lost parent. This is one way for a child to cope with the pain of the parent's loss. Unable to bear the shock of the loss, the survivor incorporates the dead person within his mind, thus keeping the parent alive in spirit. The child becomes an adult overnight. He talks, walks and acts like the dead person. Without prompt intervention, this can result in serious consequences for the whole family.

A case study: A fourteen-year-old girl, the fourth of five children in the family, was extremely close to her loving but domineering father. One day, tragedy struck—the father suddenly died from a heart attack. He had been the only breadwinner, and the family was thrown into utter chaos. The girl did not mourn her father at the funeral because she was so angry at him for abandoning her at such a tender age. Unable to accept the catastrophic loss, she kept him alive inside herself by incorporating his spirit into her mind. She immediately assumed her father's role and took charge of the household affairs. Soon, she was barking orders to everyone at home, including her mother, exactly the way her father had done. When the grieving younger brother began to fail in school, she boxed him on the ears and attempted to straighten him out. When he grew up, he harbored traumatic memories of his childhood association with his sister. As the years passed, all the other family members, too, resented the girl for her bossy behavior, without realizing that she was merely playing the role of her father. It kept on snowballing until the girl ultimately became estranged from her mother and all her siblings. Then, when her own daughter turned fourteen, she relived her childhood trauma and became terribly depressed. This is a classic example of how one tragedy in a family reverberates through generations.

Bob Kamath, M.D.

Part II: Progression of Stress

CHAPTER SEVEN

Burying and the Saturation Point

I n Chapter One, we read about how the three functions of the conscious mind—thought, emotion and action—are directed by the information in the hidden mind. We saw how, over the course of time, burying painful emotions in the hidden mind can lead to stress disorders. In addition, burying can disrupt functions of the hidden mind, resulting in serious consequences. In this chapter we will study these phenomena in greater detail.

1. What is in your hidden mind?

All the information one has gathered over his lifespan is neatly saved in numerous files, embedded in various folders in the hard drive of the hidden mind. After each piece of sensory input is received, the conscious mind asks the hidden mind a question about that input, and the hidden mind gives the necessary information so that the conscious mind can react appropriately. For the purposes of our discussion, we need to know eight of these folders in the hidden mind.

A. The "Memory" folder. This is a huge memory bank or reference library, which holds the memories of hundreds of thousands of past incidents, events and situations of our lives. The "Memory" folder stores information in layers. Some information is readily available, other information is not so readily available (subconscious), and still other information is not available at all (unconscious). If you hear the word "grandma," the image of your grandma will appear on the screen of your mind, along with emotions related to her. If you smell fresh bread being made, very old memories of your mom making bread in her kitchen might come up on the screen of your mind. These particular memories have been in the hidden mind. Every time the conscious mind receives a sensory input (a sound, sight, smell, taste or touch), it asks this folder, "Do you recognize what this is?"

B. The "Belief" folder. This folder holds various beliefs, opinions, views and ideas (BOVI) about different aspects of life, which we have learned from our elders as well as from various life experiences. The primary purpose of these beliefs is to decide whether a sensory input is good or bad for us. All our conscious perceptions are rooted in this folder. If someone asks you about another person, you might say something like, "Oh, yes, I know him. He is a good man," or "I know that mechanic. Don't even think of taking your car to him." Every time the conscious mind receives a sensory input, it asks the "Belief" folder, "Do you know if this sensory input is good for me or bad for me?"

Even one faulty belief can ruin one's entire life. For example, a young woman who erroneously believes that expressing emotion is a sign of weakness can suffer from serious bouts of depression and anxiety throughout her life. The same person could prevent future episodes of depression and anxiety just by giving up this one erroneous belief. In my everyday practice, I see a wide spectrum of irrational or faulty beliefs in my patients which have led to their serious life problems. One of many ways therapists help patients is to correct the faulty perceptions that have created stress for them.

Every faulty perception comes with a heavy price tag. A fifty-five-year-old white woman, believing that all foreign-trained doctors were incompetent, stayed in treatment with a local white doctor, who misdiagnosed her serious psychiatric condition and gave her the wrong treatment for over ten years. After spending more than two hundred thousand dollars on fruitless treatments and enduring unnecessary suffering, she finally agreed to see the local "foreign-trained" doctor. With proper treatment, she recovered from her ailment within one month.

C. The "Wisdom" folder. This is the highest faculty of our hidden mind, which tells the conscious mind to do the right thing in response to a life situation. As primitive man evolved into civilized man, this was the last folder to be installed, and so it is the first to break down when one is under stress. The "Wisdom" folder has seven essential files in it:

1. "Lessons Learned" from various life experiences
2. "Knowledge" of objects in the world
3. "Judgment" about people and situations, as well as the right responses to them
4. "Reasoning" related to cause and effect
5. "Insight" into human behaviors and life situations
6. "Moral values," such as, "thou shalt not," which form our conscience and thus control our weaknesses and base instincts
7. "Noble Virtues," such as generosity, forgiveness, charity, kindness, empathy, etc., which elevate us to the highest human potential

When wisdom guides our thoughts, emotions and actions, we do the right thing. We are then considered to be wise. There are few long-term negative consequences to wisdom-driven actions. When the conscious mind becomes disconnected from the "Wisdom" folder, we lose touch with reality, as well as from all that civilized man stands for. Our actions are then said to be stupid or evil. Every time the conscious mind receives a sensory input, it asks this folder, "What is the right thing to do in response to this situation?"

Later, we will see how burying painful emotions in the hidden mind can disconnect the conscious mind from the files in the "Wisdom" folder, leading to stupid or evil behaviors on the part of some stressed people.

Bob Kamath, M.D.

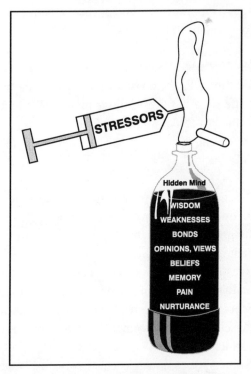

Picture 22: The hidden mind has many folders.

D. The "Personality Weaknesses" folder. What society considers personality weaknesses are deep-rooted relics of the primitive man within us. This folder also represents one's darker side, or demons. It generally contains seven files:

1. "Lust" for sex and wealth
2. "Hatred," or rage, which often leads to violent ac tions
3. "Greed," which often leads one to commit fraud
4. "Arrogance," which creates enemies
5. "Jealousy," which leads to pathological comparing and competing
6. "Possessiveness," or entanglement, which leads to controlling and manipulative behavior

7. "Insecurity," which leads to ostentation, boastful
   ness and financial problems

When a person's thoughts, emotions and actions are guided
by these personality weaknesses on a regular basis, civilized society
refers to him as criminal, evil or stupid, depending on his actions.
Rape, murder, theft, deceit, robbery, kidnapping, child molestation,
fraud and other heinous behaviors are rooted in these primitive traits.
Much of our time and energy is devoted to protecting ourselves from
these antisocial elements in society. In fact, the most interesting
shows we watch on television are those in which good guys win over
bad guys.

Sometimes, even highly moral people fall prey to one or
more of these weaknesses and get into serious trouble with the law.
An otherwise decent man who seduces innocent little girls under the
influence of lust is an example of stupid or evil behavior, devoid of
the benefit of wisdom. Actions driven by one or more personality
weakness are at the root of some of the bad events and most of the
bad problems of life. When a sensory input activates a personality
weakness, the conscious mind asks this folder, "What evil or stupid
acts can I indulge in to satisfy my socially forbidden desires?"

E. The "Bonds" folder. This folder holds our positive and
negative bonds with different sense objects. These bonds are memories of good and bad events and situations associated with sense
objects, especially people. When we lose the sense objects, the bonds
break down, releasing good and bad memories into the conscious
mind. As we studied in a previous chapter, bonds play a major role in
grief and stress. When we lose someone we love, the conscious mind
asks this folder, "Let me review, one last time, all the good, bad and
indifferent memories I have of the lost person."

F. The "Instincts" folder. This folder holds basic, deeply
rooted sexual, aggressive and territorial instincts, which we share
with all animals and insects. These are instinctual drives that moti-
vate us to procreate and find sexual gratification, to commit aggres-
sion against others, and to establish personal territory. These drives

are generally concealed by the façade of social etiquette. However, under the right conditions, they can become activated. Sexual instinct can become activated by exposure to a highly sexually charged situation, such as, for a man, being in a room alone with a helpless and vulnerable woman. The rape of innocent young women by soldiers is an example. When this instinct is activated, even a highly moral person can lose his inner restraint and commit immoral acts. Aggressive instincts can be activated by traumatic incidents, leading to serial murder, abduction and rape. The territorial instinct can become activated when one's security is threatened, or whenever one experiences euphoria associated with victory or success. When the territorial instinct is activated, a person might develop domineering behavior with everyone around him: "I am bigger than you," "I am smarter than you," "I am richer than you," "I am more powerful than you," etc. Such primitive, self-inflating behavior is known as the alpha syndrome ("I'm one up on you"). When the conscious mind gets an appropriate sensory input, it asks the "Instincts" folder, "Is this the right opportunity to be sexually, physically or territorially aggressive toward other human beings?"

G. The "Pain" folder. This folder is especially installed, usually during childhood, for people who cope with their overwhelming stress by burying their painful emotions in the hidden mind. By and large, these buried emotions are outside our daily awareness. When this folder is overfilled, painful emotions start filling the balloon, or the conscious part of the mind, and can also spill over into other folders in the hidden mind, thus interfering with their functions. When a current event reminds us of something that is in this folder, those painful emotions resurface into the conscious mind. This causes the balloon to inflate, and serious stress symptoms develop (the double whammy). A current painful situation makes the conscious mind ask this folder, "Are you carrying any buried painful emotions similar to the ones I am feeling right now?"

Some deeply buried, painful emotions are difficult to retrieve. How, then, do we know they are there? They show up in the form of a behavioral pattern. For example, a man who was traumatized as a child by being abandoned by his mother might become clingy and controlling toward his wife. This behavior is the clue to his unconscious fear of abandonment. He is aware neither of his odd behavior nor of the connection between it and his childhood trauma. Such odd behaviors, rooted in emotional scars, are known as emotional baggage.

H. The "Nurturance" folder. This folder holds memories related to the nurturance received in childhood. If one has had a happy and contented childhood, his "Nurturance" folder is said to be full, and he lives a happy and contented life. If his childhood was deprived of love, kindness, empathy and warmth, his "Nurturance" folder will be partially or fully empty. Just as a starving person constantly seeks food, people with empty "Nurturance" folders hunger all their lives for attention, love, kindness and praise. This often results in their displaying attention-seeking or love-seeking behavior (ASB) in their relationships with others. Many of these people are trapped in abusive relationships. They are willing to suffer an extreme degree of physical, emotional and sexual abuse just for a little bit of love and attention. When a sensory input comes into the conscious mind, it asks this folder, "What kind of behavior can I indulge in to be noticed and to get the maximum attention, love, kindness, praise and appreciation?"

We often see a severe form of this behavior in disorders such as borderline narcissistic and histrionic personality disorders. These are people who display a flair for drama in whatever they say or do. Many borderline and histrionic people cash in on their attention-seeking talents by becoming Broadway or movie stars or entertainers. Some become shameless exhibitionists. As more people in our society grow up without having filled their "Nurturance" folders, we see an increasing display of attention-seeking behavior. This explains why there are more people out there in society today disrobing in public, wearing revealing clothes or embellishing their bodies with attention-drawing tattoos, piercings, hairstyles and other primitive markers. These days, everyone seems to want to be noticed.

When the buried, unmet desires, needs and cravings suddenly resurface in one's mid-thirties or mid-forties, the midlife crisis is the result. During the midlife crisis, a person attempts to fulfill these unmet desires and needs by, for example, indulging in an extramarital affair. In other words, he tries to fill up his empty "Nurturance" folder all at once. We will study this phenomenon in greater detail later.

2. Any sensory input can activate a file.

Let us review briefly how the different files and folders become activated, leading to corresponding actions. Looking at the picture of a hungry child can activate the "Generosity" file in your "Wisdom" folder, causing you to make a donation to the charity that put out the picture. If you get a phone call from a con artist promising you a huge profit for a small investment, the "Greed" file in your "Personality Weaknesses" folder can become activated, making you invest money in a worthless business scheme. Finding a photograph of a long-lost lover could bring up fond memories of those good old days from the "Memory" folder, making you feel happy, warm and fuzzy again. Hearing the sound of a helicopter could bring up bad memories of a combat that took place many years ago from the "Pain" folder, causing one to shut himself up in his basement to keep his balloon from popping. A new business in town might kindle the territorial instinct in the "Instincts" folder of the owner of the only competing business, leading him to renovate and redecorate his place of business. Reading about the opening of a new abortion clinic in town could activate the anti-abortion belief in one's "Beliefs" folder, making him join a boycott group outside the facility. I think you get the idea. This kind of activation process goes on twenty-four hours a day.

3. The habit of burying usually starts in childhood.

The habit of coping by burying painful emotions usually starts in childhood, as children have difficulty in understanding, processing and expressing their painful emotions. Some traumatized children quietly bury their painful emotions and continue this habit as adults. When these adults are questioned about their childhoods, they respond by saying, "I have no memory of my childhood. It is all a blank." They may or may not relive their traumatic experiences as adults, depending upon whether they continue to be exposed to other similar traumas.

Children who are unable to bury any more begin to display physical, mental, behavioral and emotional symptoms. According to which symptoms predominate, these children are diagnosed as having attention deficit hyperactivity disorder (ADHD), bipolar disorder, oppositional defiant disorder and the like. They are often treated with drugs, simply because drugs work fairly promptly and it is too difficult for untrained or inexperienced people to figure out why children behave this way.

Common to all these children is the fact that they have been traumatized by life circumstances, and they simply do not know how to cope with their painful emotions. Since they do not have sophisticated verbal or emotional skills, they block off or bury their emotions, and when they can no longer bury them they just act them out. Instead of saying, "I can't take this bullshit anymore!" they act out. They cut themselves in an attempt to release the pain from the tense balloon; they run away from home; they get into fights with their caretakers or teachers; they become argumentative, etc. When these children become adults, they continue to bury or act out, instead of coping through appropriate means.

4. Burying during adulthood. ("I just want to forget about it!")

Under extremely trying circumstances, it is not uncommon for people to start burying in adulthood. An otherwise normal person might cope with the diagnosis of cancer by burying his or her emotions. How do we know this is the case? Well, these painful emotions can resurface during one's annual check-up with his doctor, causing the re-inflating of the balloon and the return of severe stress symptoms. A well-adjusted woman might cope with her husband's infidelity by burying her hurt and anger, and these emotions can resurface later and pop her balloon.

How do people bury their painful emotions? When upset about something, some people say to themselves, "This is too upsetting for me, so I will not think about it and I will not talk about it. I will not let this thing bother me. I will be strong. I will divert my attention to something else. I will do my best to forget it." The painful emotions are thus transferred from the mind/balloon to the hidden mind/soda bottle. The balloon shrinks, the brain chemicals go back almost to their normal state, and the stress symptoms more or less disappear. The person feels calm once again. He believes he has handled his stress well, when, in fact, all he has done is to transfer his emotions from his conscious mind to his hidden mind. Once in the hidden mind, the painful memories are more or less forgotten.

Picture 23: Burying emotions shrinks the balloon and calms us down.

This process of forgetting—handling emotions by being strong, as most people prefer to call it—is known as bottling up, or burying. Psychiatrists use the word "repression." Repression is not the same as suppression. In suppression, one is fully aware of how he feels but he chooses not to disclose it, whereas repression, like denial, is a defense mechanism by which the mind protects itself from experiencing intolerable pain. Sometimes burying is also loosely referred to as internalizing. Colloquially, burying is called "sweeping it under the rug," "putting it on the back burner," "pushing it down," "putting it out of one's mind," "blowing it off," and by other, similar phrases. A person fools himself into believing, "Hey, I'm okay! I handled this upsetting situation very well. I have calmed myself down. I was strong through the entire ordeal." As you can see, this is only self-deception. Burying gives fairly immediate relief from emotional pain, and this quick relief further reinforces the habit of burying. In the long run, however, burying is bad news for its practitioner.

5. Burying is facilitated by distractions, pleasurable activities and drugs.

A. Distractions. Burying is greatly facilitated by distractions such as vacationing, cruising, taking skiing trips, trekking, bungee jumping, etc., which take a person's attention away from the source of his stress. Through these and other multitudes of mindless activities—exercising, jogging, taking hot baths, driving around aimlessly, watching movies, listening to music, etc.—people try to forget their pain. Once the painful emotions go underground, the person feels better. That is why you will find hordes of people who swear by these so-called anti-stress activities. The problem with these activities is that they do not address the painful emotions in the mind that are causing the stress symptoms. If one is upset with his boss, jogging ten miles a day is not going to solve the job problem.

B. Pleasurable activities. Some people try to cancel out their emotional pain by indulging in pleasurable activities. These potentially dangerous distractions facilitate the burying process. Drowning one's sorrow in alcohol, getting stoned with illicit drugs, numbing the mind with tranquilizers, smoking incessantly to blow off one's worries, gorging on food eight times a day, obsessively engaging in promiscuous sex and gambling round the clock give the sufferer some temporary relief and distraction. The painful emotions settle down in the hidden mind. However, getting drunk is not going to solve any problem a man has with his wife. He will have to face the music sometime in the future.

C. Psychiatric drugs. As we read earlier, the prompt control of the symptoms of stress disorder that is available through drugs gives the stressed-out patient a false sense that all he needs to do is take a pill a day. He neither gives up his habit of blocking off emotions nor learns appropriate ways to cope. The result is that the painful emotions that popped his balloon in the first place are buried in his soda bottle, if there is still room. Or, after another bad event, when the drug coating outside the balloon can no longer protect it from the emotional pressure that has been building up, the balloon may pop again, resulting in a breakthrough episode. This reality— that drug treatment actually greatly facilitates burying, just as alcohol and street drugs do—is yet to be acknowledged by psychiatrists.

6. The saturation point

As we have seen, the hidden mind does not have a limitless capacity to store painful emotions. As long as one can bury emotions in the hidden mind, he is free from stress symptoms. But sooner or later, the soda bottle becomes saturated. The saturation point is that point in a stressed-out patient's life when he is no longer able to bury his painful emotions in his hidden mind. The hidden mind/soda bottle says to the conscious mind/balloon, "I don't have any space left to store the garbage you are giving me. From now on, keep the garbage yourself!" From this point onwards, the incoming painful emotions start re-inflating the balloon, resulting in a steady worsening of stress symptoms (Rule #1). People who are stressed out (except for those with the double whammy) trace the onset of their stress symptoms to the saturation point. If you ask any stressed-out person, "When did you first notice your anxiety (or depression)?" he will say something like, "Well, maybe about five years ago." What this means is that the hidden mind finally became saturated about five years ago, and the balloon started re-inflating shortly thereafter.

Is Your Balloon About to Pop?

Let us now study the consequences that follow when the saturation point is reached.

———◆•◆•◆———

CHAPTER EIGHT

Low Stress Tolerance Syndrome

1. Low stress tolerance syndrome.

  A. After reaching the saturation point, the balloon starts to re-inflate. Hitherto—that is, until it reached the saturation point—the hidden mind acted like a shock-absorbing system. But after the saturation point is reached, the incoming painful emotions have no place to go, and they start accumulating in the balloon. The conscious mind/balloon begins to re-inflate. As it re-inflates with painful emotions, the brain chemicals begin to change and more and more stress symptoms reappear (see Rule #1): irritability, snappishness, sleeplessness, sleepiness, anxiety, tension, sadness, poor concentration, racing of thoughts, memory problems, aches and pains, headaches, mood swings, etc.

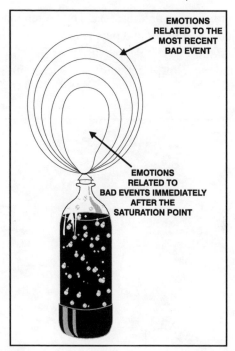

Picture 24: The balloon re-inflates, and stress symptoms get worse over time.

The number and severity of stress symptoms depends upon which complex of emotions (fear, sadness, anger or guilt) is in the balloon, and how many of them are present; that is, how big the balloon has become. When people at this stage become upset, they stay upset for longer and longer. As the balloon gets closer to its breaking point, these people become increasingly intolerant of any additional sensory input. This inability to tolerate any more stress is known as *low stress tolerance syndrome.* This is the third stage of stress. Since people can no longer bury their painful emotions, they now resort to the tactic of blocking off, or denial. As per Rule #2, most, if not all, of these people have little or no awareness of the painful emotions in their balloons. Their total focus now is on their stress symptoms.

B. How do we know this is happening? Listen carefully to people in this unfortunate predicament. They often make this type of statement: "I just can't be around people any more. When I am with people, I get very nervous." "People piss me off." "Some years ago, nothing bothered me. Now, I get upset at the least little thing." "I can't

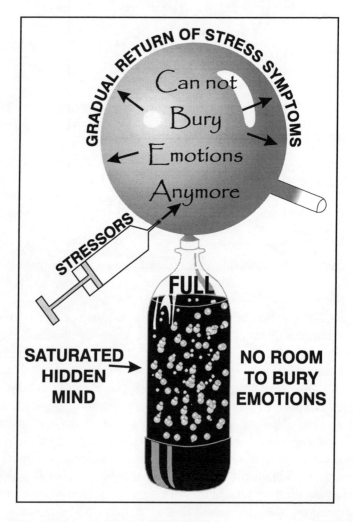

Picture 25: Low stress tolerance syndrome: both the bottle and the balloon are full

take things as the way I used to." "Nowadays, when I get upset, I stay upset. It takes me a long time to calm down." "I am irritable all the time. I explode at least thing. I never used to do that before. I just snap at people for no good reason." "I can't stand noise or ruckus any more." "I can't concentrate on anything." "My memory is not as sharp as it was some years ago. I don't remember what I did ten minutes ago." "I used to be a patient person. Now I have no patience at all." "I just want to be left alone. I cannot take excitement any more." "My mind is constantly filled with worry, with all kinds of thoughts and emotions. I just can't get rid of them." "Sometimes I feel completely shut down. I go into la-la land." "I have no energy to think or do anything." "I just can't turn my brain off." "My PMS is getting worse all the time." "I feel mentally exhausted. I want to sleep all the time." "My mind is going constantly, zigzagging here and there, from one thing to another. I can't concentrate on anything." "I feel panicky, even when I am doing nothing; even when I am just watching television!" "I used to read a lot. Now I can't finish even one page." Different people complain of different set of symptoms, largely depending on what painful emotions are present in their balloon.

Patients who did well on medications for a while report, "I did well on medications for a couple of years, but they don't help me any more. I have become immune to them." "My depressive bouts are lasting longer, and the intervals between them are getting shorter." "It does not take much to make me feel depressed any more. Sometimes I get depressed over nothing." Some people say, "I am anxious and depressed, even though I am on two antidepressant drugs and two tranquilizers."

These patients are fixing to have a breakthrough episode. The balloon is so full that if you blow even a little painful emotion into it, it will pop immediately. These people are often referred to as fragile, brittle, delicate or burnt out. Their relatives and friends frequently remark, "When you are with him, you feel like you are walking on eggshells!" or "He is like a ticking time bomb. You never know when he is going to go off." This condition is just one step away from a full-blown stress disorder, such as major depression, bipolar disorder, or panic disorder.

Some people in this state explode from time to time, provoked by minor events, as if to release the inner tension. People with "road rage" belong in this category. Others report having frequent weeping spells. They say, "Now I cry at the drop of a hat." It is as if the mind/balloon is making attempts to release its inner pressure by "leaking" tears that have built up over the years. Children in this predicament often try to cut themselves, as if to release their inner pain. Feeling physical pain seems to somehow reduce the emotional pain, just as emotional pain is often made tolerable by being converted into a physical pain.

C. The sources of painful emotions. Where are these painful emotions coming from?
1. The first source of painful emotions is unresolved issues. As we read before, almost all bad events lead to bad problems. One might think that he has coped with a bad event by burying the emotions related to that event; however, the aftermath of the event is still with him, and these unresolved problems keep bringing in painful emotions. For example, one might have dealt with the pain of divorce by burying; however, the pain related to the custody battle, financial settlement, etc. keeps coming in.
2. The second source is the ordinary life stress we all face on a daily basis—stress related to job, family, money, health, etc. These stresses are newer sources of painful emotions.
3. The third source is one's reactions to the stress symptoms themselves. When one suffers from persistent sleeplessness, anxiety, pain, etc., he becomes upset about them. Now, "reactive" painful emotions, such as the sense of helplessness and frustration, are added to the balloon.
4. The fourth source is the various stupid mistakes people make because of the conscious mind's disconnection from the "Wisdom" folder. Stressed-out people often make one mistake after another that any sensible person would consider stupid. That is why once a person's hidden mind has reached the saturation point, the course is steadily downhill. The balloon keeps getting bigger and bigger, exponentially, and the symptoms get worse as time passes.

2. How people try to protect their full balloons from popping.

A. Denial. Denial means not acknowledging one's painful emotions or the stressors that have brought them on. The person tries to block them off from his awareness. It is a sort of pretension. "I am not upset" and "I have no problems" are two mantras repeated constantly by people practicing denial. Obviously, denial protects them to some extent from experiencing their emotional pain. People whose balloons are already full are more likely to deny than those whose balloons are empty. In fact, the bigger the balloon, the greater the denial. This means that the sicker a person is, the more likely he is to deny.

1. Temporary denial, which protects us from the shock of a very stressful event, is common and normal. That is why denial is often referred to as a defense mechanism. When we see a terrible event on TV, say, the blowing-up of the Twin Towers, our immediate reaction might be, "Oh, no! It can't be! It must be a movie!" We often hear shocked people say things like, "Is this really happening? Pinch me!" or, "Tell me I'm dreaming. Tell me this is not happening." Here, denial gives us breathing time to absorb the shock of the event. After the reality hits us, we admit to ourselves that it was a terrible experience. We react to the situation with appropriate emotions, deal with them and move on with life.

2. Most people who have low stress tolerance syndrome are not aware that they have been upset for some time over past life-events and problems (Rule #2). When faced with a new stressor that inflates the balloon even further, they try to cope with it by indulging in denial ("I am not upset. I have no problems.") In fact, to throw people off the track, they may even exaggerate how wonderful they feel. They often say such things as, "I feel wonderful! Things could not be any better in my life. That is why I don't understand why I have all these horrible symptoms." These people are hurting like hell in their minds, and they are miserable from many stress symptoms: sleeplessness, tiredness, anxiety, depression, loss of appetite and the like. Everyone around them can see it. Inevitably, a question arises in the naïve or unsympathetic observer's mind: "If everything is so wonderful in this person's life, how come he feels like shit?" However, we cannot ignore the horrible tragedies these people have been through and how much they are hurting. They have no choice but to stop their emotional pain by hook or by crook.

Picture 26: Denial blocks off painful emotions from one's awareness.

Some examples of denial:

A young man hadn't slept in two weeks and had lost twenty pounds in that time. He said, "My wife left me two weeks ago, but I don't miss her at all. It's all for the best!" If it were all for the best, he wouldn't be feeling so miserable.

A thirty-five-year-old woman became terribly depressed and anxious immediately after she married a bum. This was the third bum she had married, and she was determined not to divorce him. When asked if she was upset about her husband, she replied, "Not at all! He is a wonderful man. So what if I have to live in a shed? I love him!"

A middle-aged woman, married to an alcoholic for twenty-five years, complained of depression, anxiety and aches and pains all over her body. She had had these symptoms for twenty-four years, and she had been making the rounds of different doctors for over twenty years for a dozen different maladies. It was obvious to her doctors that she was trapped in a bad marriage. But when asked about her husband, she replied, "My husband is a wonderful man. He drinks and sometimes becomes violent, but that does not upset me at all. We have a wonderful marriage. When he does not drink (which was not often!), he is a wonderful man. I love him!"

3. Denial has many shades. At one extreme, a person in denial can be completely unaware of his painful emotions ("I feel nothing!") A person suffering from sudden panic attacks usually falls in this category. At the other extreme, one might be fully or partially aware of his emotions or problems but unwilling to openly acknowledge them in front of others. An alcoholic's blatant denial of his drinking problem is an example of this. Subtle forms of denial are very common. A young woman may say, "My husband and I haven't made love in six years. We are very close. In fact, we are best friends. We simply don't have time for sex!" A depressed grown-up incest victim may say, "My father was a great man. I loved him, even though he had sex with me when I was growing up. He meant no harm. That was his way of showing me affection. Who doesn't make mistakes? He had a heart of gold! I have forgiven him." As a person becomes sicker and sicker, his denial gets more and more blatant and bizarre. There are instances in which a person has lived with the dead body of his loved one for over a year, denying the death of that person.

4. Denial interferes with the awareness and expression of painful emotions. These are two essential coping mechanisms that shrink the balloon. I have seen people who, while weeping uncontrollably during their interviews, claimed that their tears were due to an allergy, and not because they were sad. A few vain women have told me, "What good would weeping do? It would only mess up my mascara!" Healthy people are always in touch with, aware of and able to acknowledge their inner emotions, as well as the outer realities of their lives.

Bob Kamath, M.D.

5. Denial usually breaks down when a listener pushes the "empathy" button. The opposite of denial is acknowledgement and admission. In denial, one does not want to know; whereas, in acknowledging, one says, "I know," and thus he admits to his problem. Denial breaks down when a person talks to an individual whom he trusts and perceives as compassionate, empathic, supportive, non-critical and non-judgmental. People can usually respond to someone who acknowledges their pain and makes genuinely empathic remarks, such as, "You must be hurting like hell!" "You are going through some rough times, aren't you?" "You must be feeling devastated by what happened to you." This will result in the sufferer's breaking down, crying, sobbing and expressing his emotions to the empathic listener. If you want to help a stressed-out friend, don't just give him a lecture ("Stop feeling sorry for yourself!" "Enough of this pity party!") Instead, just push your friend's empathy button and let him or her boohoo a little.

B. Withdrawal from society. Many people suffering from low stress tolerance syndrome instinctively know that their balloons are ready to pop. They become intolerant of sensory stimuli such as the noise of children or dogs, driving on high-density highways, watching horror movies, listening to the evening news, being in crowded grocery shops and football stadiums. So they become increasingly withdrawn from activities, especially social activities, which have the potential to upset them. Withdrawal is their defense against any sensory input that might pop the balloon. In other words, they try to limit sensory input by shutting down the pump. Unable to tolerate the tumultuous nature of full life, many of them sleep a lot and become recluses. They actively avoid parties and gatherings. They stop inviting people to their homes for entertainment. They become less and less productive at work. They look increasingly stressed to the workers around them. Unable to focus on their work, many start making mistakes, and their productivity goes down. Over time, they become dysfunctional at work as well as at home. Some of them refuse to go to work. Psychiatrists refer to this syndrome as agoraphobia without history of panic disorder. Some of these people are diagnosed as having social phobia, or social anxiety disorder.

C. Psychopathic withdrawal. Some single people with low stress tolerance syndrome lead reclusive lives, regardless of where they live. They carve out a world of their own with no contact with the outside world and gradually drop essential activities from their daily routines, such as shaving, bathing, eating, moving their bowels and cleaning their rooms. These people, who have regressed to the "primitive man" mode of functioning, are grandiosely referred to as having social breakdown syndrome. In other words, they have become hermits. (As one patient put it, "If you are rich, they call you a recluse. If you are poor, they call you a goddamn hermit!") They are often referred to as asocial, social misfits or misanthropes.

Some of these people can become dangerous to society, such as the Unabomber, who mailed pipe bombs to scientists across the country, maiming or killing them. Some of these dangerous misfits become kidnappers, serial killers, serial rapists and the like. These are socially inept people who try to satisfy their sexual and aggressive instincts by indulging in despicable acts. A warped, idle mind is, indeed, the devil's workshop. Most of these psychopaths are described as loners. When married people commit these crimes, they are usually so disconnected, even from their own families, that they practically live in their own inner, demoniacal world.

3. Diagnoses of minor mental disorders are often made at this stage.

If the stressed-out person seeks psychiatric help at this stage, he will get one of many minor diagnoses, depending upon which symptoms are predominant. If one complains primarily of depressive symptoms, he will get a diagnosis such as Dysthymic disorder (minor chronic depression). If he complains mainly of tension, nervousness and anxiety, he will get a diagnosis of generalized anxiety disorder (GAD, or low-grade chronic anxiety). One who displays minor mood swings is labeled as having Cyclothymic disorder. One who reports diffuse aches, pains and "trigger points" will get the diagnosis of Fibromyalgia. One complaining of forgetfulness and distractibility will get a diagnosis of attention deficit disorder. One who complains of severe tiredness or exhaustion will get the diagnosis of chronic fatigue syndrome. Some are diagnosed as suffering from chronic post-traumatic stress disorder (PTSD), some with high blood pressure and others with irritable bowel syndrome. Some people who display highly abnormal behaviors are branded as having a personality disorder. You get the idea.

Almost all these people deny that they now have, or have had in the past, any stress in their lives. If, by fluke, they admit to having any stress, they minimize its importance. Common statements I hear go something like this: "Oh, this is not stress. My mom had it. It's my genes. It is a chemical imbalance"; or "Of course I have some stress. Who doesn't? I am handling it quite well." A careful review of their past histories, however, tells a whole different story. Most of them have experienced many extremely stressful events in the past, and/or they have been trapped in a chronic, difficult-to-solve life problem, such as a bad marriage, a bad job, a financial problem, etc. They have coped with their life situations stoically ("being strong"). By the time they see a psychiatrist, if they do at all, their bottles have become saturated and their balloons are inflated to some degree.

4. Some phenomena related to low stress tolerance syndrome.

A. Premenstrual tension can be an early stage of low stress tolerance syndrome. Women who suffer from premenstrual tension syndrome (grandiosely referred to as premenstrual dysphoric disorder) suffer severe stress symptoms just prior to menstruation: irritability, angry outbursts, depression, mood swings, anxiety, tension, violent impulses and the like. (You must remember that the symptoms depend upon the particular complex of emotions in the balloon.) After menstruation, these symptoms diminish or go away. Almost all the women in this predicament have inflated balloons to start with. If we examined their past histories, we would find many traumatic events and problems, all of which they dealt with by burying ("I just didn't dwell on it"). Their soda bottles are full, and the balloons are somewhat inflated.

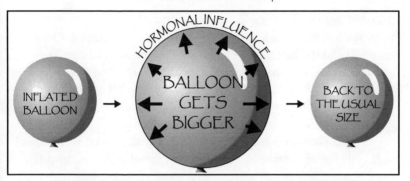

Picture 27: PMS is a type of low stress tolerance syndrome.

During the premenstrual period, fluctuating female hormones negatively affect the brain chemicals, resulting in the aggravation of stress symptoms. It is as if the balloon becomes even more inflated than it was. After the hormonal influence abates, the brain chemicals go back to their previous state and the symptoms decrease. If these women are untreated, almost all their balloons pop sooner or later, and they end up with stress-related disorders of one type or another. This explains why they respond fairly well to the judicious use of antidepressant medications on a temporary basis. However, most of these women have a strong need to blame their problems on hormones rather than stress, so they go on prolonged, fruitless searches for hormones and exotic drugs to help them. Their gynecologists readily oblige them with any antidepressant drugs they ask for. Convincing them that counseling with the right therapist could help them get over their PMS is an almost impossible task. Ignorance and stigma are powerful obstacles, indeed!

B. Post-menopausal and post-hysterectomy depression.
Some women develop depression and anxiety following menopause. The most important aspect of this is the fact that the woman feels she is less of a woman now that her reproductive years are behind her. In menopausal women, the hormonal decrease, their children's leaving home, the loss of their youth, etc. can be contributing factors in inflating the balloon. In patients who have undergone hysterectomies, we cannot blame the hormonal decrease, as many women suffer de-

pression even with their ovaries intact. In both these types of cases, histories would reveal that the soda bottles were saturated a long time ago and the balloons were already full because of past events and problems. Menopause or hysterectomy was the last push from the pump, which inflated the balloon just a little bit more. Or perhaps some buried emotions resurfaced, causing the balloon to inflate.

   C. Adult children of alcoholics. Children who were raised in families in which one or both parents drank heavily often suffer from chronic depression and anxiety. Many of them cope with their symptoms by drinking alcohol since they learned this coping method from their parents, and they are also genetically prone to alcoholism. Most of these people report having to deal with neglectful, hateful or violent parents. Painful emotions related to numerous stressful events were buried in the hidden mind: shame, anger, hurt, sadness, help-lessness, terror and the like. Some serious cases report incidents such as having been chased by a drunken father with a loaded gun, having to sleep in a cornfield at night to avoid being killed and many other horror stories.

5. Burying can disconnect the mind from wisdom.

   A. Buried emotions often disconnect the conscious mind from the "Wisdom" folder. The basic function of the "Wisdom" folder in the hidden mind is to guide or direct us to do the right thing. Buried painful emotions often disrupt the connection between the conscious mind and the "Wisdom" folder. This disconnection brings on strange or out-of-character behaviors in some stressed-out people. It is important to know this fact, because stressed-out people often create even more serious stress for themselves by their increasingly irrational or even bizarre behaviors. In my practice, I see an incred-ible number of stressed people displaying stupid behaviors that are clearly indicative of their mind's disconnection from wisdom or common sense. Here are some examples of such behaviors: a young, stressed-out single woman with few financial resources who mar-ries an unemployed bum, without taking the long-term financial and personal consequences into consideration; a young single man with a small income who gets a tiny raise and immediately buys a big house with a swimming pool; or a stressed-out, unemployed single woman who keeps having one illegitimate child after another. The vast majority of my stressed-out patients report committing actions that are blatantly stupid and whose inevitable, disastrous consequences they were unable to foresee. In people with psychoses, the disconnection of the conscious mind from the "Reasoning," "Judgment" and "Insight" files in the "Wisdom" folder results in bizarre behaviors.

If the conscious mind disconnects from the "Lessons Learned" file in the "Wisdom" folder, one repeats his past mistakes. If it disconnects from the "Knowledge" file, his naiveté gets him in trouble with predators. If it disconnects from his "Judgment" file, he will act in stupid ways. If it disconnects from his "Reasoning" file, he will act irrationally. If it disconnects from his "Insight" file, he will be baffled by his own behavior, as well as the behavior of others. If it disconnects from his "Moral Values" file ("thou shall not"), he will indulge in antisocial or immoral behavior. If it disconnects from his "Virtues" file, he will act like a self-centered narcissist. In my daily practice, I see evidence of the disconnection of the conscious mind from wisdom in many different stress-related clinical syndromes.

B. Buried emotions can interfere with the proper functions of memory. Most stressed-out people suffer from progressive memory loss. They report difficulty in recalling names and dates. They mislay their keys and laptop computers, forget important appointments and lose their wallets and jewelry. Their concentration diminishes. Many wonder if they are developing Alzheimer's disease. Some people develop serious amnesia, known as dissociative reaction or fugue state. Most people suffering from amnesia give a history of having been severely stressed out over several painful issues.

A case study: One fine morning, a fifty-six-year-old woman from Connecticut found herself in Los Angeles, California. She had no idea how she had ended up there. She had no memory of what had happened over the past two weeks. Her history revealed that she had been burying many painful emotions related to her husband's ongoing incestuous relationship with her three daughters. Obviously, the buried emotions finally disconnected her conscious mind from her memory bank.

Bob Kamath, M.D.

Picture 28: Buried emotions can block wisdom off from mind.

C. Buried emotions often block the conscious mind from accessing its knowledge. Many highly intelligent, stressed-out people report feeling like idiots. Their thinking slows down. Their minds lose their sharpness. They talk and walk slowly. Their ability to make decisions diminishes, as their conscious minds are not able to access the necessary information from their "Knowledge" files. They cannot explain where all their knowledge has gone. This is known as psychomotor retardation. We often see an extreme form of this phenomenon in severely depressed people. Some people with this type of severe cognitive impairment are diagnosed with pseudo-dementia (false dementia).

D. Some stressed-out people show very poor judgment.
When the mind becomes disconnected from the "Judgment" file,
stressed-out people may become involved in business deals that are
obviously harebrained or plain fraudulent. This is particularly evident
in manic or hypomanic states. Many such people make such a mess
of their finances that they end up in jail or file for bankruptcy. Some
otherwise decent people become involved in the sexual abuse of children, extramarital affairs, bank robberies and other stupid behaviors.
After they get well with treatment, they are full of remorse. They say,
"How could I have had such a lapse of judgment? I can't believe I
got involved in all this mess!"

A case study: Here is a story I heard on National Public
Radio. A successful fifty-six-year-old financial adviser became
progressively more and more stressed over several years. Unable to
take his emotional pain any longer, he decided to commit suicide.
He bought a handgun to kill himself, but he just could not bring
himself to do it. Sixteen months later, in broad daylight and without
any premeditation, he put on a ski mask and held up a local bank.
He collected $8,000 and quietly left the bank. When the police came
to arrest him in the parking lot of the bank, he surrendered without
resisting. He was found guilty of bank robbery and sentenced to six
years in prison. The judge refused to accept his plea of not guilty by
reason of insanity. Had the judge and the man's attorney and psychiatrist known of the phenomenon of the lapse of judgment owing to
the disconnection of one's conscious mind from his "Wisdom" file,
he could have gotten a lighter sentence. The proof that this disconnection was the source of his action lies in the fact that the man had
plenty of money of his own, had never violated the law before, had
never planned the robbery, never tried to escape, had been planning
suicide for several years and could not explain why he even did the
robbery. In my practice, I have seen countless people who have done
stupid stuff like this and said, "I have no idea why I did it!" Some
people refer to this situation as asking for help. If this is true, what a
bizarre way to do so! Decent people who indulge in shoplifting fall
in this category.

E. Stressed-out people can lose their reasoning powers.
We see this in many severely depressed people. They feel that life is
all doom and gloom, and no one can reason with them and convince
them otherwise. Some depressed people say, "I know I will lose my
job. I will lose all my life's savings. My wife will leave me. I will be
in the streets pretty soon, and I will be a homeless person!"

A case study: An intelligent but stressed-out young man
became terribly upset when his girlfriend broke up with him. This
was one of several breakups in his life. When he called the girlfriend
to make up with her, she told him not to call again. Unwilling to take
no for an answer, he kept calling again and again, even though she
became more irate with him each time. He became so stressed over
the whole thing that it was beyond his reasoning power to understand
that the more he called her, the less likely she was to come back to
him. It became obvious that his conscious mind was disconnected
from his "Reasoning" file. Very soon, he began to stalk her. Unable to reason with him, the ex-girlfriend finally reported him to the
police and obtained an ex-parte order against him. He continued to
harass her. Only a psychiatrist's intervention prevented his incar-
ceration. In therapy, instead of asking, "What did I do to end up like
this?" he kept harping, "Why did she do this to me?" Only after he
realized that his tendency to be clingy and controlling in his dealings
with his girlfriend had caused her to dump him did he get recon-
nected with his "Reasoning" file.

**F. Many stressed-out people lose insight into their own
behavior and that of others.** A man who is stressed over his financial problems takes his frustration out on his supportive wife. After
taking his verbal abuse for a while, she leaves him, saying, "I will
return when you have cooled down a little." The man becomes even
more upset with his wife and accuses her of being unsupportive of
him, when all he was doing was "trying to put bread on the table."
This man has no insight into the fact that his consistently rude behavior was the cause of the breakup of his marriage. He keeps saying,
"What have I done to deserve this treatment? I don't know why she
left me."

G. Disconnection of the mind from moral values results in out-of-character behavior. We encounter instances of perfectly moral people indulging in blatantly immoral behaviors, such as shoplifting, cheating on their spouses, soliciting sex from children on the Internet, sexually abusing children, swindling customers, abusing street drugs or even committing murder. Disconnected from their "Moral Values" files, all their actions have come under the influence of their personality weaknesses: lust, greed and the like. After they are caught, these people look back in guilt, shame and remorse and exclaim, "I can't believe I did all those immoral things! What was I thinking?"

H. A stressed-out virtuous person behaves in a crass manner. When the mind becomes disconnected from the "Noble Virtues" file, a person behaves in a crass manner. Often you hear his relatives say, "Some years ago, he was so kind, generous, forgiving, charitable, loving and whatnot, but now he is just the opposite!" After they get well, these people say, "For the life of me, I don't know why I was a horse's ass all this time. I must have stepped on a lot of toes with my obnoxious behavior!"

CHAPTER NINE

The Breaking Point

1. The breaking point: "I just can't take it anymore!"

A. A precipitating event finally pops the balloon. Some people's balloons finally pop, triggered by a new bad event or problem. This triggering event or problem is called the precipitating factor. A *precipitating factor* is the straw that breaks the camel's back. It can be a major bad event, such as the death of a loved one, or even a minor event, such as the loss of a wallet. If the precipitating event is big, it can pop even a small (only slightly inflated) balloon. If the precipitating event is small, it can pop a full balloon. At the *breaking point*, changes in brain chemicals lead to the so-called chemical imbalance. The mind/balloon, flooded with painful emotions, now feels, "I just can't take this pain any more!" Stress symptoms finally crystallize into a fairly well-defined stress disorder. Depending upon which symptoms are predominant, these people now are given more serious diagnoses: major depression, panic disorder, bipolar disorder, psychotic disorder and the like.

B. Stress disorder depends upon the individual's genes and emotional complex. The major disorder a patient comes down with depends upon his genetic background and the specific emotional complex that dominates his balloon. If the balloon is dominated by the fear complex, the patient will come down with an anxiety disorder ("fight or flight" response). If the balloon is dominated by the sadness complex, he will come down with major depression or bipolar disorder ("grief" response). If the fear and anger complexes are both dominant, he will come down with a serious psychotic disorder ("attack" response). When the guilt complex dominates, it usually complicates the above disorders. As a result, in psychotic disorders or mood disorders with psychotic features, we see irrational guilt and remorse ("God is punishing me for all my sins"). In reality, most people suffering with a stress disorder have symptoms related to almost all these complexes, as they are all related to each other like links in a chain.

C. A gene is like a seed. The cumulative effect of stress often leads to complex interactions between the altered brain chemicals and the genes, resulting in stress disorders, such as depression, anxiety disorder and high blood pressure. A gene is like a corn seed: just as exposing a corn seed to moisture and warmth causes it to sprout in a few days, exposing genes to altered brain chemicals causes them to sprout into a stress disorder. And just as a seedling cannot be made into a seed again, once the gene sprouts into a disorder it is difficult to undo the damage. If stress is like moisture and warmth, then drugs are like weed retardants. Unless one keeps the seed dry and cool, it will keep sprouting again and again, even if one applies weed retardants. The point is that learning to cope with stress is as important as taking drugs.

It should be noted here that a patient's genetic history is not always available or reliable. A more reliable guide is the emotional complex in his or her balloon.

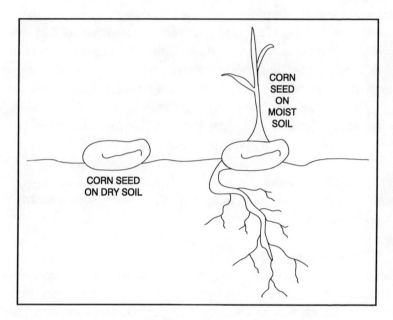

Picture 29: Under stress genes sprout stress disorders.

2. The gradual inflating of the balloon, leading to the breaking point.

Because their balloons have inflated rather gradually, many patients are at a loss as to why they have become sick, seemingly without provocation. They have no idea that their balloons have been inflating gradually over the years and have finally popped because of a minor or major stressful event. These people are now in the fourth stage of stress, the stage of stress disorder.

Is Your Balloon About to Pop?

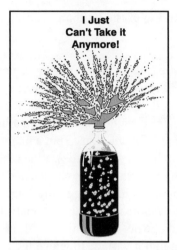

Picture 30: The Breaking Point: the stage of stress disorder.

A case study: A middle-aged woman became severely depressed following the death of her second husband, to whom she had
been married for six years. (Her balloon popped.) Her first marriage,
which lasted for sixteen years, was marred by severe verbal and
physical abuse. She had coped with it by denying (making excuses)
and burying (not thinking about it). By the time she had finally
divorced that husband, eight years previously, her bottle was full and
her balloon was almost full. She suffered from chronic low-grade depression and anxiety for many years. It was only because her second
husband was supportive and kind to her that she was able to tolerate
her symptoms and go on with her life. When the second husband
died suddenly, the stress of his death caused her balloon to pop, and
she came down with a major depressive episode, with delusions and
hallucinations (psychotic features). Her diagnosis now was "acute on
chronic depression" with psychotic features. She was hospitalized
and medicated heavily. Continuing with her medications, she went
back to her previous stage of stress, the low stress tolerance stage.
Even with medication, this woman could have breakthrough depression if she were hit by another minor stressor. She could greatly
reduce the chances of getting sick again by learning to shrink her balloon in counseling or by self-therapy.

3. The sudden inflating of the balloon, leading to the breaking point.

A current stressful, triggering event can cause the sudden resurfacing of buried emotions related to a bad event in the remote past. This means that the balloon gets a burst of painful emotions from the pump (a current triggering or precipitating event), as well as a blast of buried painful emotions from a major past trauma (fizz from the vigorously shaken soda bottle). When this happens, the balloon expands rapidly and one suffers sudden and severe stress symptoms, far out of proportion to the triggering event. This blast from the past is known as the *double whammy.* Invariably, one is at a loss to explain how and why he developed his terrible stress symptoms. This condition also has a minor variety, in which the patient's symptoms are not so severe.

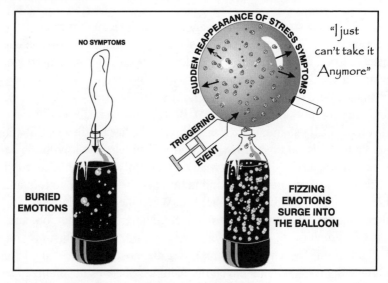

Picture 31: The minor double whammy: buried painful emotions can resurface suddenly.

A case study: A twenty-year-old woman had been anxious and depressed for about a month, since her parents had filed for divorce. Her history revealed that she had grown up witnessing her parents fight constantly. She had coped with it by burying her emotions. Now her parents' divorce shook her soda bottle and brought up buried emotions, resulting in mild anxiety and depressive symptoms.

Sometimes, buried painful emotions resurface in a fury, resulting in the popping of the balloon and precipitating a major disorder, such as major depressive disorder or panic disorder. This is especially true if the patient's balloon was already full. Most people suffering from the double whammy are not aware of the past trauma's role in their current misery. It is the job of the therapist to explain this to the patient. More than eighty-five percent of emergency visits to my office are due to a double whammy.

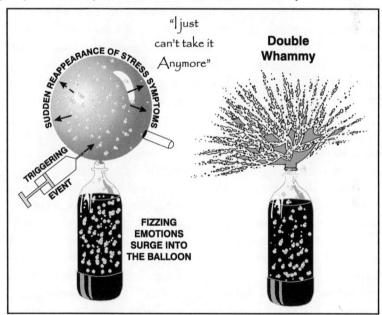

Picture 32: Major double whammy can pop the balloon.

Just prior to the blast from the past, some of these people's balloons might have been almost empty. This means that the hidden mind had not reached its saturation point, and the balloon was not inflated. The good news is that many such people do well with timely counseling with a perceptive therapist. The balloons of others might have been full, due to the hidden mind's having reached its saturation point some time before. In this case, the stress disorder can be serious. Such patients need multiple medications to control their symptoms: anti-anxiety drugs to control overwhelming anxiety, antidepressant medication to coat the balloon and an atypical antipsychotic medication to put the lid on the soda bottle.

A case study: A young woman who had completely forgotten the trauma of her sexual abuse as a child suddenly developed a massive panic attack after discovering that her eight-year-old daughter had been inappropriately touched by the woman's current boyfriend. She was terribly upset over her daughter's sexual abuse (the triggering event, coming from the pump); but this bad event also caused a resurfacing of the long-forgotten trauma of her own childhood sexual abuse by her stepfather (fizz from the soda bottle). Unable to withstand the double whammy, her balloon rapidly inflated and popped. The massive panic attack resulted in a visit to the local emergency room and subsequent hospitalization.

A case study: A middle-aged man became depressed and suicidal two weeks after being promoted to the position of manager upon his boss's retirement (triggering event). Over the course of thirty years, the man had become extremely attached to his boss. Even though he missed working with his boss, he was happy for him. He said that he was happy with his own promotion as well, and he was completely baffled by his serious symptoms. He said, "I have everything going for me. For the life of me, I can't figure out why I feel so depressed." The real reason for his suicidal depression was discovered in the interview. When he was eight years old, the patient had witnessed his father's accidental death from electrocution. Now, forty-two years later, the loss of a father figure triggered the resurfacing of the buried traumatic emotions related to his father's tragic death. This was a heavy-duty double whammy, which popped his balloon, resulting in suicidal depression. How do we know this? Well, once the patient became aware of what was really happening to him, he grieved over both losses, shrank his balloon and got on with his life.

A case study: Here is another interesting story. A forty-year-old woman, the mother of two boys, woke up one fine morning and felt an irresistible desire to shoot herself in the head. Her husband found her in bed, sobbing uncontrollably and holding a loaded gun to her head. She was brought to my office in an emergency. When asked why she wanted to die, she said she did not know. The only precipitating event was that, one week earlier, her eighteen-year-old son had left home to join the Navy. She said she was happy for him, as that was all he wanted to do.

Further digging revealed that she herself had been in the Navy nineteen years earlier. She met a Navy man and fell in love with him. One cold, snowy weekend, while they were enjoying themselves in a warm motel room in a big city, away from the Navy base, she told her lover that she was pregnant. At this, her lover got up, put on his uniform, and told her, "I'll be back shortly." He disappeared into the wintry night, never to be heard from again. Bewildered, she waited for two days for him to return, but the lover neither called nor returned. She quietly buried her grief and rage in her hidden mind, quit the Navy, moved in with her parents in a distant city and moved on with her life as if nothing had ever happened. Later, she married another man, and they raised her son together. Now, nineteen years later, the occasion of her son's joining the Navy brought up a tsunami of buried emotions, leading to the popping of her balloon. The resurfacing grief could not get out of the balloon because of the rage that came up with it, and the pain of it all was so great that she just wanted to end her misery by shooting herself in the head. She got well after she expressed her rage and disappointment in a few therapy sessions, completed the long overdue grief and moved on once again with her life.

The reader should note that these people would have ended up being on multiple drugs for the rest of their lives had they not received timely help with a few insightful sessions. All these people's balloons were relatively small (only slightly inflated) before the double whammy hit them. The majority of patients already have rather big balloons before they experience the double whammy, so they end up on multiple drug treatments for years to come—especially if they don't receive any therapy.

4. Some double whammy phenomena

A. Acute post-traumatic stress disorder is a double whammy. In this condition, a person suddenly re-experiences recently or remotely buried traumatic memories and suffers serious stress symptoms. Invariably, there is a clearly identifiable, current triggering event. The soda bottle fizzes furiously and the balloon pops. "Flashbacks," anxiety, depression, panic attacks, extreme withdrawal, etc. are common.

A case study: A twenty-five-year-old single woman became sick after an older man pulled the strap of her bra at a party. Two years earlier, she had been traumatized by a serious attempted rape by another man at another party. She had buried the emotions related to that event. The current bad event shook her soda bottle, and the buried emotions fizzed up in a fury. As a way of coping with the tremendous pressure in her balloon, the woman became mute, bedridden and non-responsive for several days. She required prolonged therapy to help her deal with the old trauma. One might ask, "Why did this particular patient need prolonged therapy?" In cases where this is needed, one may find that the bottle was already almost full and the balloon inflated before the first trauma occurred. These PTSD patients were already compromised before the trauma.

B. Chronic post-traumatic stress disorder is a double whammy in slow motion. The resurfacing of emotions does not have to happen as suddenly as in the above case. One might chronically suffer from numerous stress symptoms as a result of the slow resurfacing of traumatic childhood memories and emotions, merely in the course of watching one's own children grow up. This is like the bubbles floating up from the bottle into the balloon, slowly but continually. I have known many a parent suffering in this way from a multitude of low-grade symptoms—depression, anxiety, headaches, sleeplessness, mood swings and the like—and perpetually wondering what is happening to him or her. As their children reach a certain age, the parents relive the traumas they suffered at that age. Chronic post-traumatic stress disorder is common in people who have had rough childhoods, as well as in people who have suffered sustained periods of a high level of stress, such as serious, long-drawn-out combat. Soldiers required to bury their terror under fire often suffer from chronic post-traumatic stress disorder upon their return to civilian life. At least some cases of Gulf War syndrome must belong in this category. In these people, even the noise of a firecracker, a helicopter or a popping balloon is enough to bring on serious stress symptoms. The balloon inflates every time the fizz comes up from the soda bottle.

The fallout from chronic post-traumatic stress disorder can be devastating to family members living with the patient. A young man witnessed the deaths of several friends in Viet Nam, and was himself badly injured. His bottle became saturated and his balloon was full (low stress tolerance syndrome). Upon returning home, he was diagnosed as having chronic post-traumatic stress disorder. He became increasingly hostile, violent, hateful, irritable and abusive toward his wife and seven children. He drank heavily and refused to get help. Years later, because of the sustained nature of the stress of living with him, his wife and all seven children developed serious psychiatric disorders: major depression, alcoholism, drug addiction, panic disorder, bulimia, etc. Several of them attempted suicide.

C. The therapy-induced double whammy. Many patients get much worse immediately after starting therapy with an inexperienced therapist and end up hospitalized. This is because aggressive and indiscriminate probing by the therapist causes buried painful emotions to resurface suddenly. To be asked, in the very first session, such a question as, "Tell me everything you remember about the sexual molestation by your uncle when you were eight years old," can be devastating to some patients. In effect, the therapist has shaken up the soda bottle too vigorously and the patient's balloon, already full, has popped from the surging blast of fizz from the soda bottle. Many such patients become suicidal. Many others refuse therapy thereafter. I have seen countless patients who ended up being unnecessarily hospitalized because of a therapist's rough handling. To illustrate how serious this problem can be, even without vigorous probing, let us study just two cases.

A case study: A thirty-four-year-old woman came to see me complaining of severe panic attacks, of three months' duration, brought on by her daughter's turning eight. This woman had been molested by her uncle, starting at around age eight. In her session with me, I carefully avoided discussing the childhood sexual abuse. However, in the course of our talk, to emphasize a certain point I was making, I said, "Trust me." The patient blanched and became visibly sick. She left my office feeling worse than when she had come in a few minutes earlier. When she returned three years later, she explained what had happened to her during the first visit with me. Her uncle always told her, "Trust me," before he molested her. My innocent comment had shaken her soda bottle and spewed the fizz into her balloon so badly that she had a massive panic attack during the interview. It took her three years to muster enough courage to come back for her second appointment!

A case study: A forty-five-year-old woman suffering from severe panic disorder came to see me after five years of futile and traumatic treatment under various doctors and specialists. She had been hospitalized several times in the local hospitals and was given antipsychotic drugs, with frightening side effects. With education, medication and counseling, she got well and stayed symptom-free for five years. Thinking that it was time to start reducing her medication, I asked if she would consider gradually doing so. She fell silent for a while, and then said she was scared to do so. I did not press the issue. A few minutes after she left my office, she called me, frantically saying she was having a severe panic attack. This was her first panic attack in five years. She had pulled off the highway and was thinking of going to the emergency room. It was obvious that her bottle had been shaken, bringing up traumatic memories of past treatments, triggered by my suggestion that she consider reducing the dosage of her medications. I cannot overstate the need for doctors and therapists to be careful about what they say to their patients.

D. The double whammy resulting from trivial events. The resurfacing of emotions, good or bad, from the remote past can be triggered by even a minor sensory input: a sound, word, smell, touch, sight, gesture, smile or frown, look, glance, taste, season, cloud, dog, cat, TV show, song or, for that matter, any object that is even remotely connected to the past good or bad event. The person might not have a clue why his old memories have resurfaced. These people often make such comments as, "I don't know why, but I felt sad all day yesterday. Nothing happened to make me feel that way." It is the job of the counselor to teach patients to become increasingly aware of the connection between a current sensory input and the appearance of a stress symptom.

E. A good event can also cause a double whammy. Even a genuinely good current event can cause the double whammy, thus spoiling the happiness of the occasion. The perfectly happy occasion of a second wedding to a wonderful person can bring up buried memories of a horrendous first marriage to, and divorce from, a bad spouse, resulting in depression, anxiety or marital problems. I have seen many a second marriage thus ruined by excess baggage from the first. So we must look beneath the surface to know exactly how a given "good event" affects someone.

F. The "anniversary reaction" is a double whammy. In the so-called "anniversary reaction," one suffers from severe stress symptoms on the anniversary of a bad event, say, the death of a child or a parent, the diagnosis of a serious illness, a divorce, etc. Clearly, this is caused by resurfacing buried emotions.

G. The "holiday blues" are a double whammy. Holiday blues are often due to resurfacing emotions related to bad childhood memories from around Christmastime. Many people suffer from depression as the Christmas holidays approach. They wonder, "This is supposed to be a happy time. Why am I feeling sad?" Most of these people report that they do not recall anything bad happening during Christmas while they were growing up. The key to this mystery lies in the fact that the patient was so used to all the nonsensical stuff going on in the family that he did not think of it as bad. He had nothing else with which to compare his situation. But during every Christmas, his family was in turmoil for one reason or another; so all the buried memories related to Christmas in his hidden mind are painful.

Every Christmas, they resurface and make him feel bad.

H. Borderline personalities suffer from rapid-fire double whammy. In a serious psychiatric disorder known as borderline personality disorder, the patient experiences wild mood swings, frequent panic and depressive attacks, angry outbursts, suicidal ideas and gestures, difficulty in tolerating intimacy, inability to get along with others, seeking closeness and rejecting it, impulsive acting-out and many other highly uncomfortable and often self-destructive behaviors. These people have been through serious stressful events and situations in their childhoods—sexual, physical or emotional abuse, emotional abandonment and deprivation. In a person with this disorder, his balloon is always full, and it receives continual blasts of fizz from the soda bottle, triggered by even minor everyday events. In other words, the capacity to hold down the fizz in the bottle is almost nil because of the tremendous emotional pressure in the bottle. Thus, the balloon pops frequently. These people like to cut themselves with knives and blades, as if they are trying in their own primitive way to release their inner emotional tension. Somehow, experiencing physical pain seems to relieve emotional pain somewhat. (We read elsewhere how the mind releases emotional pain by experiencing bodily pain.) Another reason why such people cut themselves is to hurt the internalized parent figure. In other words, driven by their inner rage, they are trying to hurt the "parent" in them. In addition to this, in a vain attempt to fill their "Nurturance" folder they indulge in serious attention-seeking behavior (ASB). This behavior is geared toward getting love, empathy and concern from people around them, including their therapists and psychiatrists. These patients often threaten suicide and make superficial attempts to indicate their suicidal intention. Because of their unpredictable behavior, most therapists dread treating such people.

A case study: A thirty-year-old woman with a borderline condition called me shortly after she left my office, threatening suicide by jumping off the bridge that crossed the Mississippi River. She had been in a good mood when she left the office a few minutes earlier. When I asked what had happened between our meeting and her phone call, she was not able to explain. Suddenly, it occurred to me that as she was leaving my office, I had been distracted by a phone call and failed to shake hands with her. This apparent "rejection" triggered the resurfacing of all her past rejections, resulting in the instant popping of her balloon. When I apologized to her for not shaking hands before she left my office, she calmed down. I used this opportunity to give her some insight into the roots of her suicidal behavior.

I. Postpartum disorder is a double whammy phenomenon. In this condition, shortly after the birth of a baby the new mother experiences severe depression, anxiety, obsessive thoughts of a violent nature or even psychosis. The baby's birth triggers buried painful emotions related to her traumatic childhood, her younger siblings and her own parents. These emotions are spewed up into the balloon, and they pop it. The severity of the symptoms depends upon the nature and amount of the resurfacing painful emotion. The patient can experience resentment and violent or homicidal thoughts and impulses against the baby and/or the baby's father. In turn, these obsessive, violent thoughts create severe fear and guilt, resulting in the balloon's inflating even more, and this can bring on panic attacks as well. The perfectly happy occasion of the birth of a baby is thus ruined. When questioned directly, the patient might deny any childhood issues. However, a skillful therapist will not fail to obtain useful information about the mother's relationship with her own siblings and parents, her feelings about being a mother and the like. Most of these women report a highly ambivalent relationship with their own parents. The hormonal imbalance associated with childbirth almost certainly contributes to the problem. Prompt treatment with reassurance, education, insight, medication and counseling controls the symptoms. Postpartum depression could also happen in men due to the resurfacing of painful childhood emotions.

J. "Road rage" and "going postal" can be a double whammy gone berserk. Some people's hidden minds are so filled with compressed rage that they are ready to explode at the least provocation. Most of them are walking around with overfilled balloons that are ready to pop. These people are truly sitting on a powder keg; all it takes is a stray bullet to blow them sky high. "Road rage" and "going postal" are but two examples of the furious explosion of both the balloon and the bottle, resulting in a "rage reaction." Men who kill their wives in a rage, women who run over their unfaithful husbands with their cars, people who commit murder or suicide, people who hold their families hostage, people who threaten to jump off radio towers or bridges and who commit suicide all belong in this category. A real or imagined insult, rejection, punishment or injury is enough to explode the powder keg in their hidden minds. In all these cases, the conscious mind is completely out of contact with the wisdom in the hidden mind.

K. Bad dreams and nightmares are a double whammy.

Dreaming is a normal function of the mind. It serves the purpose of reviewing all the information we have piled up on the floor of the mind in the course of the busy day, and filing it in appropriate folders for future use, while the mind is resting at night. While it is being reviewed, the information appears on the screen of the sleeping mind. Sometimes, the information appearing on the screen of the mind might trigger a buried, bad memory, which resurfaces in the dream. This results in bad dreams or nightmares. When the contents of a dream are merely painful, the dream is called a bad dream. Dreaming about the death of someone dear or about grieving over a dead person are examples. In a bad dream, one experiences emotions related to the sadness and guilt complexes. Dreams that are full of violence and terror are called nightmares. In a nightmare, one experiences painful emotions related to the anger and fear complexes. In some nightmares, we experience fear-related emotions, such as terror; for example, when we dream of someone chasing us and wanting to kill us. In a nightmare filled with anger-related emotions, we might dream of killing someone else. Dreams are the mind's way of expressing buried painful emotions.

Almost always, a daytime triggering event precedes the dream or nightmare. For example, one might have talked about his dead mother with his sibling during the day. That night, he dreams of his mother and wakes up crying. Often, not knowing the beneficial effect of dreams, people become upset over bad dreams. When

I tell them that even bad dreams are good for them, their perception changes and they smile with relief. I use this opportunity to encourage people to learn to express their emotions if they wish to avoid bad dreams.

L. The midlife crisis is a type of double whammy

1. In the midlife crisis, buried unmet needs, desires and wishes from childhood suddenly resurface. In the so-called midlife crisis, it is not the buried emotions that resurface but the buried desires, dependency, needs, cravings, wishes and yearnings from our childhood days, which went unmet. These unmet needs were quietly denied, forgotten and buried in the "Nurturance" folder in the hidden mind. A precipitating event, such as a chance meeting with an old flame or a heartfelt compliment from a person of the opposite sex, can set this process in motion. When the unmet desires and needs resurface, one experiences an intense need to fulfill them. The consequences, though, can be great, and often disastrous. The midlife crisis is responsible for the breakup of many marriages. In a midlife crisis, one's desire to get love and attention is so great that it disconnects the mind from the restraints of one's own moral values, resulting in out-of-character behavior.

2. Spouses are often clueless. The reason for this so-called crisis occurring in one's late thirties or forties is that it is beginning to dawn on vulnerable men and women that they are "over the hill." They think, "I'd better catch up with whatever I missed in life." During the crisis, a person intensely craves to be admired, loved, worshipped, attended to, appreciated or taken care of by a person of the opposite sex. Married men and women may find someone outside their marriage who seems to meets their needs. They find their spouses totally unable or inadequate to meet these almost insatiable needs. In such cases, the spouse is usually clueless and indifferent to his or her troubled spouse's needs. Often, the sufferer of the midlife crisis has been emotionally distant from the clueless spouse for some time, because of their failure to renew the bonds between them. Thus, they have grown apart.

3. Consequences of the midlife crisis. Once the affair begins, fireworks explode in the mind's sky, and bells and whistles go off in the head. Rivers of adrenaline and oxytocin begin to flow. The person feels giddy. A lot of hanky-panky and cloak-and-dagger stuff begins to take place. Some people are able to keep the affair under wraps (pun intended); but when the cover is blown, the shit begins to hit the fan. Separation and divorce may follow. Others, unable to handle their gnawing guilt, confess their misdeeds to their naive spouses and make a big mess of everything. This can lead the balloons of both spouses to pop. Still other people make plans to leave their marriage. They now "want some space" to think things over. They rent someplace so that they can carry on their nefarious affairs in perfect privacy.

Sometimes, when the affair is with an unstable character, such as a borderline or narcissistic personality, one may have to deal with "Fatal Attraction"-type behavior: blackmail, stalking, manipulation, threatening conduct or controlling behavior. Most extramarital affairs triggered by a midlife crisis last for about eighteen months. However, thousands of people quietly and successfully manage their affairs for decades or "till death do us part." Some unsuspecting spouses discover an affair only after the death of their spouse. This can be devastating for them. Marriage to the "other person" following a divorce is usually short-lived, as it is based on false premises, deceit and mistrust. As soon as the new couple gets married, the fireworks stop. Rivers of hormones dry up and the bells and whistles fall silent. The new spouse hangs onto his or her partner for dear life, fearing that now it might happen to her (or him)!

One unfortunate consequence of the midlife crisis is that some of its victims are misdiagnosed as having bipolar disorder and are put on medications for years to come. This happens because their symptoms—sexual misadventure, euphoria, poor judgment and the like—are mistaken for symptoms of bipolar disorder. Even though the midlife crisis is a clearly identifiable psychiatric syndrome, it is not yet accepted as such by the psychiatric community.

A case study: A middle-aged woman, unhappily married to an alcoholic, met an old boyfriend at a barbecue party. The ex-boyfriend said and did things that kindled a great deal of happiness in the woman's heart. This chance meeting suddenly brought to the surface intense unmet desires and cravings to be loved, admired and adored. The woman had buried these needs as a child and suppressed them as an adult. Her parents had split up when she was three years old, and her stepfather had given her no love. Her alcoholic husband paid little attention to her needs. The sudden re-acquaintance with an old flame rekindled her buried desires and needs, and she went on to have a tempestuous affair with him.

A midlife crisis does not have to hit during the middle of one's life. It can come at any time in adult life. In modern times, the midlife crisis is an increasingly common phenomenon, due to the fact that millions of children are growing up without their basic emotional needs being met on account of parental neglect and self-centeredness. The net result of the midlife crisis is that spouses are traumatized, families broken and children put through hell. This cycle repeats itself in the lives of the children and their grandchildren. Again, the ripple effect continues.

4. The midlife crisis has many other forms. Not everyone going through a midlife crisis has an extramarital affair. Many become involved with social causes, crusades against social evils, movements, litigations, conflicts, wars and the like in order to fulfill their insatiable needs to be noticed, appreciated, adored and empowered. Some even become heroes or movie stars, while others end up on the garbage heap of history.

Finally, the influence of early traumas can be seen in the lives of many notable figures in all professions. Col. T.E. Lawrence, a.k.a. Lawrence of Arabia, is a classic example of a hero motivated by childhood issues. The entertainer Madonna is another example of greatness stimulated by childhood deprivation and trauma.

We should remember that all of us carry our excess emotional baggage with us, wherever we go and whatever we do. I guess that is what makes people, as well as life, interesting!

———◆•◆•◆———

CHAPTER TEN

Persistent Stress Symptoms

In the first chapter, we read that stress symptoms are *transient* in people who are good at coping with stress and shrinking their balloons. We also read about how, after the hidden mind reaches its saturation point, the balloon starts to inflate and stress symptoms return. Now these stress symptoms become *persistent*, as the person is no longer able to shrink his balloon by burying. Persistent stress symptoms indicate an inflated balloon or popped balloon. Every stressed patient must become familiar with these symptoms in order to understand and cope with his disorder. The persistent stress symptoms are the brain's way of alerting us: "Your hidden mind/soda bottle is already full. Now your balloon is getting filled up. Do something!" They are the signals of the brain's alarm system. As we have read, persistent stress symptoms are just the tip of the iceberg. Buried in the soda bottle, filling the balloon and causing those symptoms are painful emotions related to numerous extremely bad events and problems.

In the chapter titled "Pain in the Brain," we studied how each emotion complex—fear, sadness, anger and guilt—causes a unique set of stress symptoms. You can figure out roughly what emotions you have in your balloon by noting what symptoms you have. Often, however, by the time a patient sees the psychiatrist, he has emotions related to two, three or four complexes, which result in a wide range of stress symptoms.

For the purposes of our discussion, we can re-categorize persistent stress symptoms into four convenient groups: physical, emotional, mental and behavioral. All psychiatric stress disorders include all four of these sets of stress symptoms, but in different permutations and combinations. For example, anxiety disorders have primarily physical symptoms, while depressive disorders have primarily grief-related symptoms.

1. Physical stress symptoms.

Persistent physical symptoms are of three types:
A) Pain, somewhere in the body, for which doctors have found no cause.
B) Dysfunctions of certain body organs, for which no cause can be found even after extensive testing. Doctors often refer to these as "functional" symptoms.
C) General body symptoms, for which there appears to be no physical basis.

A. Pain somewhere in the body is rooted in unexpressed emotional pain. Pain somewhere in the body for which doctors cannot find a cause can show up in the form of headache attacks, chest pain, stomach pain, back pain, muscle and joint pains or pain anywhere else. When the patient suffers persistent physical pain for which no physical cause has been found, it is invariably rooted in unexpressed emotional pain (hurt), caused by one or more serious bad events in the past. Without exception, the patient's focus on his physical pain is so great that he has absolutely no clue about his inner emotional pain. The longer the patient has suffered pain, the harder it is to help him through psychological insight. In most of these patients, the emotional pain is deeply buried. In some of them, the physical pain serves the purpose of keeping their minds off their emotional pain. In others, the pain serves them well, getting them attention, sympathy, money or disability payments.
      1. Stress-related pain can be helped at an early stage. The sooner these people get help after the onset of pain, the quicker the results.

A case study: Here is an example of timely intervention that helped. A thirty-eight-year-old married woman was admitted to hospital for severe pain of one week's duration on the lower right side of her chest. In spite of repeated shots of morphine over two hours, she kept doubling up in bed with pain. She screamed and yelled uncontrollably until, finally, psychiatric help was sought. During the interview, I found out that the woman's father had died a week earlier, in the same hospital, from an abscess of the right lung. She had helplessly witnessed his suffering and had been terribly upset over the sight of a big tube sticking out of his chest, which apparently caused him a great deal of pain. Now she was experiencing the same type of pain in the same area of the chest. Clearly, she had a lot of unexpressed emotional pain in her balloon related to her father's suffering and death. Once she broke down and sobbed over the whole painful episode, her balloon shrank, her pain went away and she went home within an hour after the interview, completely free from chest pain.

2. Once pain becomes chronic, it is extremely difficult to get rid of. Many patients do not seek psychiatric help in time because of ignorance about the mind-body connection, the stigma attached to mental disorders and a closed-minded attitude. Instead, they go on fruitless medical wild goose chases, get addicted to pain medications, become disillusioned and depressed, and finally, after their pain becomes chronic, they wind up disabled. Chronic pain syndrome is extremely difficult to treat, since by the time these patients come to the attention of psychiatrists, they have made the rounds with many specialists and have a great deal of emotional and financial investment in their pain. Their symptoms get them attention, sympathy, money and other secondary gains. The primary gain was the partial relief from converting their emotional pain to physical pain.

A case study: Here is a classic example: A fifty-six-year-old widow, the mother of two grownup boys, was referred to me by her frustrated doctor for unremitting, severe pain in the right upper abdomen, which is the liver area. The pain had started suddenly about two years earlier. Unable to tolerate it, the woman initially tried high doses of addictive pain medications. When the pain medications did not help, she went on a medical wild goose chase and saw many specialists. Her liver biopsy came back normal. A surgeon opened her abdomen, and, finding nothing to explain the pain in the region of the liver, he removed her gall bladder. Following her recovery from surgery, the pain became even worse. She underwent another surgery, this time on her back, to cut the nerve supply to the affected part of the body. When this surgical procedure also failed to control the woman's excruciating pain, she went to the Mayo Clinic. There she underwent surgery on her spinal cord to cut off the nerve fibers that carried the pain message from the abdomen to the brain. This did not diminish her pain even a bit. At the Mayo Clinic, she saw a psychiatrist, who gave her a diagnosis of chronic pain disorder, which stands for stress-related pain. However, being a drug-oriented doctor, he did not get a detailed psychiatric history from her. She was put on an antidepressant medication.

In our interview, I obtained the following information: twenty-two years earlier, her husband had been diagnosed as suffering from terminal cancer of the liver. He complained of severe, unremitting upper-right abdominal pain. He was sent home to die with a lot of pain medication. However, the pain medications did not help him at all. He screamed and yelled in pain, day in and day out. Unable to tolerate his suffering, his wife locked him up in a room. She tried to protect her two boys from this trauma by stuffing their ears with earplugs. She quietly stuffed her own pain in her hidden mind by "being strong." After her husband's death, she moved on with her life and raised her two boys as if nothing had happened.

Two years before our interview, the day before the pain in the woman's right upper abdomen started, she received a phone call from a local hospital. Her thirty-year-old son was in the hospital with a broken leg following a major motorcycle accident. When she rushed to the hospital to see him, he was in bed with his leg dangling in the air, held up by a rope over a pulley. He was screaming in pain at the top of his voice, begging for pain medications. Memories of her husband's screams of pain twenty-two years earlier must have suddenly resurfaced in her mind. That night, she became agitated and she slept little. By the next morning, the liver area of her abdomen was in great pain. It was then that she began her medical wild goose chase.

At the end of the interview with me, the patient wanted to know what I had found out. I explained how she had buried her painful emotions related to her husband's pain and suffering by "being strong." Her son's accident had brought up the old emotional pain in the form of abdominal pain. The woman let out a deep sigh, became tearful and fell silent for a while. She appeared somewhat stunned by this unexpected insight. She had been expecting me to say that she had a chemical imbalance. Then, regrouping her denial (self-deception), she said, "I don't see how this could be. How could my mind cause me to have severe pain like this?" My explanation about the mind-body connection, and how emotional pain often shows up as physical pain, made no impression on her closed mind. I pointed out that her pain did not go away even after they had severed the nerve supply to her abdominal area, but even this made no impression on her. Finally, it dawned on me that this sudden insight was a little too much for her to accept, since she had already invested so much time, money, effort and suffering in search of a physical cause for her pain. Admitting to a psychological basis for her pain would mean losing face with herself and everyone around her. She declined to make another appointment with me, saying she did not think counseling would help. I had to accept the reality that I could not save them all.

3. The mind of every headache victim has gallons of unshed tears. A careful evaluation of victims of recurrent headache attacks, whether they are sufferers of cluster headaches or migraines, reveals that they never expressed their emotional pain by shedding tears in response to one or more painful events in either the remote or recent past. In other words, when the body was trying to lower its blood pressure and the volume of blood in the head by shedding tears, these patients fought back, held in their tears and refused to let nature take its course. Now, even a small painful event or sensory input can severely dilate the blood vessels to the head, bringing an increased blood flow into the head, as if the frustrated body is trying to squeeze out the unshed tears at the slightest opportunity. Almost all these patients have such a deep emotional investment in keeping their headaches "physical" and not "mental" that it is practically useless to attempt to convince them otherwise. Headache sufferers are some of the most unaware patients in my practice. They are constantly in search of a new medication that will help their headaches. Therapy to help them shrink the balloon is not for them. You will hear them say, "Nothing ever stressed me. Now, headaches come on whenever the weather changes. It is worse during the allergy season," or some such statement, which indicates that the patient has no clue about what is inside his or her balloon.

4. Fibromyalgia is common in stoic-natured people. A careful evaluation of Fibromyalgia sufferers reveals that their primary coping mechanism is to bury their emotions by "being strong" in the face of adversity. Their emotional pain manifests in micro muscle spasms, which choke off the blood supply to the nerve endings in the muscles, resulting in aches and pains all over the body. Some of these people have "trigger point" pain spots. Most are not psychologically savvy. Their pain is real, but its roots are in the balloon and the soda bottle. The best therapy for these people is to join a support group. Certain antidepressant medications can help alleviate their pain to some extent.

B. Organ dysfunction symptoms. Dysfunctions related to different body organs are common in stressed people.

Heart: rapid heartbeat, skipped heartbeat, elevated blood pressure, low blood pressure, fainting.

Lungs: rapid breathing, fullness in the chest, deep breathing, difficulty breathing, sighing, shortness of breath.

Gastrointestinal tract: stomach knot, nausea, vomiting, diarrhea, gas in the stomach, heartburn, belching.

Muscles: twitching, spasms, pain, tension, jaw-clenching, paralysis, trembling, shakes, aches, restlessness.

Skin: blotches, hives, redness, warmth, chills, itching, pain, goosebumps, numbness, sweating, hot flashes, tingling, burning.

Eyes: blurred vision, watery eyes, tearfulness, redness, itching, blindness.

Genitourinary system: sudden incontinence, frequent urination, burning sensation while urinating, impotence, delayed ejaculation.

Ears: dizziness, deafness, pressure.

Throat: choking, difficulty in swallowing, dryness.

In some disorders, physical symptoms are severe. These organ-related symptoms are often part of a severe form of anxiety known as panic disorder, although they can also occur with depressive disorder and other so-called somatization disorders. In panic disorder, when the patient's balloon pops he suffers from episodes of severe symptoms related to one or more of the body organs: fast heartbeat, shortness of breath, dizziness, choking sensation in the throat, knot in the stomach, vomiting, diarrhea, skin blotches, hot and cold waves over the body, etc. The patient suspects a serious illness related to the organ involved—heart attack, stroke, gall bladder attack, low blood sugar, brain tumor and the like—and he goes on a medical wild goose chase. A careful review of his history will reveal a clear precipitating event, as well as many underlying bad events and problems. Of course, most people deny these problems outright. It is as if a pregnant young woman were to deny ever having had sex, or even knowing what a man looks like. Then there are patients who complain of one specific symptom, such as hearing loss, blindness, choking of the throat, paralysis of a limb, impotence, etc. Again, careful exploration will reveal that the patient has focused on just the most distressing symptom and excluded the others. Some of these symptoms are labeled by doctors as conversion symptoms, meaning that a hidden emotion is converted into a body symptom in a surreptitious attempt to express it.

A case study: A middle-aged man complained of the sudden onset of impotence. An extensive physical examination did not reveal any basis for his impotence, and he was referred to me by his family physician, who suspected an emotional basis. In the interview, the man revealed that his impotence had started shortly after his new boss was appointed. His new boss was an ex-military man, who intimidated the patient by using profane language and threatening gestures. The patient felt emasculated by his boss. This became apparent every night in the bedroom. After much encouragement from me to be assertive with his boss, the patient decided to tackle him. One day, when he found his boss alone in a small room, the patient closed the door behind him and grabbed the boss by the throat. Using the same filthy language that his boss usually used, the patient told him to back off or he would soon get what was due to him. The thoroughly shaken boss promised to behave himself. The next day, I received a phone call from the ecstatic wife, thanking me for curing her husband's impotence. Of course, I had never advised the patient to confront his boss the way he did! Nevertheless, the problem was solved.

C. Generalized body symptoms. Some common general body symptoms are tiredness, weakness, exhaustion, fatigue, sleepiness, sleeplessness, malaise, low-grade fever, flu-like symptoms and "just not feeling good." It is as if the brain chemicals have become burnt out by the ongoing battle with the emotions. Some of these patients, who focus on physical exhaustion alone and do not admit to other symptoms, are given the diagnosis of chronic fatigue syndrome. Invariably, they have other stress symptoms as well, but they do not admit to them. If someone were to interview these people with their guard down, they would give histories of many painful life events and problems. They have coped with these problems by burying their emotions, and by the time they see a doctor for their fatigue, it is too late. Most of these people are incapable of insight. Their disorders are permanent, and they get worse from year to year. Medications and supportive treatment are the mainstays of their treatment.

2. Persistent emotional symptoms.

A. Emotional symptoms that are brought on by the painful emotions related to stressors. These include loss of interest, feelings of gloom and doom, sadness, despair, irrational guilt, anxiety, etc. These emotional symptoms are brought on by painful emotions that have inflated the balloon over a period of time. They are seen in depressive and anxiety disorders.

B. Emotional symptoms related to the suffering itself. When stressed-out people express painful emotions, such as helplessness, hopelessness, frustration, despondency and the like, these emotions are usually related to the patients' reactions to their current illness, and so they are secondary in nature. These "reactive" emotions disappear as soon as the patients begin to get help. The fact that

Bob Kamath, M.D.

they are now doing something to alleviate their misery, along with reassurance by a doctor, gets rid of their hopelessness, helplessness, fear and frustration. This explains why most people feel better immediately after they start treatment, even before the medications have had time to work.

3. Persistent mental, or cognitive, symptoms.

Cognitive stress symptoms are related to the thinking process. They include worrying, forgetfulness, inability to recall names and incidents, difficulty concentrating, slowed thinking, mental exhaustion, inability to make decisions, disorientation, a sense of unreality, out-of-body experience, suspicion, distrust and delusions. These mental, or cognitive, symptoms steadily worsen as the balloon becomes bigger. As we read elsewhere, many of these people are inappropriately diagnosed as suffering from Attention Deficit Disorder.

4. Persistent behavioral symptoms, which can get people into serious trouble.

Common persistent behavioral symptoms are irritability, agitation, angry outbursts, arguing, pacing, hand-wringing, crying, yelling, fighting, screaming, shouting, slamming the door, hitting the wall, assault, reckless driving, withdrawing (avoiding people), promiscuity, not getting out of bed, drinking alcohol, abusing drugs, abusing family members and the like.

A. Behavioral symptoms are more common in angry, immature people. Obviously, these symptoms are indicative of a troubled mind. They are prominent in stressed children and adolescents, as young people express themselves more by acting out than by speaking out. Immature adults who are unable to speak out also frequently show their inner tension by acting out. Adults with behavioral symptoms should be considered potentially dangerous. They can be hateful, hostile, obnoxious, mean, angry and violent. These behaviors are often part of a personality disorder, and when such a disorder co-exists with other serious disorders (a dual diagnosis), such as bipolar disorder, major depression or psychosis, the result can be disastrous. Many people who act out get into serious legal problems.

B. Passive-aggressive behavior. One is said to display passive-aggressive behavior when he expresses his inner displeasure or anger by means of a passive act, such as not keeping an appointment, not showing up for a family occasion, not going to work, not fulfilling a promise or obligation, not paying back a loan, etc. Some angry spouses punish their partners by withholding sex. Passive-aggressive behavior can do as much damage to one's relationships with others as overt violence. Psychiatrists often deal with this type of behavior in their practice, with patients not showing up for confirmed appointments, not paying their bills, dirtying the carpet in the waiting room, throwing cigarette butts and garbage in the parking lot, etc.

C. Other elaborate acting-out behaviors may include having an extramarital affair, going on vacation without one's spouse, buying big-ticket stuff without the spouse's knowledge or permission, otherwise spending money recklessly without consulting the spouse, taking up a job in distant city without shifting one's household, etc. In these cases, the acting-out person has some unexpressed anger toward the spouse, which he or she is unable to speak about.

5. Some people try to cash in on their symptoms

A. Disability syndrome. Sometimes, patients knowingly (consciously) or unknowingly (unconsciously) use persistent stress symptoms to get sympathy, support, love, attention, money, etc. When they do this knowingly, they are labeled malingerers. When the motive is not so conscious, this phenomenon is known as secondary gain motivated behavior. Since the sufferer obtains some type of psychological or financial benefit because of his symptoms, he is not much motivated to receive treatment or get better. Thus, if I am collecting disability payments from an insurance company because of my anxiety symptoms, I will report no improvement of my symptoms, regardless of what treatment I have received, as this would mean losing my monetary benefits and having to return to a job I hate.

   A case study: A fifty-eight-year-old woman who had been receiving disability payments for over twenty years on the grounds of some vague physical complaints received a letter from the Social Security Disability Department, requiring her to undergo a routine evaluation so that her current health status could be assessed. After examining her, the naïve physician said, "Congratulations! You are in robust health. There is not a thing wrong with you." As the doctor left the room, he heard a thud. When he turned to see what had happened, he saw the patient on the floor. Apparently, she had fainted. The physician was forced to hospitalize her for further investigation. The woman stayed in the hospital for over two weeks, complaining of one stress symptom or another and costing Medicare several thousand dollars. No matter what the doctor did, the patient kept telling him she was not feeling any better. She agreed to leave the hospital only after the doctor assured her that he was going to pass on to the Social Security Department her three-inch-thick medical record, showing how sick she was.

   B. Compensation neurosis. People who are injured at work often do not feel better until they receive adequate compensation for their pain and suffering. This type of secondary gain syndrome is called compensation neurosis. The people who have this syndrome are usually insecure by nature, and they invariably have a list of grievances against their employers. They harbor anger and hate against an employer or supervisor for real or perceived injustices done to them. Often, these people give histories of some higher-up having made a derogatory remark just before or after the accident occurred. Some are fearful of getting fired when they return to work. They also report that they did not receive proper attention or sympathy from the supervisor at the time of the accident, were not sent a get-well card while recovering and so on.

By the time these people consult a psychiatrist, they have already retained a lawyer. In treatment, they usually do not take medications as prescribed, do not keep their appointments for physical or talking therapy and report no response to the medications or therapy given for their main symptoms. They have no incentive to get well, as they would then have no claim for compensation. For the doctors, treating such patients is like telling a psychotic death-row inmate, "As soon as you are certified as not psychotic, we will strap you to the electric chair and cook you till you're done." No matter how many shots of antipsychotic drugs you might pump into the inmate, he will not give up his craziness. These patients' symptoms improve dramatically as soon as they have received their compensatory payments.

A case study: A fifty-five-year-old truck driver received a minor injury to his neck as a result of a damaged side mirror on his truck. The injury missed his carotid artery by a millimeter. After the skin laceration healed, the patient continued to have a number of physical symptoms, such as blurred vision, numbness of the face, weakness of the tongue, etc. He did not respond to any of the treatments prescribed by his neurologist, including nerve medications. Unable to find a physical cause, the neurologist finally referred the man to me.

In the interview, I found out that the patient had worked for a local truck company for over thirty years. This truck company was now in the process of downsizing and was laying-off truck drivers one by one. The man was certain that if he returned to work, he would lose his job and that he would not find another job at his age. As long as he stayed sick, he was, by law, guaranteed his full salary and benefits. So, regardless of what treatment I gave him, he came back to report, "I am worse than ever."

Then, one day, he walked into my office looking quite cheerful. He said he was doing just fine. Surprised by this wonderful change in his demeanor, I asked what had happened. He replied, smiling, that he had just been diagnosed with cancer of the stomach, and that the Social Security Department had declared him totally and permanently disabled. Now that he was guaranteed a paycheck and did not have to go back to his old job or risk being fired, he felt great. The fact that his stomach cancer would kill him in six months seemed far from his insecure mind. This man would rather die than be without an income!

C. Stress symptoms are sometimes abused in order to control and manipulate others. Sometimes, people who are insecure in their relationships with their significant others keep hanging onto their stress symptoms to control and manipulate them. No matter what the doctor does, their symptoms do not get any better.

A case study: A thirty-five-year-old woman who suspected her husband of infidelity started to have severe panic attacks. Her husband thought that her panic attacks might have something to do with their strained relationship, and he became extremely solicitous and supportive in response to her suffering. In spite of high doses of medication and regular psychotherapy, the patient reported little improvement. It soon became clear that she was scared to declare any improvement, as that could jeopardize her improved relationship with her husband.

Patients often use such symptoms as dizziness, weakness in the legs, headaches, chest pain and shortness of breath to control others, obtain sympathy, avoid responsibilities and escape punishment. Usually, an enabler is involved. Once these symptoms become well established, both parties need to receive counseling to control them.

6. The stress equation

None of us can completely avoid experiencing painful emotions, no matter how good we are at managing stress in our lives. All we can hope for is to keep the input of these emotions to a minimum, and their output to a maximum. In the final analysis, it is the total amount of painful emotion remaining in the mind/balloon that determines how severe our persistent stress symptoms are. The word "amount" represents the total number of painful emotions combined with their severity. Here is an attempt to quantify this equation:

TPE - (BE+EP+CE) = SSS.

In this equation, TPE represents the total number of painful emotions that have appeared in the mind/balloon. BE represents the buried emotions in the hidden mind/soda bottle. EP is the expressed emotions. CE is the cancelled-out emotions. Thus, the total painful emotions minus the sum of buried emotions, expressed emotions and cancelled-out emotions leaves a balance, which is whatever remains in the mind/balloon. This balance decides the SSS, or the severity of persistent stress symptoms.

CHAPTER ELEVEN

The Medical Wild Goose Chase

In this chapter, we will study how people react when their stress symptoms become persistent and how this creates more prob lems for them. Once stress symptoms become persistent, they are baffled and scared by them, especially the physical symptoms. They have made no connection between their symptoms and accumulating painful emotions in their mind. This fear of strange symptoms and the consequences of the behavior that follows it add to the already accumulating painful emotions, causing the balloon to inflate even more. Thus the stress symptoms become even worse.

People react to each set of symptoms—physical, emotional, mental and behavioral—somewhat differently. The reactions depend upon the type, severity, suddenness, rate of recurrence, and many other factors related to the symptoms and to the sufferer. Everyone is unique in the way he reacts to stress symptoms, but when they are persistent, self-help and the medical wild goose chase (MWGC) are two common reactions. Most people try to help themselves as well as they can before making the rounds of doctors; but self-help invariably fails or makes things worse, as the stress symptoms become persistent. Let us review some of the self-help steps people take.

1. People try self-help before starting MWGC.

A. Over-the-counter and under-the-table medications. If the physical symptoms are minor—headaches, sleeplessness, stomachaches, tension, etc.—people try to help themselves with over-the-counter medications, such as pain relievers, sleeping aids, antacids, muscle relaxants, etc. The vast majority of television commercials we see today promote such products. These remedies are almost completely useless, except temporarily. People may also resort to taking nerve medications borrowed or stolen from relatives or friends. This has become a rampant problem in society. In fact, drugs are sometimes stolen from patients by nurses and pharmacists. I have lost count of the honest patients who tell me, "My sister-in-law came to visit me. After she left, I discovered that all my nerve medications were gone!" Or, "When I went home from the pharmacy and counted my pills, I found I was twenty-nine pills short."

B. Pleasurable and mindless activities. We have already read about how people indulge in pleasurable, useless activities to cope with their stress symptoms

2. The medical wild goose chase.

A. The medical wild goose chase is due to ignorance of the mind-brain-body connection. When self-help fails and more dreadful physical symptoms start re-appearing one by one, the patient wonders what is happening to his health. Now his imagination runs wild. He starts visiting doctors and hospitals, and soon he is on an endless medical wild goose chase. I believe that hundreds of thousands of people in America are in this predicament at any given time. In my opinion, after the greed of the medical establishment, the medical wild goose chase is the most important cause of the health care crisis in America today. Here is a description of the steady downward path some people take.

B. The medical wild goose chase usually begins with a visit to the emergency room. If the physical symptoms are serious, alarming or of sudden onset, as is the case in panic disorder, the patient suspects a serious disorder, depending upon the organ involved: heart attack, stroke, bleeding ulcer, gall bladder attack, appendicitis, asthma, brain tumor, allergic reaction, low blood sugar and the like. Scared to death, the patient runs to the emergency room and is tested extensively—and expensively. Often, he spends a night or two in the intensive care unit. After this brief hospitalization, patients are often discharged with such dubious diagnoses as minor heart attack, seizure disorder, transient ischemic attack (also known as TIA, or temporary loss of blood supply to a part of the brain)—all in the absence of any convincing medical evidence. Forever thus labeled, they live in fear of having another episode, and they keep taking a variety of unnecessary medications, such as digoxin, blood thinners, anticonvulsants and the like, for years to come. The regrettable fact is that the average medical doctor, including the emergency room doctor, has little awareness of the role stress plays in the onset of the patients' symptoms.

C. Visits to one's personal doctor. If the symptoms are somewhat scary and recurrent but not too serious, the patient visits his personal doctor. A thorough physical examination and a battery of tests are done, all drawing a blank. The patient is slightly relieved, but also baffled. "If everything is all right, how come I have all these scary symptoms?" When the good doctor asks, "Are you under any kind of stress?" the usual flippant reply is, "Oh, no! None whatsoever!" or "No more than any one else," or "I handle my stress well. This cannot be stress." A more indignant reply might be, "I am not imagining this, Doctor. I am not crazy! This is for real, okay?" The naïve doctor buys into this denial, and goes on ordering more tests. He does not want to risk either losing the patient or being sued by him. It is a win-win situation for the health care providers.

D. Visits to specialists. As symptoms get worse and become recurrent or chronic, patients start to visit medical specialists: the neurologist, cardiologist, ear, nose and throat specialist, gastroenterologist, allergist, lung specialist. You name it! Often, the patient is hospitalized many times, and insurance companies are milked to the maximum. Test after expensive test is ordered. MRI scans follow C/T scans. Angiograms and cystograms are done. Endoscopies and laparoscopies are performed. Sometimes, surgical procedures are performed. Yet nothing physical is found to explain the symptoms. The curious thing is that the specialists keep prescribing one drug after another, some of which are nerve medications, while telling the patient that there is nothing wrong with him. Perhaps the doctors suspect an underlying nervous condition, or perhaps they are hoping for a placebo effect. Or, more likely, they feel they must do something to justify the huge bills they have charged. By now, most patients are justifiably disheartened, disillusioned and demoralized.

E. Visits to famous medical centers. Disappointed, many patients undertake pilgrimages to well-known medical centers, such as the Mayo Clinic, believing that their local doctors must have missed something. When the hot-shot specialists at these medical centers also find nothing, you can imagine how hopeless and helpless the patient feels. Some, especially those who have good insurance policies, go back again to the same institution or to similar one with a greater reputation. In other words, they redouble their efforts, vowing to "get to the bottom of this."

3. Complications of the medical wild goose chase.

A. Medical trauma. Many medical wild goose chasers become traumatized by the grueling ordeal associated with this futile chase. Unexpected complications from medical tests and from unnecessary surgeries sometimes develop, such as bleeding, infection, nerve damage, collapsed lung, peritoneal adhesions, etc. The patient feels angry, disgusted, frustrated and disappointed with the medical profession in general, and with his personal doctor in particular. Even the doctors begin to get frustrated. Disgusted doctors often make matters worse by saying unkind things, such as, "Lady, I don't know what your problem is! It certainly is not physical. It must all be in your head. I think you should see a shrink." Patients interpret such off-the-cuff, hostile remarks to mean that they must be going crazy, or that the doctor believes they are lying about their symptoms, with some ulterior motive. Feelings of fear, anger, helplessness, hopelessness and abandonment are common. People who were traumatized by abandonment earlier in their lives can become extremely sick immediately after such an interaction. Thus repeatedly traumatized, these people never trust doctors again.

B. Medication phobia. As we read before, nowadays, antidepressant medications are widely and sometimes indiscriminately prescribed by just about any licensed medical doctor. Some patients, especially those with anxiety disorders, become severely sick from antidepressant medications inappropriately prescribed by well-meaning but inexperienced doctors. Patients with anxiety disorder are particularly sensitive to antidepressant medications, and most doctors are unaware of this fact. After a few bad experiences, many patients develop medication phobia (fear of medication). They get sick at the very sight of medicine, can become very ill after taking even a miniscule dose, and often run to the emergency room, believing that they have had an allergic reaction or panic attack. In my practice, these are the most difficult patients, as, being the sickest of the sick, they are the ones who would most benefit from medications, yet they are the ones who most fear them. Unless the psychiatrist is thoroughly aware of this condition, he, too, can contribute to the patient's phobia by being irate with him or by starting him on too large a dose of medication. Patients with this problem need a great deal of education, understanding and support. I tell my medication-phobic patients, "A drug is only as good or bad as the doctor prescribing it." These patients do well when a doctor starts them on miniscule doses of medication and gives them permission to raise the dose at their own pace. A small dose of anti-anxiety medication can be used to calm the nerves while the patients increase the dosage of the antidepressant. This takes a little longer than the usual course of medication, but in this way, almost all patients can be desensitized to their medications.

Bob Kamath, M.D.

Picture 33: The medical wild goose chase is a disillusioning experience.

C. Rare Disease Syndrome is a complication of the medical wild goose chase.

Some medical wild goose chasers develop Rare Disease Syndrome. They delude themselves into believing that they have some type of dreadful, obscure disease that all the specialists have missed. Many manage to locate doctors in bigger cities who specialize in rare diseases, such as Lyme disease, chronic fatigue syndrome, chemical allergies, Fibromyalgia (no longer rare) and the like, and they pursue their fruitless search with these doctors for many years to come. By the time they come to the attention of a perceptive psychiatrist, it is too late to help them. Their minds are already made up.

D. Demoralization is the end point of the medical wild goose chase.
Gradually, the patient becomes disillusioned over the consistent lack of results from medical checkups and tests, the accumulating bills of doctors and hospitals, the hostility he meets from his boss and co-workers for frequently missing work, and the lack of or diminishing support and sympathy from family members, who by

now are sick and tired of the ever-elusive sickness. In the end, these patients have nothing to show for all the money and time they've spent and the trouble they have taken. Despair, disillusion and demoralization are the end point of the medical wild goose chase.

E. Maybe they cried "Wolf!" once too often. Many chronic medical wild goose chasers are unjustly labeled as malingerers, hypochondriacs, hysterics, chronic complainers and the like by frustrated and uninformed doctors. Emergency room doctors dread their visits. The problem with this is that when such patients show up with real medical problems, doctors might not take them seriously and thus miss life-threatening disorders.

4. Causes of the medical wild goose chase.

Why do so many people go through this harrowing experience? The reasons are obvious.

A. The patient has no clue. Most people indulging in MWGC have no knowledge of the mind-brain-body connection. You often hear them say, "This is not in my head. I am not imagining this!"

B. Stigma. The patients feel a dire need to prove that their symptoms are physical, not mental, since, to them, "mental" means that one is a certified nut case.

C. **The doctor has no clue.** In the absence of any physical cause, the doctor is unable to explain the symptoms. He is not aware of the mechanism of persistent stress symptoms and is not informed about the fact that unexpressed emotions can result in frightening physical symptoms.

D. Health insurance companies are ignorant of the nature of stress symptoms. Insurance policies usually pay all expenses for "physical" symptoms, but not for "mental" symptoms.

E. It provides distraction. The medical wild goose chase keeps the patient's mind away from all the personal problems that brought the illness on in the first place. Besides, as per Rule #2, the more severe the stress symptoms, the less one is aware of his inner, painful emotions. That is why these patients say, "Nothing else is bothering me. I am just upset over these darned physical symptoms."

F. There are secondary rewards. As we have seen, some people secretly enjoy the sympathy, concern, attention, pity, time off work and disability payments that go with this whole shebang.

5. Emotional symptoms can make some people feel out of control.

People suffering from emotional symptoms—sadness with uncontrollable crying spells; ongoing feelings of helplessness, hopelessness, gloom and doom; and uncontrollable anxiety and panic attacks—become scared that they no longer have any control over their emotions and their minds. This fear adds more emotions to the balloon, making the symptoms even worse. If the need to be in control of one's emotions is great, as is the case with some "control freaks," the patient can feel quite out of control. Some, unable to tolerate the loss of control, may even attempt suicide. Some of them succeed, while others botch it badly. By now, most of these patients feel, "I just cannot take this any more!"

6. Mental symptoms make people suspect a serious brain disorder.

Patients who suffer mostly from mental, or cognitive, symptoms—forgetfulness, inability to recall events or names, inability to concentrate, confusion, etc.—begin to suspect that they are suffering from Alzheimer's disease, a brain tumor or Attention Deficit Disorder (ADD). They have their brains scanned and their heads wired for electrical waves, and they undergo different types of neuropsychological testing. Many of these people take a variety of vitamins, food supplements and herbal medicines (remember garlic pills?), hoping that their memory will get better in time. People who suspect that they have Attention Deficit Disorder start to take prescription drugs or street drugs to control their symptoms. Drug companies have been so successful in "raising awareness" of the medical profession of the "epidemic of ADD" in the U. S. that now millions of people are on stimulant drugs, mostly amphetamines, just so they can cope with their everyday life! The only thing that is wrong with the majority of these people is that their bottle is saturated and their balloon is ready to pop. Some patients' cognitive symptoms can become so bad that doctors give them a diagnosis of pseudo-dementia (false dementia).

7. Behavioral stress symptoms make people feel guilt and shame.

Patients suffering primarily from behavioral symptoms—irritability, short temper and violent outbursts—become shameful, guilt-ridden and angry at themselves for not being able to control their own behavior. They are caught in an unending cycle of misbehavior, guilt, remorse, and more stress, more misbehavior, more guilt, shame, remorse, and more misbehavior. Their balloons grow bigger because of the accumulating emotions of guilt, shame and remorse. Many end up quitting their jobs or abandoning their families; others end up losing their jobs, spouses and families.

8. Personality disorders result from reactions to trauma and deprivation in childhood.

Some people, as a result of their heroic attempts to adapt to chronic early-life traumatic events and problems—abandonment, rejection, excessive criticism, physical, sexual and emotional abuse, emotional deprivation, absence of parental figures, etc.—develop what are called *personality disorders*. Their personalities are the human equivalents of stunted Bonsai trees, which have been subjected to the sustained stress of twisting, bending and pruning, as well as being deprived of water and nutrients. People with personality disorders—called borderline, histrionic, narcissistic, antisocial, dependent, schizoid, etc.—are seriously emotionally stunted in certain ways as a result of their mal-adaptation to severe early-life stressors, traumas and emotional deprivation. In the past, they were referred to as immature personalities. Except for the antisocial personalities, who suffer no guilt or remorse, these people are highly vulnerable to stress disorders, just as Bonsai trees are highly vulnerable to disease. The antisocial personalities take the route of chemical abuse in order to damage themselves and the society they hate. They then develop more stress as a result of their involvement with the legal system.

Over one-third of the American population suffers from a partially or fully developed personality disorder of one type or another. Since these people are "immature" by nature, they tend to communicate by means of acting out or acting up, as children do, rather than by speaking out or speaking up. They have poor control over their impulses and demand excessive attention and nurturance from others, which leads to attention-seeking behavior (ASB). Some of them suffer from hypersensitivity to rejection and criticism, "authority hang-ups," perfectionism and other quirks. Their warped thinking and personality quirks create major interpersonal conflicts in their dealings with others. They often entangle therapists in their intrigues and shenanigans—suicide attempts, attention-seeking behaviors, aggressive or passive-aggressive acting out, and alcohol and drug abuse—which lead to serious conflicts and consequences. Because of these and many other factors, people with personality disorders are extremely difficult to treat. Psychiatrists specializing in the treatment of such people fully understand how delicate and sticky they can be, so they give their own brains a coating of "Teflon" before they become involved with them. Without arming themselves with such a coating, naïve psychiatrists and therapists often get sucked into the black hole of treating these people, and they become stressed themselves. It takes a highly skilled botanist to rehabilitate a Bonsai tree and bring it back to nature.

Picture 34: This forty-year-old Bonsai tree has wonderful personality!

CHAPTER TWELVE

Some Common Stress Disorders

L et us now look briefly at the outlines of a few common stress disorders using the model of the mind we have studied so far. Most of these disorders are amenable to symptomatic treatment with drugs. However, in order to prevent their recurrence, education and supportive or insightful counseling are needed to shrink the balloon. Symptomatic treatment means controlling the symptoms of the disorder with drugs. If the drugs are withdrawn, in the majority of patients whose balloons have popped at least once, the symptoms will return sooner or later. Also, if the patient receiving drug treatment does not learn to keep his balloon shrunk, he will suffer from breakthrough episodes when his balloon inflates from time to time because of ongoing life events and problems. This means that the emotional pressure inside the balloon will break through the drug coating over the balloon. When this happens, additional drugs may be needed to coat the balloon or to reduce the pressure coming from the bottle.

1. Three broad categories of disorder are associated with stress.

A. Stress-related physical disorders. Stress can be the source of physical illnesses, such as high blood pressure, irritable bowel syndrome, ulcerative colitis, heart attacks, asthmatic attacks, stomach ulcers, Fibromyalgia, chronic fatigue syndrome, migraine headaches and many other disorders that are not yet recognized as resulting from stress. Discussion of these disorders is beyond the scope of this book.

B. Disorders caused by bad habits that are used to cope with stress. As we have read, many stressed people indulge in smoking, drinking alcohol, overeating, having illicit sex and other vices, which can lead to serious physical disorders such as cancer, AIDS, heart and lung disorders, etc. The majority of all hospitalizations are related to diseases that these habits have caused or to which they have contributed. A separate book would be needed to deal with this topic.

C. Stress-related psychiatric disorders. Some common disorders in this category:

1. Prominent physical symptoms without any physi cal findings
2. Mood disorders (major depression, bipolar disor der)
3. Anxiety disorders (panic disorder, generalized anxiety disorder, obsessive-compulsive disorder and post-traumatic stress disorder)
4. Psychotic disorders (free-standing or associated with mood disorders)

2. Seemingly serious physical symptoms with no medical findings.

In the chapter titled "Persistent Stress Symptoms," we read about three types of symptoms in this category: pain somewhere in the body, organ dysfunction and general body dysfunction. Many patients in this category are given diagnoses of hysteria, somatization disorder, conversion disorder, atypical panic disorder, etc. As we have seen, these symptoms often stand for something the patient is trying to communicate non-verbally. Some such symptoms are paralysis, blindness, deafness, loss of speech, numbness, pain somewhere in the body, dizziness, muscle twitching, seizures, exhaustion, loss of taste and smell, fainting spells and many other similar symptoms. Repeated physical examinations and tests reveal nothing to explain these symptoms.

The main treatment for all these patients is counseling to shrink their balloons. A small dose of anti-anxiety or antidepressant medication, given on a temporary basis, might help greatly. As a rule, the shorter the duration of the symptoms, the better the results from counseling. The longer the symptoms have persisted, the harder it is to get rid of them, because secondary gain issues—sympathy, disability income, freedom from punishment—will have complicated the problem. The unfortunate fact is that many people end up on medication for years because very few health-care providers have either the time or the expertise to explore their minds for just one hour.

3. Mood disorders: unipolar and bipolar disorders.

Mood has to do with how one feels. If a person feels excessively elated, he is referred to as manic. If he feels excessively sad, he is referred to as depressed.

There are two broad categories of mood disorder: unipolar (or one-poled) depression, in which one suffers from depressive bouts only; and bipolar (or two-poled) depression, in which one suffers from depressive bouts (downs) and at least one manic (up) or hypomanic (mildly up) spell.

A. Unipolar depression through stages of stress. Depression means a feeling of being "down." Not only is the person's mood down, but almost all his bodily functions are also down. He feels as though his whole body is operating on a run-down battery. Just as decreased voltage in a house's electric power supply slows down all its appliances—air conditioner, fan, refrigerator, etc.—decreased voltage in the brain due to a chemical imbalance results in a reduction of the person's energy and causes all mental and bodily functions to slow down: interest in one's usual activities, sleep, appetite, concentration, hope, enthusiasm, memory, stress tolerance, thinking capacity. Sometimes, depressed people sleep more to avoid sensory input into their balloon. Sometimes, they eat more, especially if they are chronically depressed, in order to counter their accumulating emotional pain. Some people try to counter their emotional pain by drinking alcohol or taking street drugs. Let us see how depression progresses through the various stages of stress.

1. Depression, at stage two of stress. Some people are depressed because something bad is going on in their lives. The balloon has inflated temporarily. They might be grieving over a loss or going through anticipatory grief over the expected death of a loved one. They might have a specific life problem, such as a job problem. Once they have dealt with the offending issue, these people feel better. Such people are said to be suffering from adjustment disorder with a depressed mood. It is best to avoid medications in these cases unless the symptoms are intolerable. For example, a seventy-eight-year-old man, grieving over the death of his wife of fifty-five years, might need a mild medication to help him sleep and eat better until he completes the grieving process.

2. Depression, at stage three of stress. This is the low stress tolerance stage. In people at this stage, the hidden mind/soda bottle reached its saturation point a long time ago. The balloon has gradually inflated, and it is now almost full. These people have developed depressive symptoms over a long period of time. In other words, they now have a case of chronic depression, or Dysthymic disorder. They have low-grade depressive symptoms. Even a small bad event, the proverbial straw, can break this camel's back, resulting in a major depressive disorder. This is now labeled as acute on chronic depression. Medication is often warranted in these people.

3. Major depressive disorder (MDD), at stage four of stress. In major depression, the symptoms are more persistent and severe. Even in this case, symptoms can vary from mild to severe. In its extreme form, the emotional pain is so bad that one constantly feels, "I just can't take it any more!" Suicidal ideas are common in severe cases.

Severe major depression is often precipitated by a painful event. The balloon pops as a result of an external event or because of resurfacing emotions, as in the double whammy. In general, suicidal ideas and impulses are far greater in depression brought on by the double whammy because of the suddenness and fury of the depressive symptoms. Almost all these patients need medication to control their depressive symptoms before they can start to shrink their balloons.

4. Major depression with psychotic or anxiety or obsessive pain features, at stage five of stress. In this type of depression, the patient not only suffers from serious depression, but he also has symptoms of another disorder as well. In other words, the balloon has had a second or even a third breaking point, which results in the activation of genes that cause a disorder other than the original depression. These patients can have psychotic symptoms, such as delusions ("I think my stomach is rotting") or hallucinations ("Voices are telling me that I am a bad person"). Or they could have panic attacks or obsessive thoughts ("I have this bad thought that I might hurt my child"). Or they might have severe pain somewhere in the body (headache or backache), which complicates the depression. Invariably, patients with symptoms of multiple disorders need treatment with two or more medications. Shrinking their balloons through self-help or counseling is mighty difficult!

5. Complications of depression. If major depression is not treated, it can lead to suicide attempts or completed suicides. In some cases, the patient becomes a recluse in order to avoid further stress. Many patients who are treated improperly commit suicide because of increasing feelings of hopelessness ("None of these medications helped me. I must be a hopeless case"). Other improperly treated patients develop medical trauma and medication phobia.

6. Drug treatment. When symptoms are treated correctly with the judicious use of antidepressant drugs, they gradually improve over four to six weeks in the majority of patients. This is the main rule to follow: *Start small. Build slowly. Give high doses as*

Bob Kamath, M.D.

they are needed and can be tolerated.

If psychotic symptoms are present, antipsychotic drugs are required to control them. Since antipsychotic drugs "put the lid on the soda bottle," they are eminently useful in depression that results from the double whammy. If the patient has concurrent panic attacks, these should be controlled quickly with high doses of anti-anxiety drugs, or else the balloon will pop again due to feelings of helplessness and hopelessness engendered by the panic attacks. In cases of depression complicated by panic attacks, when the treating doctor does not control the patient's symptoms aggressively, the suicide rate is extremely high.

If the patient has obsessive thoughts of a violent, blasphemous or sexual nature, it is important to educate him about the nature of these thoughts and to reassure him that such thoughts are quite the opposite of what he truly thinks, and that he will never act upon them. Serotonergic antidepressant drugs take about fifteen to twenty-five weeks to decrease obsessive thoughts. Reassurance, reasoning and education do it much faster.

If the depressed person has severe pain of recent origin somewhere in the body, it might respond to one insightful session. Chronic pain does not usually lend itself to such a quick fix. It is important that the pain be acknowledged and treated with appropriate pain medication. Patients with associated pain often respond better to drugs working on the norepinephrine system (Nortriptyline, Imipramine) or to drugs working on both serotonin and norepinephrine (Effexor, Cymbalta).

7. Education. I believe that education is as important as drug treatment. It is necessary to explain to the patient the process by which he came to this state of affairs. When the patient understands this well, then, far from getting worse, he feels better. For one thing, just knowing what is happening to him helps him to feel better. Not knowing is far more stressful than knowing. Secondly, he feels better knowing that his doctor knows what is going on, and how to take care of it.

8. Counseling or therapy. Patients who are receiving drug treatment at stage three, four and five of depression are better off waiting for six weeks before being referred for counseling. In the state of mind the patients are in, they can't figure out much, anyway. Besides, an inexperienced therapist might shake up the bottle too vigorously and pop the balloon again, just as the balloon was being coated with an antidepressant drug. Just as we don't put patients through physical therapy until the fractured bone is healed in a cast, it is best to wait until the "cast" over the balloon dries before the patient starts talking therapy. It is also advisable that the therapist not deal with issues in the bottle at this stage; that is, issues that existed before the Saturation Point was reached. It is best to use the same principles we applied for Onion-peeling Journaling: painful emotions in the balloon are explored slowly and in layers, going backwards from the most recent painful issues. The issues in the bottle are left untouched unless absolutely necessary.

B. Bipolar disorder (BD) through the stages of stress.
This is the disorder of mood swings, or highs and lows. Thanks to the drug companies, we are now on the verge of becoming a bipolar nation.

A significant degree of mood swing, known as mood instability, is common in stressed people. This does not qualify them as being bipolar. To be diagnosed as being bipolar, one must have a sustained high spell that lasts for several days or weeks. However nowadays, this diagnosis is given to people who have rapid-cycling mood swings (highs and lows several times a day, week or month). Some people have highs and lows at the same time. These patients are labeled as mixed bipolar. Many of these syndromes are clearly complications arising from drug therapy. Antidepressant medication given for the treatment of major depression or other conditions can bring on a manic spell in some patients, whether or not they have family histories of bipolar disorder.

A high spell is the mirror image of depression: increased energy, interest, productivity, memory, hope, activity, happiness, optimism, grandiosity, euphoria or elation. It is as if the brain chemicals are saying, "All right! We've had it with these toxic, painful emotions. We can't take this crap any more! We're going to fight back. We are going to war. We are going to storm and overwhelm the toxins by 'shock and awe' tactics!" The result is like the household

Bob Kamath, M.D.

voltage going up from the usual 120 volts to 300, 400, 500 or even 600 volts. Imagine what this would do to all the household appliances! The puny fan would revolve a thousand times a minute, the light bulbs would get blindingly bright or burn out, the refrigerator would freeze and the air conditioner would make the room freeze. The more voltage there is in the brain, the more severe the manic symptoms. Depending on the severity of the disorder, one can experience additional symptoms, as we will see below. Following such a "high," most manic patients burn out and crash into depression.

All manic patients have been through serious stressful events and problems over a period of time. As in the case of major depression, either their gradually-inflating balloons popped one fine morning or they popped because of a sudden double whammy. Let us study bipolar disorder through the stages of stress.

1. Mood swings, at stage two of stress. When a person is going through rough times, he might experience significant mood swings, especially if there is a family history of bipolar disorder. This person's balloon is inflated, but he is fully aware of what is going on. I would avoid treating this patient with medications. Instead, I recommend a few intense therapy sessions to deflate his balloon immediately. He should be encouraged to express his emotions and solve his problems.

2. Bipolar disorder, at stage three of stress. Most patients with mood swings at this stage are diagnosed as suffering from a mild type of bipolar disorder, known as Cyclothymic disorder. These people have minor ups and downs. The soda bottle was saturated some time ago, and the balloon is filling up gradually. These people can also benefit from counseling, but most of them prefer drug therapy (the easier route), as they have no clue that they have been burying their emotions all their lives. A mood-stabilizing drug can quickly take care of the mood swings. Another syndrome associated with stage three of stress is hypomania, a condition in which one feels euphoric, energetic and enthusiastic; he is talkative, hyperactive, and full of ideas. If this person has a history of having had a major depressive episode, he is considered to belong to stage four.

3. Bipolar disorder, at stage four of stress. At this

stage, the balloon has popped. There are several likely scenarios: the patient may be suffering from hypomania and have a history of major depressive spells (bipolar II); a full-blown manic syndrome (bipolar I); a mixed manic-depressive spell; rapid-cycling bipolar illness, etc.

a) Bipolar II disorder. Patients in this state of mind rarely get into serious trouble. They might overspend, but they rarely do things that are blatantly stupid. Their judgment, reasoning and insight are still relatively intact. Treatment with a mood stabilizer is indicated. If the patient has depression with a history of at least one hypomanic spell, an antidepressant drug might need to be added, at least temporarily.

b) Bipolar I. Mania, or the manic episode, is a condition in which the patient has more serious symptoms, such as grandiosity ("I will run for president; I can do anything and get rich"); reckless buying sprees; excessive generosity; excessive talking; extremely high energy level; racing thoughts; an inability to focus on a given task because of racing thoughts; reckless driving; trying to do good to the world; marked sleeplessness. This is a syndrome of excesses. Soon, the patient piles up debts, gets into accidents or runs afoul of the law. Many of these patients end up in jail or file for bankruptcy. Unidirectional hostility toward the spouse or a parent is common. This particular symptom is rarely, if ever, found in any other psychiatric syndrome.

In mania, the patient's mind is often significantly disconnected from the files in his "Wisdom" folder: "Judgment," "Reasoning," "Insight," and "Moral values." With the loss of these higher faculties, the patient's mind runs on his personality weaknesses, resulting in impulsive and stupid behaviors. Treatment with a powerful mood stabilizer, with or without hospitalization, is mandatory.

4. Bipolar disorder, at stage five of stress. The manic episode at this stage is a very serious condition. The patient has a full-blown manic syndrome, as described above. In addition, he has psychotic symptoms, such as delusions of grandeur ("I have a billion dollars in my bank account"); messianic complex ("I am Jesus!"); extreme hostility and violence that is usually directed toward one particular person in the family; severe agitation; auditory or visual hallucinations (visions of God or angels) and the like. Some of these people are so "high" that they are labeled as suffering from delirious mania. Hospitalization and aggressive treatment with major mood-stabilizing as well as antipsychotic medications are mandatory.

5. Complications of untreated hypomanic episodes are relatively few: financial problems arising from excessive spending and the resulting problems with the spouse. The complications of untreated manic episodes are more serious: writing bad checks usually leads to legal problems; reckless borrowing and spending leads to bankruptcy; reckless driving leads to traffic tickets; unidirectional hostility toward the spouse can lead to violence, followed by divorce; overconfidence at work can lead to being fired from one's job. Some manic patients suddenly switch to profound depression. It is as if the brain chemicals have suddenly lost the wind in their sails. The realization, at some level of the mind that one has created a big mess leads to the brain chemicals saying, "Well, our strategy of 'shock and awe' did not work. We admit defeat."

In the manic episode with psychotic features, more serious complications can arise. In the delirious state of mind, the psychotic manic can commit a violent crime against family members, or even against strangers. The list of possible serious mishaps arising from delirious mania is unending.

6. Drug treatment. Excellent mood stabilizers are now available to rapidly control manic symptoms. Taking these drugs is like installing a stabilizer in the electrical system, which lowers the voltage when it gets too high and elevates it when it gets too low. Regardless of whether the patient is in a manic or a depressive state, he must be on a mood stabilizer. In a depressed state, he might need an antidepressant drug in addition to the mood stabilizer. Most mood stabilizers are also antipsychotics.

Many hypomanic and manic patients like being high for obvious reasons. They don't like how the mood stabilizers make them feel—normal. They like the adrenaline rush that often goes with hypomania and mania. Many of these patients quit their medications soon after getting better (or worse, they think). For psychiatrists, these are some of the most challenging cases. Most manic patients think they are smarter than the psychiatrist treating them (which may or may not be true), so they second-guess the doctor, or even try to tell him what the best treatment for them is.

7. Education. It is almost impossible to educate patients who are in the hypomanic or manic state. They all know more than the doctor. Once they have been stabilized, they can be educated—for about ten minutes. After that, they are the masters of the universe. To drill into their heads how their painful emotions caused their chemical imbalances, which in turn caused all their current problems, takes months or years, as their denial is very strong and the desire to be manic is overwhelming.

8. Counseling is mighty difficult with hypomanic and manic patients until their symptoms are well controlled. After stabilization, they may need counseling to deal with recent events and problems. Again, use the principles of Onion-peeling Journaling. In addition, the therapy should be geared toward re-linking their minds to their "Judgment," "Reasoning" and "Insight" files. Therapy should also help them to take care of the various problems they have created for themselves in the manic state of mind.

4. Anxiety Disorders

A. Panic disorder (PD)

1. Symptoms of panic disorder. This is the most frightening of all stress disorders. A person who thinks he is in relatively good health suddenly experiences many physical symptoms, which terrify him because he does not know why he has them. Some of these symptoms can be very scary: chest pain, a crushing feeling in the chest, fullness in the chest, racing heart, flip-flopping of the heart, shortness of breath, choking sensation, tingling sensation in the hands and around the mouth, trembling of the hands, hot and cold waves all over the body, profuse sweating, nausea and vomiting, diarrhea, dizziness, passing out, seizures, a feeling of being closed in, blurred or tunnel vision, feeling as though one's head is about to explode, mental confusion, a sense of unreality, out-of-body experience, feeling the hands turning into claws and many other strange symptoms.

Because these symptoms are unexpected and the victim does not know what causes them, he becomes extremely scared. The fear adds to what is already in the balloon, the symptoms become even worse, and new symptoms appear. These additional symptoms, brought on by one's reaction (fear) to his first, or primary, symptoms, are known as secondary symptoms. They usually last from two minutes to about twenty minutes. After the attack is over, the patient feels completely exhausted.

When panic attacks are frequent, the diagnosis of panic disorder is given. In panic disorder, the balloon has popped, either as a result of having gradually inflated and reached its breaking point or as a result of the double whammy. In the former case, after the patients feel better with treatment, they all admit that they noticed more and more symptoms of anxiety over a period of time, as their balloons gradually inflated. In the case of the double whammy, the panic attack is sudden and without any warning; hence, these patients react with more fear. Repeated panic attacks over several weeks mean that the patient has a panic disorder. This is different from an incidental panic attack, which one might suffer in a traumatic situation.

In panic disorder, a brain center by the name of the locus ceruleus is implicated. When the brain chemicals reach the breaking point, they plead with this brain center, "Give this person such a scary warning that he will never forget it. Scare the hell out of him!" In other words, a panic attack is the body's warning signal to the mind: "Your brain is overstuffed with painful emotions. Stop denying! Get them out of your system."

2. Consequences of fear. Fear of dying, being seriously ill or going crazy causes a person who is having a panic attack to run to the nearest emergency room. By the time he reaches the ER, the panic attack is over. The ER doctor checks the patient and does some obligatory tests, and they all come back normal, as can be expected. The patient is baffled. Now his imagination runs wild. Depending upon which physical symptoms are predominant, he suspects brain tumor, stroke, heart attack, asthma attack, gall bladder attack or seizure, etc. Many patients now begin the medical wild goose chase. Readers have read about this disastrous course in the chapter titled "Medical Wild Goose Chase."

Let us now trace panic disorder through the various stages of stress.

3. Panic attack at stage two of stress. A relatively healthy person under severe stress may have a panic attack. This person's soda bottle is not full. The attack is a warning signal, a wake-up call, telling him to take care of something that is inflating his balloon. Once he shrinks his balloon he feels better, and, if he learns how to keep his balloon shrunk, he might never have another panic attack. Counseling, with or without the temporary use of mild tranquilizers, usually takes care of the problem. This condition is labeled adjustment disorder with anxious mood.

4. Panic attack at stage three of stress. As noted above, at this stage, the person's balloon has been inflating gradually, and he has had many persistent anxiety symptoms: tension, nervousness, worrying, difficulty falling asleep, restlessness, sweating, trembling, etc. This state is referred to as generalized anxiety disorder. By now, most people are on some type of nerve medication. If the balloon is nearly full, they experience frequent panicky feelings. Once the balloon pops because of a bad event, they suffer a massive panic attack. If the balloon pops again and again, they are diagnosed as having panic disorder. Now they are in stage four.

5. Panic attack at stage four of stress. As in the other disorders, the balloon pops, either because of a bad event (causing the patient to graduate from stage three to stage four) or a double whammy. Immediate control of the anxiety with rapid-acting anti-anxiety medications, such as Xanax (alprazolam) or Ativan (lorazepam), is indicated, unless the patient has been having panic attacks for years and is now relatively comfortable with them. Patients can benefit from taking antidepressant medications, with or without anti-anxiety medications. An antidepressant drug known as Wellbutrin (bupropion), which works on the dopamine system in the brain, not only does not help with panic attacks, but it can make them worse.

When the balloon pops because of a double whammy, the panic symptoms are severe. Aggressive treatment with a quick-acting anti-anxiety medication is mandatory to prevent complications such as depression and agoraphobia (fear of being in crowds). Such patients respond well to atypical, or even typical, antipsychotic drugs, which put the lid on the soda bottle and prevent the fizz from escaping into the balloon.

6. Panic attack at stage five of stress. At this stage, the person has developed many serious complications as a result of the trauma of panic attacks. These may include:

a) Agoraphobia. This term is not accurate, but it serves the purpose. Agoraphobia means "fear of the marketplace." In reality, it means the sufferer fears certain situations in which the sensory input is too great, and so he avoids them like the plague in order to protect his full balloon from popping again. This results in his avoiding noisy and crowded places, such as supermarkets, football stadiums, church congregations, etc. Some patients are afraid of having a panic attack in public and thus making fools of themselves. Some avoid any situation where they might have another panic attack with no one around to help them. They avoid expressways, bridges and other inaccessible places. Some people avoid flying, going to strange places, driving anyplace alone and the like. Some avoid cars or restaurants, because that is where they had their first panic attacks. If they are untreated, many of these people end up as recluses. Many are completely home-bound. To avoid sensory input, they pull down the screen and sit quietly in a darkened room.

b) Depression. Repeated panic attacks create feelings of helplessness, hopelessness, dejection, despondency and other painful emotions related to the sadness complex. Now patients can reach a second breaking point, precipitating a major depressive episode. This is a deadly combination, indeed. In these cases, suicidal attempts are common unless the treating doctor is pursuing aggressive treatment of both disorders and the patient has a lot of trust in him or her.

c) Hypochondriasis. Many people become so scared by their panic symptoms that they become sensitized to them, and keep anticipating them. Even a minor symptom remotely resembling a panic attack creates severe fear, resulting in a panic attack. To prevent this, the patients become obsessed with their bodily symptoms. They go to doctors even when their symptoms are minor, as if wanting to take care of them before they lead to a panic attack. A skipped heartbeat, a feeling of fullness in the chest, or slightly blurred vision is enough to make them rush to the nearest emergency room. Many keep suspecting that they have some type of dreadful disorder that the doctors have missed, and repeated reassurance does not calm them. They make the rounds of doctors, year after year, wasting money on unnecessary tests.

d) Medication phobia. As we have seen, anxious patients are extremely sensitive to antidepressant medications. When given big starting doses of these medications, they react severely and their anxiety escalates. Most doctors who prescribe antidepressant medications are unaware of this fact. The result is that the patients claim they are allergic to medications and refuse to get any treatment. The long-term complications from this avoidance of treatment are mind-boggling.

e) Chronic anxiety. Many patients remain chronically anxious in spite of treatment. This is especially so in patients whose balloons popped after gradual inflation (stage three of stress). With treatment, these people go back to the third stage, and remain anxious forever, suffering from breakthrough panic attacks from time to time, when under stress.

f) Medical trauma. Patients with panic disorder are more likely to suffer from medical trauma, because they experience a greater number of frightening physical symptoms than people with any other stress disorder. They are clueless as to why they have these symptoms, and so they are too willing to subject themselves to potentially dangerous tests and surgical procedures. They always manage to find doctors who are, likewise, too willing to put them through these tests and surgeries. Hospitals and doctors are having a ball on account of these patients. In the end, however, all that they are left with is medical trauma, medical bills and the three big Ds that go with it: disgust, disillusionment and demoralization.

7. Treatment with drugs. If the panic attacks are severe, it is imperative that the doctor immediately medicate the patient with powerful anti-anxiety medications, to control the symptoms of panic disorder, prevent them from coming back, and stop the fear/helplessness/panic attack cycle. Too often, doctors withhold addictive anti-anxiety medication for fear of creating addiction in the patient. These doctors are completely unaware of the seriousness of this disorder and the debilitating complications that follow without prompt treatment.

After the symptoms have been brought under a fair degree of control with benzodiazepine, very small doses of an antidepressant medication in the serotonin or norepinephrine category can be started. Usually, this is one-eighth to one-tenth the recommended dose. This dosage can be increased gradually over six weeks until the optimum dose is reached. It takes over eight to twelve weeks to receive any benefit from these medications. Patients should be informed about this time lag, and the doctors should prepare them to expect panic attacks, off and on, during this period. Once they feel good, anti-anxiety medications should be gradually withdrawn by a one-sixteenth reduction of the daily dose every two weeks. It might take six months to a year to take them off the drug completely—and that, too, not without a fight. Patients see these anti-anxiety drugs (Xanax, Ativan) as their life-savers, which they really have been. Because they work rapidly, the patients come to have more faith in them than in the antidepressants, which take over eight weeks to kick in. The problem with anti-anxiety medications is that the body develops tolerance to them, so, after a while, they do not help. Furthermore, even when they are withdrawn extremely gradually, the ensuing withdrawal symptoms might remind the patient of his panic attacks, scaring him severely and bringing on more attacks. A great deal of education and reassurance is needed to get patients off of these medications.

8. Education. This is highly effective in patients who suffer from panic disorder, as fear is a great motivator. Unlike manic patients, who like their "highs," these patients hate their panic attacks. They are anxious to know why they have them, and reassured to know that they are caused by stress and not by a serious physical illness. Patients need to be educated about the disorder, the slow response to antidepressant medications, the recurrent nature of the disorder and other relevant factors. They need to be educated about the balloon/soda bottle concept.

9. Counseling. This consists of helping the patient

to identify the events that precipitated the disorder, so he can become able to deal with the painful events and problems before the disorder manifests. Onion-peeling Therapy can ensure the gradual shrinking of the balloon. All issues that existed prior to the saturation point are best left alone until the balloon is completely empty. By then, in any case, it will be pointless to examine them.

B. Obsessive-compulsive disorder (OCD)

1. Obsessive thoughts lead to compulsive acts.

We can call this the broken-record disorder. When afflicted with this disorder, the patient experiences repeated thoughts of a particular nature, which do not go away. These recurrent "bad thoughts" are referred to as obsessive thoughts. They are generally the exact opposite of what one consciously thinks, and so they are highly upsetting (stressful) to the sufferer. Therefore, he either suffers from serious anxiety in reaction to these thoughts or indulges in repetitive actions to counter them. These uncontrollable, repetitive acts are known as compulsive acts. There are numerous different types of obsessive thoughts. Most sufferers of OCD are so ashamed of their thoughts that it takes a high level of skill to make them confess that they have them.

All these people have issues buried in their hidden minds, which resurface when triggered by some precipitating event. These issues are related to some childhood trauma, which remains buried until it comes up in the form of an obsessive thought. Obsessive thoughts are mild and temporary at stage two of stress; more persistent and moderate at stage three; more severe at stage four; and extremely severe at stage five, when they are associated with panic attacks and depression, and, in some cases, psychosis.

A case study: A thirty-two-year-old woman suddenly developed an obsessive thought that she might run someone over while driving her car. Consequently, she worried about every little bump in the road that she experienced while driving. She would pull the car over and look back to see if there was a dead body in the road. Before driving five miles, she would already have stopped the car more than ten times. Her history revealed that when she was a child, she had lost a younger sister in a hit-and-run accident. She had buried the trauma that was related to this tragedy and moved on. Just prior to the onset of her symptoms, she had read about the hit-and-run death of a child in the community. This was the double whammy that precipitated her OCD.

Here are some varieties of OCD:

a) Blasphemous thoughts. In this case, one has recurrent thoughts of a blasphemous nature, which upset the sufferer a great deal. Usually, the sufferer is a highly religious person, perhaps a pastor or deacon. A blasphemous thought could be "God is the devil," "I want to have oral sex with Jesus," "The Bible is a fraud" or some such highly upsetting thought. Unable to get rid of these thoughts, the sufferer becomes scared, guilt-ridden, and increasingly anxious and depressed. Some develop frank panic attacks, or they avoid going to church or reading the Bible. Since there is no corresponding repetitive behavior except avoidance, these people become depressed because of their helplessness, hopelessness, sinfulness and guilt; or they become anxious due to their fear of being punished by God for their mental transgressions and doubts.

b) Thoughts of insecurity. In this type of OCD, one has recurrent thoughts about some type of danger to his safety. These people feel insecure when they are at home. They keep checking the door again and again to see if it has been securely locked, or they keep checking the gas stove to make sure that it is not leaking and about to explode.

c) Thoughts of excessive scrupulousness. Some people experience excessive scrupulousness. They become obsessed with the fear of making a mistake. They double-check everything they do; insist on returning to people whatever they owe, immediately and without fail; and make lists so they do not forget what they are supposed to do. In extreme cases, this can lead to bizarre behavior. For example, a man went to the local police station saying he should be arrested for not completely stopping at the stop sign.

d) Thoughts of dirt, germs and chemicals. People with these obsessions are concerned about being contaminated by dirt, germs or dangerous chemicals. They constantly wash their hands and keep everything absolutely clean. Their histories invariably reveal buried memories of some incident in the remote past that scared them to no end.

e) Thoughts of infidelity. People with this obsession keep thinking their spouse is being unfaithful. This is usually brought on by a relatively minor incident that shocked the sufferer mildly. In the history of almost all these people, one parent was unfaithful to the other, and the discovery of the infidelity caused major trauma to the patient when he or she was a child.

f) Violent thoughts. Some people become extremely upset when a violent thought enters their conscious minds, such as, "I want to cut my husband's throat," "I want to squeeze my child's neck until he is dead," "I want to poison my wife," etc. These types of violent thoughts are fairly common in postpartum disorder. One can imagine how fearful, guilt-ridden and ashamed these people feel. Most develop panic attacks or depression from the emotions these thoughts cause them to experience.

2. Drug treatment. This consists of giving the patient SSRI drugs such as Prozac, Zoloft, Paxil, Luvox and Anafranil. As usual, these drugs should be started in small doses and increased gradually to avoid aggravating the patient's anxiety. They take much longer to help OCD—twelve to twenty-four weeks—than to help depression and anxiety, and they need to be given in larger doses. Furthermore, these drugs do not completely control the obsessive thoughts; they simply decrease their intensity, making them more tolerable.

3. Education. The most important part of education is teaching the patients to accept that these unpleasant thought are completely opposite to their real thoughts, and that they never result in violence. The patients cannot blame themselves for the tricks that brain chemicals play on their minds. When this reality dawns on them, they stop feeling scared and blaming themselves. This reverses the cycle of bad thought leading to fear, leading to guilt, leading to depression. Then, the patients need to learn about the balloon and the soda bottle.

4. Counseling. There is no need to write any more about counseling here, except to say that Onion-peeling is the best course to take. However, if one can gently bring up the buried trauma that the obsessive thought is rooted in, the patient can benefit greatly from the insight. OCD does not have to be of lifelong duration. Shrinking the balloon can effectively reduce the severity of its symptoms. Much depends on how smart and open-minded the patient is.

5. Psychotic disorders

Psychosis is the most serious form of stress disorder. A person who is psychotic is said to be out of touch with reality; that is, he is not able to discern what is real and what is not in relation to some specific issue. Thus, his beliefs and perceptions of a particular situation become distorted, causing him to suffer from delusions or hallucinations. Because of this, many psychotic patients can indulge in bizarre behavior. The history of such a person would reveal that he had been through many traumatic events and problems, which he coped with by burying. His balloon has finally popped, just as it does in all other stress disorders. His brain chemicals are in a state of imbalance, and his conscious mind has been disconnected from certain files in the hidden mind—"Reasoning," "Judgment," "Insight" and "Belief," for example. Patients suffering from psychosis have buried emotions related to the fear complex (fear, insecurity, dread, terror) and the anger complex (anger, rage, resentment, jealousy). Such thoughts as "Someone is trying to kill me," "Someone is trying to hurt me" or "Someone is following me" are indicative of this fear and insecurity. Violent behavior is seen in some of these people as a result of the anger-based actions they perform in an attempt to protect themselves from their imaginary persecutors. The delusion of persecution often leads to increased fear; this, in turn, leads to severe anxiety and panic attacks. The frustration, helplessness and hopelessness associated with the fact that no one believes in their delusions often lead to depression and suicidal ideas. Some disorders in which psychotic symptoms can appear are schizophrenia, bipolar disorder and major depressive disorder.

A. Delusions. As we saw earlier, delusions are the distorted perception that something is happening when it is not. For example, a psychotic person might think that his wife was systematically poisoning his food, even though this idea was blatantly contradicted by his absolutely robust health. One cannot reason with such a person; it is fruitless to say, "If she is poisoning you, how come you are so healthy?" We have all heard of people who are fearful that the Mafia, the FBI or the CIA wants to kill them. It is pointless to reason with them, as they are disconnected completely from their "Reasoning," "Judgment" and "Insight" files. The variety of delusions that psychiatrists encounter is too great to list here.

B. Hallucinations. These are sensory perceptions of things that do not exist in reality. The person might see objects, hear voices, smell a scent, feel a touch or have a bad taste in his mouth. These people are so thoroughly withdrawn from the external world that they manufacture sensory input in order to feel alive. Their sensory perceptions are real to them. Some may act on these perceptions. They might indulge in some bizarre act, claiming, "My voices told me to do it." In a court of law, such people are found not guilty by reason of insanity. Because the actions of these people are disconnected from their "Wisdom" folder, and because they are based on delusions and hallucinations, they are invariably described as bizarre.

When someone has a sensory perception that he or she knows to be unreal, that is not a hallucination. For example, a woman who recently lost her husband might wake up at night and see him standing near her, or she might smell his odor. She knows these perceptions are not real, and are caused by her mind's resistance to let go of the lost husband. They are called false or pseudo-hallucinations.

C. Complications. Some common complications of psychosis are panic attacks, depression, legal problems, hospitalization and loss of job and family.

D. Drug treatment. Excellent antipsychotic drugs are available to reverse the chemical imbalance and get rid of delusions and hallucinations. Not only do these drugs put the lid on the bottle, but they also reconnect the conscious mind with the "Wisdom" folder to some extent. However, most patients who have suffered from psychosis remain extremely brittle, as this is more serious than other stress disorders. Many psychotics refuse treatment outright, saying that what they are experiencing is not a delusion or hallucination, but reality. Because of their disruptive behavior, many end up in jails or psychiatric hospitals. Their treating doctor must be a psychiatrist in order to get the best results, as well as to anticipate, avoid and deal with the serious side effects associated with antipsychotic drugs. Doctors who are not familiar with these side-effects should refrain from treating psychotic disorders.

E. Education. This is an important adjunct to treatment. The patient will feel better knowing that his disorder is stress-related and that it is a serious chemical imbalance. However, it is pointless to try to educate patients while they are in a psychotic state of mind.

F. Counseling. This is difficult, at best, as the patient believes that he is all right and has no need of any therapy. Because of his mind's disconnection from the files in his "Wisdom" folder, it is usually difficult for such a person to connect with the therapist's reasoning, insight and judgment. In any case, therapy must go extremely slowly, and it must be very supportive and cautious. We cannot peel this onion; we should be satisfied if we can keep the skin intact and shining. This person is like a shattered vase that has been glued together. The therapist must be careful about how he handles the vase.

6. Stress disorders can cascade, just as painful emotions do.

Just as one painful emotion can cascade into many, one stress disorder can cascade into many others. In other words, with or without treatment, the patient might develop several successive breaking points that lead to several distinct stress disorders. A person suffering from severe panic attacks might feel progressively helpless and hopeless. The addition of these sadness-complex emotions to his balloon can lead to the balloon popping again, with the result being a major depressive episode. This is usually a serious problem, as the suicide risk is high when panic disorder and major depression are combined. A patient with panic disorder can develop agoraphobia, hypochondria and generalized anxiety. A severely depressed person might feel so fearful and insecure that he develops delusions and hallucinations. Someone suffering from persecutory delusion might become so scared that he develops panic attacks. Someone suffering from severe obsessive thoughts of violence or sex might feel so much fear, guilt and shame that he develops severe panic attacks and depression.

Here is an example of cascading: Stress leads to a breaking point, which leads to OCD, which leads to guilt (overly bad thoughts). This leads to fear (of acting on the bad thoughts), then to anxiety, then to panic attacks and then to more fear (of having panic attacks). This chain reaction results in more panic attacks, frustration, helplessness, hopelessness, despondency, despair, depression and more despair. Finally, the person has suicidal ideas and attempts suicide.

Another example of cascading: Stress leads to a breaking point, which leads to panic attacks, fear (of having more panic attacks), agoraphobia, withdrawal, helplessness, hopelessness, sadness, depression and, finally, to suicidal ideas and a suicide attempt.

It is the job of the psychiatrist to trace back the patient's symptoms, identify those that appeared first and come up with an appropriate treatment to address them. For example, when a person presents with panic attacks, the doctor has a choice of giving him a drug that works on the norepinephrine system or the serotonin system. If he knows that the patient's panic attacks are secondary to obsessive thoughts, he will choose a serotonin drug, as this will control both conditions.

Multiple breaking points, resulting in multiple disorders, mean that the patient is in the fifth and final stage of stress, the stage of despair.

7. As time passes, the balloon pops more easily and more frequently

As the years pass, it takes almost nothing to precipitate an episode of stress disorder in stressed-out people who do not learn better coping skills. Their balloons are so full, fragile and ready to pop that an insignificant event, such as the minor illness of a spouse, is enough to bring on a bout of depression or an anxiety attack, even if the balloon is fully coated with one or more medications. As time goes on, the interval between these episodes becomes shorter and shorter. These people have almost no ability to recognize a precipitating event, they are not aware of how they feel about it and they do not have the ability to verbalize their emotions. They don't see any connection between an obviously stressful event and the onset of an episode, partly because the event seems so trivial. The focus of treatment rests squarely on supportive therapy (being kind and understanding) and on prescribing medication and more medication. Creative polypharmacy seems especially designed for these patients. Some of them are on four or five different medications at the same time. They are often labeled "refractory cases," "treatment challenges" or "immune to treatment." Many are constantly on the verge of committing suicide. Most ultimately graduate to stage five, the stage of despair.

8. Medications don't shrink the balloon

Psychiatrists use several different types of medications to help people suffering from stress-related disorders. The basic idea is to reverse the chemical imbalance and bring the chemicals back as nearly as possible to a state of balance. Medications merely control stress symptoms by reversing the chemical imbalance to some extent, the way a diabetic medication controls blood sugar. They do not get rid of painful emotions (shrink the balloon). While medications push the brain chemicals to their original state, stress pushes them in the opposite direction (see picture below). If stress wins, the medications lose their efficacy. Patients can help medications work better by coping with stress better. Education and counseling are allies of medication, and they are essential for recovery. In many patients who do not wish to shrink the balloon or learn better coping skills, the balloon keeps inflating. Finally, unable to withstand the inner pressure, the balloon pops again; in other words, the pressure breaks through the coated balloon. Thus, every two or three years, these patients become "immune" to their medications, so the poor doctor has to come up with new drugs, add more drugs or send the patient for electro-convulsive therapy (ECT), also known as shock treatment. Now the patients are branded "refractory" or "treatment resistant." No wonder doctors routinely tell such patients, "You have a chemical imbalance. You will need to be on these medications for the rest of your life." Far from becoming upset about this, many wear the dubious phrase "chemical imbalance" as a badge of honor and go around bragging about it. The truth is that under the supervision of enlightened doctors, most, if not all, could gradually learn to cope better and go off of at least a few of their medications.

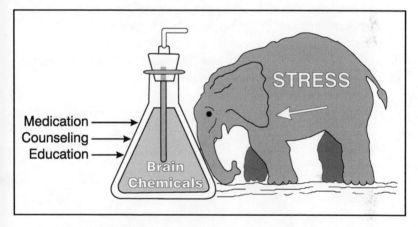

Picture 35: Medications, education and counseling vs. stress.

Let us now study how these medications work.

A. Antidepressants coat the balloon. Antidepressant medications are prescribed to control depressive and anxiety symptoms. Using the balloon-and-soda-bottle model, let us see how they work. Antidepressant medications and mood stabilizers are like a coat of paint or Teflon, which strengthens the balloon. They ease the tension in the balloon, causing symptoms to decrease in intensity or go away. They keep the balloon from popping, but they do not shrink the balloon by themselves. Some degree of shrinking happens once the treatment starts, because of the doctor's reassurance and the disappearance of fear, helplessness and hopelessness. In addition, as symptoms diminish or disappear, the stress caused by suffering also disappears.

Bipolar patients with depression need a coating of a mood stabilizer (like a primer) over the balloon before they get an antidepressant coating, as the latter can cause manic spells in patients who are not thus protected. As the name suggests, mood stabilizers cause mood swings to level off. They are also useful in controlling manic psychosis.

Sometimes, an additional medication is needed to boost the antidepressant medication; for instance, when the pressure in the balloon breaks through the antidepressant coating. This boosting is known as augmentation. There are two ways to augment: 1) add another antidepressant drug coating, which targets a different brain chemical, or 2) add lithium, or an antipsychotic drug, which gives the antidepressant a kick in the butt. The latter method works best in disorders precipitated by a double whammy.

Picture 36: Antidepressants coat the balloon.

The reader must know that antidepressant medications are not as effective in controlling symptoms of depression as drug companies claim. Given by themselves, they work in about sixty-five percent of cases. Even in those patients, they control only a majority of their symptoms—not all of them. Some symptoms, such as tiredness and poor concentration, linger on. When these drugs are prescribed with education and appropriate counseling, the percentage of patients responding to the treatment can rise to ninety or ninety-five percent. There are many specific doctor- and patient-related factors that determine how well patients respond to medications.

B. Anti-psychotic medications put the lid on the soda bottle. Anti-psychotic medications are dispensed to control delusions (believing that something is happening when it is not), hallucinations (hearing voices and seeing things) and mood swings. They ease the tension in the balloon by preventing the fizz from getting into it (repress the resurfacing emotions and memories). By thus reducing tension in the balloon, they relieve symptoms, and the conscious mind reconnects with the files in its "Wisdom" folder. In other words, anti-psychotic drugs keep the fizz in the bottle. Seriously depressed and anxious patients often need a combination of antidepressant and anti-psychotic medications (especially the newer "atypical"" anti-psychotic drugs), even though they are not psychotic, because many of them are undergoing a double whammy. This combination, which gives a chemical coating to the balloon and puts a lid on the bottle, can offer fast relief to seriously ill patients.

Picture 37: Antipsychotic medications put a lid on the bottle.

    C. Anti-anxiety medications break the anxiety/discomfort/anxiety cycle. Anti-anxiety medications, also known as minor tranquilizers ("benzos"), quickly reduce anxiety symptoms. They break the cycle of anxiety/discomfort/fear/inflation/more anxiety. The inflow of fear and helplessness caused by the suffering produced in this cycle is turned off, and once people get back their sense of control, they feel better.

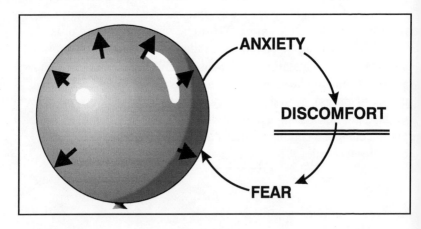

Picture 38: Anti-anxiety medications break the anxiety/discomfort/ fear/anxiety cycle.

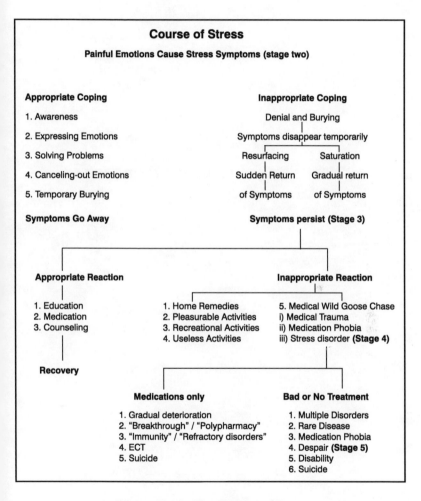

Picture # 39: The Course of Stress

Part Three: Liberation from Stress

CHAPTER THIRTEEN

How to Shrink Your Balloon

Coping means shrinking the balloon by appropriate means. Coping with stress simply means being able to calm your self down after you have become upset about something. The most important thing to do in coping is to rid the mind of toxic, painful emotions as quickly as possible, and bring back peace and tranquility. This allows the brain chemicals to go back to their original position, or near it, resulting in the disappearance of stress symptoms. People use various colloquial terms to describe coping: handling, dealing, coming to terms with, making peace with, settling the issue, getting a grip on it, etc.

In general, the lower the stage of stress you are in, the easier it is to shrink your balloon. As we read in Chapter One, when one is at stage two, *the stage of distress*, he is temporarily going through a difficult time. Since people at this stage are highly aware of their inner emotions, it is easier for them to get rid of them than it is for those who are in stage three. At stage three, *the stage of low stress tolerance syndrome*, the bottle is saturated and the balloon is inflated to some degree. At this stage, people are becoming progressively unaware of their inner emotions. At stage four, *the stage of disorder*, most people are completely unaware of the painful emotions inside their balloons. For people in stage five, *the stage of despair*, self-help is impossible because of the overwhelming preoccupation with their multiple stress disorders and the total inability to gain awareness of their painful emotions.

This chapter is for those who are capable of at least some degree of *self-awareness.*

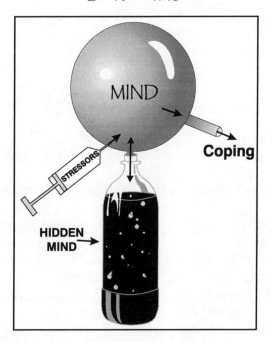

Picture 40: Coping with stress means shrinking the balloon.

1. Give up hang-ups about expressing painful emotions.

People must give up such beliefs as, "Expressing painful emotions is a sign of weakness" and "I don't want to fall apart and look ridiculous." Then, automatically, their emotions will not be held back. However, giving up irrational beliefs is easier said than done. Irrational beliefs are deep-rooted, and people need frequent reminders and efforts to overcome them. Most people who harbor such beliefs are fearful of society's ridicule, and, when they are trying to free themselves of these beliefs, they might need to prepare their close relatives and friends so that they do not become alarmed by the new, now-normal emotional responses. A spouse might need to be retrained not to say such things as, "Honey, what's the matter? Don't cry! It's all right. Everything will be okay. Calm down!" Instead, the spouse should be supportive and empathic. He or she should say,

"Honey, I know you are hurting like hell. I understand. Go ahead, let it all hang out. Don't hold back!" Accepting the fact that expressing painful emotions is the most natural thing one can do counters denial and burying, two inappropriate coping mechanisms.

2. Stop focusing on symptoms and start focusing on painful emotions.

Recognize that as long as you are totally focused on your stress symptoms (anxiety, sleeplessness, headaches, etc.) you will not be able to get in touch with the painful emotions inside your conscious mind/balloon. Instead of saying, "I don't have any painful emotions in my mind," you must learn to say, "I *must have* some painful emotions in my mind, or else I won't have these dreadful stress symptoms."

Even the most educated and intelligent people often have problems doing this. Most people with stress disorders talk only about their symptoms: "I can't sleep well," "I feel down all the time," "I am anxious," "I have no appetite." If one is absolutely clueless about his inner emotional pain and all the stressors that brought it on, self-help might not be possible for him. He might need to control his symptoms first with medications and then through therapy with an experienced therapist. Empathic interaction with the therapist will certainly raise one's awareness of his blocked painful emotions and facilitate their expression.

3. Take an inventory of all past events, problems and painful emotions related to them.

First, establish your *saturation point*. This is the point in time when your hidden mind became saturated and you first noticed your stress symptoms (your balloon started re-inflating). Then, determine a recent time when your symptoms got worse. Make a list of all the bad things that upset you from the time of the saturation point until now, in chronological order. For example, let's say that you first started having depressive symptoms five years ago. That is the point in time when your balloon started re-inflating. Make a list of all the bad stuff that has happened to you since then: your son left home, your husband got sick, you lost your job, you were fired from another job, your mother died, you were in an accident, you found out about your spouse's affair. Then make a list of the painful emotions related to all these incidents: fear, hurt, anger, sadness, disappointment, guilt and shame. You must recognize and acknowledge that they have all played a role in your current predicament. Now you are beginning to turn your focus away from your symptoms and toward your painful emotions and the bad events and problems that caused them.

4. Awareness of painful emotions evaporates them from the mind.

When upset about something, instead of blocking off the painful emotions, say to yourself, "I am really upset over this. I feel hurt, angry and sad." Don't say, "I don't let things bother me!" You need to find someone to share these emotions with as soon as possible. If you have no one, write them down on a piece of paper or in your journal. Spend fifteen minutes of your time everyday to write about things that have upset you that day. If you have become depressed or anxious suddenly, try to connect your symptoms to some event that took place just prior to the onset or worsening of those symptoms. Don't say, "Nothing happened." People do not become depressed or anxious unless something has happened to upset them.

Awareness causes painful emotions to *evaporate* and facilitates their expression. Awareness means getting in touch with the painful emotions in the conscious mind/balloon that we have blocked off and not allowed to come to our awareness. As we read before, when the balloon inflates because of the accumulation of painful emotions, we shift focus from the painful emotions to their stress symptoms. We do this for several reasons. For one thing, it distracts us from our emotional pain. Secondly, stress symptoms draw the attention of the people around us to our misery. Thirdly, stress symptoms are actually a way of releasing the pressure in the balloon—though a relatively ineffective and abnormal way.

Awareness is the antidote to the *self-deception* of denial and burying. Just becoming aware of how angry you are can stop you from acting out your anger by kicking the dog or yelling at your loved one. Raising awareness is like bringing up a page on the screen of a computer and looking at it. Admitting to yourself that you are scared, angry, sad or disappointed makes you experience the blocked-off emotional pain again. You might feel some uncomfortable symptoms, such as headache, red face, hot ears, sighing or tearfulness. The symptoms indicate that you are releasing the emotions and shrinking the balloon.

Let's say that you find yourself in a bad mood when you come home after a hard day's work. You are irritable and snappy, though you felt fine when you left home in the morning. Obviously, for some reason, your balloon inflated since you left home. If your spouse asks you, "Honey, did something happen at work to upset you?" you will snap, "Nothing!" In fact, you have blocked off the emotions related to what might have happened at work. Now, ask yourself, "What happened today to make me feel upset?" Keep searching your memory files. Suddenly, bingo! You remember the nasty phone call that upset you terribly. You were so upset that you just put it out of your awareness (blocked it off), and went on with your business as if nothing had happened. Remembering this nasty episode, you sigh deeply and curse the caller under your breath with the choicest words. Your balloon shrinks right away. Then you say to your spouse, "Yes! Something did happen at work. I was pissed off with this jerk who called me today." The next thing you know, you are your old self. The point is, at the end of the day your balloon should be as small as it was at the beginning.

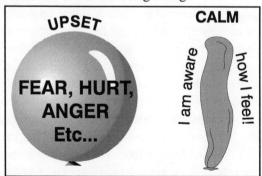

Picture 41: Awareness evaporates painful emotions.

Cultivating awareness about your inner emotions is not easy. It is an ongoing struggle that requires you to ask yourself constantly, "What am I feeling? What happened to upset me? Why am I behaving like this? Why am I having all these symptoms? Why did my balloon inflate?" Such questions can help us overcome denial, self-deception ("I am not upset!"), and self-delusion ("Everything is wonderful in my life!"). Awareness of the impact of a bad event motivates a person to experience the painful emotions related to that event, and this, in turn, motivates him to express them.

A case study: A thirty-two-year-old woman complained of the return of anxiety and depression shortly after she had come home from a two-week vacation at the Gulf Shores. Obviously, her balloon had inflated. Before going on vacation, she had been on antidepressant medication and completely symptom-free for several months. When asked directly if anything had happened to upset her while she was on vacation, she vehemently denied it. She had clearly put some painful event that happened on vacation out of her awareness. Suspecting a connection between her vacation and the reappearance of her symptoms, I casually asked about the vacation. She said she had had a wonderful time with her family at the Gulf Shores. I asked where she had stayed on her way back home, and she said she stayed with her elderly father in Oxford, Mississippi. When I asked how her father was doing, she said, without showing any emotion, that he had just been diagnosed with terminal cancer. His liver scan showed a huge malignant mass. She appeared to be completely unaware of the impact this major bad event was having on her mind. However, when I *raised her awareness* by making the empathic statement, "You must be devastated by this bad news!" her face became intensely red and she broke down and cried uncontrollably (shrank her balloon). She was going through anticipatory grief but had blocked off all the emotions, and the increased pressure in her balloon had brought on a *breakthrough* depression. Once this woman became aware of her inner grief-related emotions, I told her to go home and keep grieving over her father; thus, she would continue to shrink her balloon. She got well rapidly, without having to increase her medication.

A case study: A young man complained of severe sleeplessness, irritability, sadness, weepiness, headaches and many other symptoms, of two weeks' duration. He claimed he had no idea why he felt this way. It was clear that he had put some traumatic event out of his awareness. His history revealed that, two weeks before, a close friend had upset him by making a derogatory remark about him in front of quite a few people. When asked if he was upset about the incident, he replied, "Not really. He is my best friend. I don't think that has anything to do with why I am like this." The man was indulging in massive denial. Here is how his awareness about his inner, painful emotions was raised.

I remarked, "It must be hard to get upset with a close friend." (Empathy.)

He answered, "Yes. We have been best friends for a long time."

"How did you feel about it?"

"I just wanted to wring his neck," he said, smiling (focusing on how he wanted to react rather than how he actually felt). He tried to cover up his anger with a smile.

"You must have been very angry," I said (bringing his focus back to how he felt and raising his awareness about his anger).

"Yes." (He acknowledged his anger.)

"You must have been very hurt." (I raised his awareness about why he was angry.)

"Yes." His eyes became a little moist.

"You must have felt humiliated."

"Yes. I felt so humiliated that I wanted to die." The patient's eyes were now filled with tears.

"You were *disappointed* that your best friend had let you down like this."

"Yes. I didn't expect him to do this to me. We were so close!" Now he was crying openly. As his awareness was raised, he expressed his painful emotions more readily.

"It seems that this sad episode has changed your relationship with him."

"Yes. I don't think I can ever trust him as I did." The patient cried more, releasing his sadness. He was now grieving over the loss of trust and friendship.

"You are sad, and are grieving over the loss of a good

friend."

"Is that what I am doing?"

"Yes. See how much pain you had inside you! Your balloon was full. Because you would not acknowledge your painful emotions, you have had all these symptoms."

"I didn't realize I was so upset over this. What do I do now?"

"Constantly try to raise your awareness about whatever painful emotions you have blocked off, and get them out of your system. Grieve over your loss and move on with your life."

"Okay."

The raising of awareness is an ongoing task. As discussed earlier, most of the people I treat in my office are unaware of the connection between their painful emotions and their current stress symptoms. Much of my time is dedicated to teaching them, on an ongoing basis, the *art of awareness-raising*. Every time they call me complaining of severe stress symptoms, I ask, "What happened to make you feel this way now? (What inflated your balloon?)" The standard answer of unaware people is, "Nothing!" Within a minute or two of conversation, however, they reveal the truth: "I had a fight with my husband." "My dog died." "My friend betrayed me." Until that very moment, they had no clue as to why they were upset. In the long run, people who cultivate the art of awareness keep feeling better and better. The others remain their doctors' permanent clients.

5. Expressing painful emotions shrinks the balloon.

In coping with stress, it is important that you learn to fall apart. When upset about something serious—say, the death of a loved one—you must talk about it immediately and not postpone it until some future day. Talking, crying, sobbing, sighing, bawling, squalling, groaning, moaning, grunting, protesting, scolding, yelling and screaming in response to an upsetting event or situation are some of the common healthful ways by which we express painful emotions. This is also known as *ventilation, or catharsis*. It is as if you were opening the windows of your room wide open and letting the smoke out. To do this, you must be aware of your inner emotions ("I am aware that I am angry at this person"), willing to admit them to yourself and others ("I am so mad at him that I want to wring his neck!"), and able to express them in an appropriate manner ("I am mad at you because of the nasty comment you made about me"). Expressing painful emotions ("I'm hurt, sad, mad, disappointed; I feel guilty; I feel ashamed of myself") causes emotional tension in the mind/balloon to diminish immediately. This reverses the chemical changes that have taken place in the brain, and stress symptoms disappear one by one.

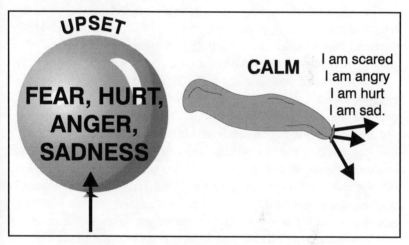

Picture 42: Expressing emotions shrinks the balloon.

A. Talking
1. Talking personally. If you are upset with a person over something he said or did to upset you, the best way to shrink your balloon is to talk with that person face to face—as long as it does not end up in a shouting match. Nothing shrinks the balloon better than getting things off your chest in an appropriate manner. To do this, you need to be assertive, not aggressive.

2. Talking over the phone. If you are scared to talk to the person face to face, use the phone. Express yourself clearly, without getting too upset. Tell the person how you feel. Do not yell or scream, but be assertive in expressing your feelings.

3. Talk to a trusted friend. If the offending person is a friend or relative and you don't want to talk to him or her, for whatever reason ("I don't want to lose him as a friend"), then talk to someone you are close to and shrink your balloon by expressing your hurt and anger. You must have complete trust in the person you talk to. You are not likely to open up to someone who is untrustworthy or who keeps giving you advice instead of just listening. A daily walk with a trusted friend offers an excellent opportunity to release your emotions on a long-term basis. Talking, not just walking, is the way to cope with stress.

A word of caution: If you have always been timid by nature, and people are used to your being that way, then becoming suddenly assertive could baffle them, resulting in serious consequences.

A case study: A mild-mannered young woman who worked for a domineering boss silently suffered much emotional pain and became stressed. After attending one of my seminars on stress, she decided to assert herself with her boss. Two days after the seminar, I received a frantic phone call from her. She was at the local state hospital, begging me to rescue her. She said that the day after she attended my seminar, she had gone into her boss's office and "just lost it." Not used to this type of "hysterical" behavior, the boss panicked and called the sheriff. After being declared as showing out-of-character behavior, the woman was handcuffed and taken to the state hospital in the sheriff's car. It took several phone calls to the hospital staff before I could have her released from the hospital.

B. Writing

1. Writing a letter to resolve a conflict with another person, or to express your feelings, is an important tool for coping. When you compose the letter, put all your raw, unbridled emotions in it, without holding any of them back. As you do this, you will feel your heart racing, your head throbbing, you ears getting red hot and your stomach knotting. These symptoms mean that you are getting in touch with your true emotions, and the increased awareness of painful emotions has inflated your balloon. The writing process will shrink it somewhat. *However, do not mail the letter.* Sit on it for a day or two. Now that you feel a little better, edit the letter and delete the expletives. Keep editing the letter until you feel it is just right. Wait a couple more days. If you still think you are comfortable with the letter's contents and tone, as well as with the consequences that could result, mail it. If not, file it someplace so that some day, you can have a good laugh about it. Remember, once you mail the letter, you will have to live with what you wrote—so be careful! If you are not sure, don't mail it. You can keep writing more letters, as if you were going to mail them. After a while, you will have no emotions left in your balloon.

      2. Onion-peeling Journaling (OPJ). If you decide to do self-therapy through keeping a journal, you need to do it in a methodical way in order to get the most out of it and avoid complications. I call this Onion-peeling Journaling. Imagine that your balloon looks like an inverted onion (see picture below). The layers represent emotions related to the traumatic events and problems that occurred from the time your balloon began to re-inflate (the saturation point of the hidden mind). The outermost layer of the onion represents emotions related to the most recent events, and the onion's core represents emotions related to the first bad event that occurred after the hidden mind/soda bottle reached its saturation point. In OPJ, you *do not* write about the issues that are buried in your soda bottle. Your primary goal is to *shrink the balloon*, not to shake or empty the bottle.

      To benefit from OPJ, you must write in your journal at least once every day, preferably before you go to bed. Also, you must be one hundred percent certain that *no one will read it*. If there is even a small chance of someone reading it, shred the paper immediately after you finish writing. If you write on a computer, delete the write-up immediately afterwards. Otherwise, you might become fearful of expressing your emotions truly. Focus on your painful emotions only. Do not write about irrelevant issues. Do not indulge in self-deception (denial). Don't write, "It was okay that I was fired from my job." Be brutally honest about your emotional pain. Tell yourself, "It is OK for me to complain, bitch and ventilate in the privacy of my house."

Bob Kamath, M.D.

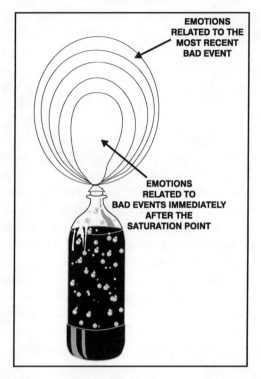

Picture 43: Onion-peeling Journaling: focus just on current issues.

Follow these steps:

A. Identify the year that your stress symptoms became per-sistent. That is when your hidden mind reached its saturation point and your balloon started re-inflating. Let's say you reached your saturation point five years ago. Do not write anything about whatever took place before that time.

B. Identify the most recent event or problem that has upset you or the issues that are currently bothering you. For example, "My current issue is that I am grieving over my chil-dren, who are living with their dad." Write down all the painful emotions related to this issue: "I feel angry at my ex-husband and his girlfriend" or "I am upset that my ex-husband sent my children to camp without consulting me." Do not write about any previous issue until you have identified all the painful emotions related to this issue and decided what course of action you are going to take.

People who are currently free from stress symptoms could keep their balloon shrunk just by writing on a daily basis current issues and emotions related to them: garbage in garbage out. As painful emotions come in, they are gotten rid of by writing them on a piece of paper and destroyed immediately; or on a computer and deleted immediately. This practice will help in raising awareness of painful emotions in the mind and counter the habit of blocking them off.

C. After you have beaten the current issue to death, go on to the next inner layer of the onion. Again, identify the events and problems in this layer and focus on the painful emotions related to these events. As you keep peeling layer after layer, your balloon will gradually shrink and you will find that your stress symptoms decrease in number and intensity. This peeling business can last for months, or even years. Keep in mind that *peeling onions makes people cry.* This is good for you. Also, keep in mind that the actual benefits of self-therapy take weeks or months to show. Finally, be aware that as you get in touch with your emotions, you might experience a temporary worsening of stress symptoms. Don't run to doctors to fix them. By focusing on these symptoms, you will be canceling out the benefits of journaling. Instead, ask yourself, "What painful emotions have inflated my balloon again?"

D. After you have completely shrunk the balloon, you might want to take a peek at the buried, painful emotions in your hidden mind. I strongly recommend that you do this under the strict supervision of a trained therapist. See the therapist once a month and do your homework on a weekly basis between visits. Bring up into the balloon the information saved in the "Pain" folder of your hidden mind. Re-open some old wounds related to abuse, trauma, etc.; become aware of the painful emotions related to these events, and write them down one by one. After you have done this for one event, go on to the next. As you do this, you are, in effect, *deleting one old file after another* from the "Pain" folder. The more you do this, the more pain will be deleted from your hard drive, the hidden mind. It is as if you are ridding the soda bottle of gas by gently shaking it, bringing a little gas up into the balloon and releasing it, again and again. Get rid of the remaining painful emotions by forgiving the people responsible for your childhood traumas. Soon, there will be no gas left in the soda bottle. This whole process of deleting files from the "Pain" folder is known as working through.

E. Dealing with the double whammy. As we read earlier, in the double whammy a recent event has shaken the soda bottle, causing the painful emotions of a buried trauma to resurface in a fury. Usually, the onset of stress symptoms can be clearly traced to an event that took place on a particular date; the patient, however, is completely unaware of this. The suddenness of the symptoms' onset and their fury are such that he might need a counselor or psychiatrist to see him through the crisis. In a milder case, one can deal with the resurfacing emotions by talking to someone or writing in his journal. If the resurfacing emotions are extremely painful, I recommend OPJ only after the patient has been well stabilized on medication and has developed sufficient insight into what is happening to him. It may be easier to use OPJ when the double whammy is chronic or minor (as when a mother is reliving some childhood trauma in the context of the growth of her own child), since in this kind of situation the buried emotions are fizzing up a little at a time.

3. Write an autobiography, a fictional story, a drama or a poem. Pour your heart and soul into it. Try to cash in on your misery! Hundreds of thousands of Americans are making a good living today by selling the stories of their shenanigans, screw-ups, addictions, chemical imbalances, misfortunes, tragedies, abuse, struggles and heroism in the face of adversity.

C. Therapy groups are helpful when one is trapped in a life situation for which there is no easy solution, such as illness—either one's own or that of a relative. The groups are of two types. The first is educational; it involves sharing information, listening to lectures, etc. The second is about healing; it involves people sharing their emotions in an intimate setting. The second type of group is far superior in its outcome, as it facilitates the expression of painful emotions, the sharing of experiences, and the building of intimacy and emotional support. It has been claimed by some authorities that cancer patients who participate in regular group therapy live longer than those who do not.

D. Individual therapy with an experienced therapist can be highly beneficial, as long as the therapy focuses on dealing with painful emotions in the balloon, solving the current life problems that create painful emotions, changing erroneous beliefs and perceptions and developing the patient's insight. The basic principles of OPJ must be followed: as far as possible, the balloon must be shrunk first, before old issues are brought up from the bottle. Counseling or therapy does not have to be long-winded and complicated. Even simple, insightful statements made by a perceptive therapist can bring about profound changes in patients, leading to the shrinking of the balloon or a change in behavior. Here are five examples out of hundreds of such cases.

A sixteen-year-old boy complaining of panic attacks was brought to my office by his father. The father did not approve of the girl the son was dating, and in the course of the evaluation, it became evident that the father was stifling his son by his controlling behavior. To help the young man, I had to get the father off his back as diplomatically as possible. One statement I made seemed to change everything instantly: "Mr. X, you speak softly but you come on like a steamroller!" When I met the father in his furniture shop twenty years after this incident, he recalled the statement and said, "That changed everything for me and my son."

A middle-aged woman worried incessantly about her eighteen-year-old son, partly because she felt guilty for not being there for him while he was growing up due to her own health problems. She worried over his choice of a girlfriend and other behaviors. A simple statement I made seemed to make all the difference to this patient: "You seem to be getting *entangled* with your son. Let him make his mistakes and learn from them."

A young woman was severely upset over her mother's constant critical comments about the way she was raising her autistic daughter. Nothing she said or did made her mother shut up. I said something that apparently changed everything: "When someone withdraws more from your emotional bank than he or she deposits in it, it is time to close that account." When I saw her six months later, she recalled how this one statement had changed everything in her life. She simply cut herself off from her toxic mother telling her, "Mom, if you have nothing positive to tell me, I would rather you don't call me."

A fifty-five-year-old woman reminded me about how she had seen me one time, twenty-five years before, after she had been devastated by her husband's infidelity. She was full of guilt over the affair, blaming herself for his misdeed. She reminded me that I had given her a piece of paper on which I had written, "You are not responsible for your husband's misbehavior." She said she kept this paper stuck on her refrigerator for the next ten years, and it helped her to cope with her guilt and grief.

A twenty-five-year-old man suffered from panic attacks following his divorce a year previously. He felt that he was a failure. Recognizing that all he needed was a reassuring word from an authority figure, I said, "You are not a failure. You will not have another panic attack. Take my word for it!" Many years later, he reminded me how I had "cured" him of his panic attacks with this one statement.

E. Start a crusade or join one that is already in progress. MADD (Mothers Against Drunk Drivers) is an example of sublimated rage. Sublimation is a method by which we channel painful emotions into a constructive activity. If you have rage about some injustice done to you by your parents or anyone else, get involved in a human rights crusade. If you have rage stemming from your own hungry childhood, get involved in a "food for hungry children" movement. The lives of virtually all crusaders are rooted in their own unresolved childhood issues.

F. File a lawsuit. When you are not satisfied with merely expressing your anger or rage, whether personally or in writing, resort to a socially acceptable action, such as filing a lawsuit. Society developed the system of justice so that individuals would not act out their anger and seek personal revenge. Since there are millions of angry people out there, millions of lawsuits are waiting to be heard in our courts. The "sue-happy" people we see all around are coping with their rage by asking for compensation from the people they think have hurt them. These days, the first thing a person asks when he has been injured in an accident is not where the hospital is, but who the best lawyer in town is. Naturally, there are plenty of ambulance-chasing lawyers around. In our society, an injured person who does not sue, no matter how insignificant his injury may be, is considered an idiot.

6. Canceling out painful emotions from the conscious mind.

There are many ways by which one can cancel out painful emotions from the mind and shrink the balloon. I list here six of these mechanisms: 1) reasoning, 2) changing one's perception, 3) putting things in proper perspective, 4) neutralizing, 5) insight, and 6) humor. People raised in functional, healthy families learn many of these "tricks" from their parents, relatives, teachers, pastors, siblings, mentors, books and scriptures. These tricks help them to cope with everyday life stressors.

A. Reasoning requires one to understand the cause and effect of his stress. By using logical or rational thinking, one is able to make some sense of a painful situation so that it becomes less threatening and more acceptable. For example, the death of a loved one becomes more acceptable when you reason that all living things have to die some day. In time, we lose everyone we love, through death, breakup or a move to a different locale. If your stocks go down in value, you can remind yourself that you knew the risks fully before you bought the stock, and it is in the nature of stocks to go up and down. If you build your house on the New Madrid earthquake fault, you can avoid panic every time the earth starts rumbling by simply reminding yourself that this is what you should expect to happen from time to time. If your sixteen-year-old son is driving on the highways, you can tell yourself that worrying about him is not going to accomplish anything. If you knowingly marry an alcoholic with a long history of legal problems, you must not then complain that your spouse has ruined your life; that is just the nature of the beast. One must keep in mind, however, that reasoning out a bad situation in order to cope with it is different from rationalizing bad behavior. For example, a man who is having an extramarital affair might try to deal with his guilt by rationalizing that it gave him a chance to make up for what he missed in his adolescence. That is not what I mean by reasoning!

Many of the proverbs in common use are meant to appeal to our reasoning. While growing up, we have all heard hundreds of such statements, made by wise elders: "You may not be responsible for being in the ditch, but you are responsible for getting out of it." "Don't waste your life being angry at your parents. They did their best under the circumstances." "Don't cry over spilt milk." And so on and so forth.

A case study: A young man, retired from the army, felt chronically guilty about the fact that his close friend had died in combat, trying to protect him. He had a long chat with his grandfather, a Korean War veteran, who reasoned with him that his guilt was irrational. The veteran told his grandson that the dead friend would have wanted him to do the same thing if the situation were reversed, and that feeling guilty was an insult to the friend's memory. The young man's guilt disappeared immediately. His balloon shrank and he felt better right away.

A case study: An elderly woman felt used and abused by her grown-up, wayward daughter, who frequently demanded large sums of money from her. In our interview, it became clear that the mother was carrying irrational guilt over the fact that the daughter had been born thirty-five years earlier as a result of rape. Once the mother realized that her guilt was uncalled-for and her actions were damaging to both of them, she got rid of her guilt and refused to send her daughter any more money.

Many stressed people have poor reasoning capacity to start with. That's why they became stressed in the first place. The minds of some stressed people who do have their reasoning powers intact can become disconnected with the "Reasoning" file because their buried emotions effectively block them off from that file. It is partly because of their impaired reasoning that abused wives keep going back to their battering husbands, mothers keep enabling their antisocial children, and wives enable their alcoholic husbands. In general, the sicker a person is the less reasoning power he has. That is why severely depressed and psychotic people are often beyond reasoning and can only relearn the art of reasoning in the course of a prolonged therapeutic relationship.

B. Changing one's perception cancels out painful emotions.

In this technique, we try to see a situation from a different point of view. A hostile and hypercritical boss can been seen as insecure rather than evil, with his behavior simply indicating that he has a need to cut others down in order to make himself feel more secure. An intrusive mother-in-law may be perceived as needy and lonely rather than nosy. A teacher, angry at you for not attending his class, does not hate you but misses having you in class.

Generally speaking, every stressful event or situation has two sides, a positive side and a negative one. One can see the glass as half full or half empty. One can see a drug, such as lithium, as a poison that can kill or as a miracle drug that has saved thousands of lives. When one's perception is dynamic, he can absorb new information and change his perceptions so that they are consistent with the reality of the current situation. In other words, he is able to change the contents of the "Beliefs" folder in his hidden mind. When one's perception is inflexible, because of rigid beliefs, opinions, views and ideas, he can easily become upset whenever the changes taking place around him are not consistent with his views. An opinionated, anti-gay politician might have to endure public embarrassment when it is revealed that her son is gay. A bigoted Ku Klux Klan honcho might lose his marbles when he finds out that his daughter is pregnant with a black man's baby. Some patients go to doctors with erroneous ideas about medications, and treating them becomes difficult when they are not able to change their faulty beliefs in spite of the doctors' best efforts to educate them. These patients lose the benefit of the medications as well as the doctors' expertise, and continue to suffer from their serious stress disorders. When our perceptions are not consistent with the reality of a situation, our actions result in great stress. Every prejudice and distorted perception comes with an expensive price tag. A person who can see his cup as half full instead of insisting that it is half empty will cope better when things go wrong. A person who looks at the plunging price of his stocks as an opportunity to buy more stocks instead of lamenting over his misfortune will do well in life. As they say, every cloud has a silver lining. In fact, something good will come out of most bad situations.

A case study: A fifty-year-old woman was distraught over a situation with her elderly parents, who were in their mid-nineties. Both of the parents suffered from early Alzheimer's disease, but they refused to be put in an assisted living facility. Every day, when the woman visited them, she found that they had not eaten well, taken their medications or bathed. When she gave them their medications, they screamed, yelled and scolded her angrily. Their relentless scolding and name-calling began to take a toll on her. She was not used to this type of abuse, as she was their only child and they had always adored her. Her balloon inflated with sadness, hurt, guilt and helplessness. She complained of severe anxiety and depression. She did not know what to do.

I asked her, "Who are these people?"

"They are my parents!" she replied.

"No. They are not your parents any more," I countered.

"What do you mean, they are not my parents now? They are my parents!" she argued back.

"They were your parents," I said, "but they are no longer your parents."

"Who are they now?" she asked, completely baffled.

"Now they are your children. They don't know what is best for them. Just as you put your foot down with your own children, you must now put your foot down with them. Just as you ignore your children's protests when you tell them what they don't want to hear, now you will have to ignore what these children tell you. Ignore their scolding and protests. Do the right thing."

A big smile of relief appeared on her previously depressed and tense face. Everything changed immediately, and her balloon shrank. Once she resolved to do what had to be done, her anxiety and depression disappeared.

C. Proper perspective cancels out painful emotions. With this technique, one looks at the bad situation from a larger perspective, and finds it not so bad after all. You might have lost some money in one stock, but you have made gains in others. Having to quit a job might make things difficult for a short time, but in the long run, it might be the best thing that ever happened to you. A student might drop out of school for a full year, but the lost year is only one of eighty-plus years in his lifespan. The bottom line is that one evaluates a situation as part of the entire picture, understanding, "I have lost a battle, but I am winning the war."

While growing up, we have heard our elders make statements that put things in perspective, such as, "Count your blessings." "Look at the man without feet, before you complain that you have no shoes."

D. Neutralizing painful emotions. In Chapter Three, we read about how, in the course of his evolution, man developed four complexes of painful emotions: fear, sadness, anger and guilt. His first coping mechanism was to form a society that would enable him to deal with fear. Life is nothing but a struggle to conquer one fear or another. A good social support system greatly reduces one's fear. Total faith in God, a higher power or destiny gives a great deal of freedom from fear of any kind. Decreased attachment to sense objects reduces the fear of losing them. Ultimately, those who conquer fear—whether the fear is of losing people, power, title, love, affection or money—become immune to stress.

When we studied the thirty-six emotions in the chapter "Pain in the Brain," we noted some ways to neutralize them. We can neutralize particular painful emotions by taking certain specific actions: anger is neutralized by forgiveness; helplessness is neutralized by taking an appropriate action to deal with whatever is causing one to feel helpless; hopelessness is neutralized by decisive action, hope and prayer; shame is neutralized by public exposure; guilt is neutralized by apologizing, seeking forgiveness, making amends, or offering compensation; sadness is neutralized by solace; humiliation is neutralized by dignity; hurt is neutralized by self-comforting or solace; frustration by patience; disappointment by acceptance;

embarrassment by dignity; terror by fortitude; hate by indifference or love; sinfulness by repentance. As with other important coping mechanisms, we often learn these ways from our parents and from religious teachings while we grow up. Great religious texts, such as the Bible, are treasures of these coping techniques. To successfully apply neutralization, one must be spiritually inclined, or in touch with his inner goodness. The reality is that some stressed people are out of touch with their inner wisdom as well as their spirituality; otherwise, they would not be stressed in the first place.

E. Insight into a difficult situation cancels out painful emotions. Insight is a look inside the mind and behavior of a person or into the facts behind a situation. Insight is nothing but the inside story. Every story has an inside story. Acquiring insight into a difficult situation helps to alleviate the emotional pain related to that situation. Insight gives us the real meaning of one's behavior.

We have all read the story of a man who dreams that he is walking with Jesus. He sees two pairs of footprints in the sand. However, during the most difficult time in his life, there is only one pair of footprints in the sand. The man thinks that they are his own footprints, and that Jesus has abandoned him during his most difficult time. Jesus gives him the needed insight: "Those footprints were mine. During your most difficult times, I was carrying you!"

A case study: An attractive young secretary, working for a stern-faced, middle-aged insurance agent, felt bad that he rarely talked with her, rarely praised her work and never made eye contact with her. She thought he was angry with her for some reason, and that she would be fired from her job at any time. However, she liked him for his generosity, uprightness and ethical behavior. In counseling, she developed insight into the problem: her boss was avoiding contact with her for fear that he might become too involved with her! He was a married man, and he did not want to fall into the same trap that many bosses do. His problem was that he feared he might like her too much. He paid her well and gave her regular raises, but kept her at arm's length. Once the secretary got this insight, she felt better right away.

A case study: A young man, who did an excellent job as a cook at a restaurant, became concerned because his boss started to give him other responsibilities, which had nothing to do with cooking. The boss had always praised him, and had called him "son." The young man became anxious and sleepless, believing that his boss might be upset with him for some reason. His wise mother gave him the insight that his boss was giving him different tasks to prepare him for a more responsible job. His balloon shrank, and he felt better right away.

F. Humor cancels out painful emotions and defuses tension.
One can laugh off one's fear, anger or frustration by making a joke about the situation that is causing these emotions; for example, by making jokes about a stupid boss. People with a good sense of humor live long. Look at George Burns, Bob Hope, Milton Berle and all the comedians. The next time your basement floods after a heavy rain, make a joke about it. "I never thought that some day I'd be able to afford an indoor pool!" There's even a funny drama about the Enron fiasco, which is now making the rounds and tickling the aggrieved ex-employees and investors.

7. Solving a bad life problem immediately turns the pump off.

To solve a nagging problem, you must be aware of the problem, willing to acknowledge that you have it, and equipped with the skill and relentless determination to solve it creatively. If you do not have the necessary skill, you must enlist the help of a professional (doctor, lawyer, accountant, etc.) to solve the problem.

Invariably, you will be required to take certain actions and make certain sacrifices—of money, time, friendship, security, etc. These are the kinds of actions you might be required to take in order to solve a difficult problem:

Take a stand. Make a move. Back off. Cut a deal. Confront. Give up. Give in. Walk away. Run for life. Change. Demand change. Let go. Make a decision. Sacrifice. Move on. Withdraw. Act decisively. Cut off. Break up. Intervene. Precipitate a crisis. Expose an injustice. Be more assertive. Be more passive. Get a third party involved. Do whatever it takes!

You must use one or more of these actions to solve the problem that is hounding you. With or without the help of professionals, the problem must be solved so that painful emotions stop coming into the mind. All toxic relationships must be ended. All interpersonal conflicts must be resolved or you must walk away from them. All relationships in which someone withdraws more from your emotional bank than he or she deposits in it must be properly balanced or terminated. Of course, there are consequences to all this, but they are always the lesser of two evils. If you stay trapped in a problem, painful emotions will keep accumulating, and sooner or later, your balloon will pop and you will become sick. You must pull the plug on the pump. Once the problem is solved, you will immediately feel better.

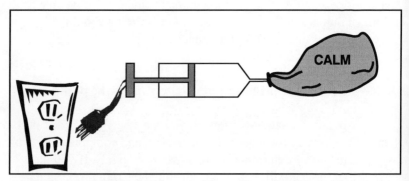

Picture 44: Solving problems is like pulling the plug on the pump.

A case study: An aggressive, insensitive and haughty hospital administrator was appointed by the hospital board over a young, inexperienced and somewhat insecure doctor. No sooner was this administrator on board than he went about like a bull in a china shop, making major changes all over the hospital. He openly put down the staff, wrote critical comments on the patients' charts, pitted staff members against each other and threw frequent temper tantrums in staff meetings. Intimidating the staff was his way of improving the hospital. All this was extremely upsetting to the young doctor, as well as to other staff members. As time passed, the administrator became more hostile and intrusive. He fired a doctor who tried to stand up to him. It was unthinkable for anyone to confront him, as anyone who did so risked being fired from his job. This problem kept inflating the insecure young doctor's balloon. As his balloon inflated, he began to lose sleep, have anxiety spells, and suffer from stomach-aches and other stress symptoms.

The young doctor finally realized that his choices were narrowed down to either leaving his job or negotiating with his boss, with the risk of being fired. Leaving the job would pose a major problem, as he had just had his first baby and had made the mistake of buying a big new house in the country. A move would be a major financial setback. But, after much soul-searching, the young doctor decided to tackle his boss and risk losing everything in order to protect his health.

He went to his boss's office and asked to talk with him. The boss asked haughtily what it was all about. Just then, the young doctor saw a wilted, almost dry zebra plant on the side table. He had seen the same plant in its lush, green glory just a week before. He asked the administrator, "I wonder what happened to that poor plant? Last week it looked so great!"

The administrator said impatiently, "Well, last Friday evening, I watered the plant just as I was leaving home for the weekend. But I was in a rush to go home, and the dirt under the plant was so dry I had to dig around it with a knife to make it absorb the water fast. I guess I cut off all the roots in the process. When I came to my office on Monday morning, it was like this."

The young doctor gently slapped his own forehead with his hand and exclaimed, "Oh, I see! I should have known better than to ask you about it. That is your style!"

The administrator's face became beet-red. His eyes grew tearful. He leaned back in his chair, took a deep breath and asked, "Is that really my style?"

The young doctor nodded. "For some time now, we all have been feeling just like that zebra plant!" Then he left the office. The administrator, wiser now, was never the same again. The problem was solved once and for all.

Sometimes, a mental conflict ("Should I or shouldn't I?") can interfere with your ability to solve an interpersonal conflict. In such cases, resolve your own mental conflict before tackling the interpersonal problem.

A case study: A forty-five-year-old man developed a case of recurrent vomiting episodes associated with severe stomachache. He was hospitalized many times over a six-year period without any benefit. He visited local emergency rooms frequently with excruciating stomach pain. He took powerful narcotics to control his pain, but none of the medications helped. He felt sick all the time. He could not work, on account of unpredictable bouts of vomiting and stomach pain. He spent most of his time in bed. After everything else failed, he decided to consult me for an evaluation.

It soon became evident that six years earlier, he had been traumatized by being fired from two different jobs, even though he had done those jobs very well. In each case, his superior had been threatened by his exceptional performance. The man harbored a lot of bitterness about these incidents. When he finally returned to work as his father's partner, he was forced to deal with the manager of his father's business—a man whom the patient himself had recommended to his father, also six years earlier. This manager did a great job of running the father's business. Now, however, threatened by my patient's return, the manager repeatedly verbally abused and humiliated him in front of colleagues. Since my client was going to inherit the business from his father, he could have fired the manager from the business. However, for reasons he was unable to figure out, he just could not bring himself to confront the manager. Instead, he became sicker and sicker. He simply played the role of a sick man and stayed away from work. It became obvious that the patient was trapped in a serious job problem: 1) he had an ongoing interpersonal conflict with the manager of the business; and 2) he had a mental conflict ("I want to fire him, but I just can't, and I don't know why"), which the patient himself was not aware of. His behavior was the only clue to his mental conflict.

At first, the patient minimized his emotional pain and the source of his stress. By the second session, he admitted to his job problem and became aware of how disgusted and hurt he felt about the whole situation. Because he was putting these two powerful emotions out of his awareness, they showed up in the form of two corresponding bodily symptoms, bouts of vomiting (disgust) and stomach pain (hurt). Next, the patient became aware of his central mental conflict: "I want to fire the manager, but I simply can't because I know how unfair and traumatic it is to be fired—especially when you are doing a great job." His empathy for the manager interfered with his ability to confront him.

Once the man became aware of the roots of his symptoms, he decided to take the middle course: to become more assertive with the manager, put the man in his place and take charge of the business. He told the manager that his days of giving abuse were over, and if he didn't like it, he could leave the business of his own volition. That saved the patient the guilt of firing him. If the manager left the job, it would be his own choice. In recognition of his talents, the patient told him that he would be allowed to continue to be the manager of the business; however, he must stop his verbal abuse, or he would be fired. The patient, then, would not feel guilty, because no owner of any business should tolerate harassment from his employee. Once he had made up his mind what to do, the patient felt empowered and his attacks of stomach pain dramatically decreased in intensity and frequency.

8. It is not easy for those who are stressed to express their emotions.

A. Deep-rooted habits are hard to overcome. The vast majority of the people I see in my office have a singular inability to express their inner emotions. In fact, even people who are normally garrulous often become mute when they are upset. Some common reasons why people don't express their emotions are the fear of being ridiculed, the belief that expressing emotion is a sign of weakness, the fear of being betrayed by the listener, guilt over their perceived disloyalty to the person they are in conflict with, shame over their role in the situation, an extreme concern with privacy and a need to be in control of their emotions. When asked how they felt about certain painful situations, some patients told me point-blank, "It's none of your business!" Some patients said, "I am afraid that if I break down, I might lose it completely." Most excuses people give for not expressing their emotions are highly irrational. A common excuse, rooted in ignorance, is, "How would expressing my emotions change anything?" Some seriously depressed people tell me, "I just cannot cry!" These people suffer from what can be called terminal emotional constipation.

Others tell me, "I cry all the time, but it does not help." In this case, the tears are a result of emotional overflow, and are not related to any specific issue the patient has blocked off. Almost all these people are suffering from unfinished grief. Here the balloon is leaking so it doesn't pop. I tell these patients, "Thank God you are weeping! I would be more worried about you if you told me that you could not shed even one tear." My advice to these people is to join the OPJ club.

B. Complete unfinished grief. In the chapter, Loss and Grief, we saw how the painful emotions related to the fear, anger and guilt complexes can interfere with the expression of painful emotions related to the sadness complex. When the grieving process is thus blocked off, the balloon remains full and the symptoms persist.

Identify any incomplete grief in your life related to death, breakup, divorce, loss of children by divorce, etc. Raise your awareness of any painful emotions in your balloon related to the fear, anger or guilt complex. First, get in touch with these emotions, and then write them down in your journal. If you are successful, you will notice that you will begin to feel sad. Now the grief has started flowing. Keep journaling until all the grief is over. When the grief work is complete, you will no longer cry at the memory of the lost loved one. Instead, you will remember that person with fondness.

A case study: A forty-five-year-old woman complained of depression following the sudden death of her fifteen-year-old daughter. She had died from acute respiratory distress caused by a severe viral infection. The woman had rushed her daughter to the emergency room, but the doctor failed to diagnose the condition. The child went into a coma early the next morning, and she died in the helicopter on her way to a medical center in a larger city a hundred miles away. The mother suffered from pangs of guilt because she thought she had not done enough to save her daughter. She also felt a lot of anger toward the ER doctor. Counseling with a local therapist did not help, as he did not deal with these two emotions. In our counseling sessions, I encouraged the mother to ventilate her guilt and anger. She came to realize that her guilt was irrational, as she had done all she could to save her daughter's life. Once these blocking emotions were removed, she grieved over the loss and recovered from her depression.

9. Some people have no problem-solving skills.

    A. Some people do not know how to go about getting help. When faced with a problem, they simply throw in the towel and walk away. They do not seem to know that there are professionals in the community to help us solve our health, financial, legal and other problems. When a marital problem crops up, many couples simply split up; when they have a problem with the boss, many workers simply quit their jobs.

    A case study: A fifty-year-old man came down with a serious case of depression because of certain stressful events and situations in his life. Instead of getting psychiatric help, he promptly quit his job and applied for Social Security Disability. When asked why he had never bothered to get professional help for his depression, he replied, "I don't have that kind of money." He then went on to reveal that he had just bought a pontoon boat worth $5,000, believing that boating would cure his depression. I can give the reader countless such examples of stupidity that defies common sense.

    B. Lots of people grow up without learning any problem-solving skills. Our problem-solving skills are often passed on to us by important figures in our childhood and adolescence. Kids who have absent parents or parents with few problem-solving skills of their own (for example, teenage parents) grow up without learning these skills. This explains why millions of people in this country today are growing up with poor problem-solving skills.

C. Trapped people have many excuses for not solving their life problems. Taking certain steps toward solving problems is easier said than done. Most people who are trapped in a life situation are not even aware of it. Those who are aware do not want to acknowledge it. And those who admit it do not want to pay the price to get out of the situation. They come up with any number of excuses why the problem cannot be solved: "I have bills to pay," "I will lose my health insurance," "I am too old to do this," "I feel too scared to change that," "I feel too guilty to do this," "I am too weak to let go of that," "I am too insecure to do this," "I don't want to hurt anyone," and what have you.

A case study: An insecure middle-aged man's health had started going downhill ever since a new boss was appointed over him, two years earlier. He lived in fear of being fired at any time. He received several unsatisfactory job reviews. No matter what he did, his boss was not happy. The man developed numerous stress symptoms and went on a fruitless medical wild goose chase. When asked if he had any stress in his life, he would say, "No!" He felt trapped in his job for several reasons: if he left the job, he would have difficulty getting a comparable job; he would lose his health insurance, seniority, etc.; he would have to dip into his savings; and so on and so forth. Unable to give up these excuses, he kept suffering the agony of his job, month after month, year after year. He had neither the skill nor the will to solve the problem with his boss, nor the self-confidence to feel that he could make it out there if he left his job, nor the willingness to give up his financial security to preserve his physical and emotional health. Most of all, he pleaded lack of money as his reason for not getting counseling to learn how to solve the problem. Obviously, his priorities were not straight. His job performance deteriorated rapidly, and ultimately he was fired. The trauma of this popped his balloon, and he was hospitalized for serious depression. Soon afterward, he declared himself "totally and permanently disabled" and applied for Social Security Disability. I just could not save this man from his determination to destroy himself.

10. Coping with emergencies by temporary burying

When extremely upset about a situation, one might have to set aside the painful emotions filling his balloon temporarily so that he can attend to the emergency situation promptly, without becoming hysterical or going into shock. He can do this by telling himself, "I must calm myself down right away. I don't want this to upset me too much. I don't want to think about it right now. I don't want to talk about it, either. I want to be strong. I want to handle this situation with as cool a head as possible." Immediately, the painful emotions, such as fear, horror, terror, etc. are transferred from the balloon to the soda bottle. The balloon shrinks, and one feels calm right away. Once the bad event is over, he can bring the emotions up from the hidden mind, break down and express them by talking, crying, sobbing, etc. Many heroes we read about in newspapers have coped with sudden crises in this way.

A case study: Driving on an interstate highway one snowy night, a young man came across a pile of wrecked cars involved in a terrifying chain accident. He saw several bodies strewn around. His initial reaction was fear and horror. However, he instantly buried his emotions in his hidden mind, shrank his balloon and calmed himself down. He pulled the car over onto the shoulder of highway, calmly called the State Troopers on his cellular phone and methodically went about saving lives. He kept himself busy reassuring the injured and giving them first aid. He experienced no stress symptoms while doing all this. Later, when interviewed by a television reporter, he said that he was no hero; he had merely done what he had to do. After he went home, he broke down and let go of his emotions without any inhibition. He talked about his experience with as many people as possible, and shrank his balloon.

Of course, for one to be able to accomplish this feat, his hidden mind/soda bottle must be fairly empty of painful emotions; that is, he must not have abused the burying mechanism to the point where there is no room left for him to bury any more emotions. If the hidden mind does not have any space in it, the balloon can become over-stretched. Then, at the very sight of such an accident, one might go into emotional shock, become hysterical, pass out in terror or crap in his pants.

CHAPTER FOURTEEN

Stress and Life Management

1. Managing stress means reducing the occurrence of stressors.

The most important goal of managing stress is to prevent the occurrence of bad life events and life problems by cultivating a wisdom-based lifestyle. The actual term should be "life management." There are basically three elements that go into good stress management.

A. We should make wise choices in managing the various aspects of life—family, relationships, finances, job, health, etc.—in order to minimize or avoid stress-producing events and problems. This requires us to follow certain sound principles in our behavior.

B. Invariably, to make wise choices one must have a good handle on the seven personality weaknesses (greed, possessiveness, hate, arrogance, jealousy, insecurity and selfish desire, or lust), which are at the root of most of our life problems. Countering these weaknesses requires us to adopt certain codes of conduct.

C. We must cultivate a spiritual attitude, which gives some degree of immunity to the negative effects of stress. This requires us to simplify our lives and reduce our entanglements with people, money, material objects and power.

Using the balloon/bottle/pump/outlet model of the mind, stress management requires us to have good control over the pump attached to the balloon. The pump represents stressors. We must learn to keep the pump's activity to a minimum. When it pumps too forcefully, we must know how to pull the plug.

2. Balancing one's quality of life with one's standard of living.

A. The key to managing the time used in earning money and the time spent with one's family is to maintain a fine balance between the two. Around the turn of the last century, most Americans equated raising their standard of living with raising their quality of life. Basic amenities, such as an indoor bathroom, a three-bedroom home, running water, etc. became the dream of every householder. By the mid-twentieth century, a car, an attached garage, a refrigerator, and a washing machine were considered essential for decent living. In the second half of the century, raising the standard of living became an obsession with most Americans. Just about everyone wanted to keep improving his lot by owning more and more material things in the mistaken belief that his quality of life would thus improve. More and more people began to make a list of "must-haves." Keeping up with the Joneses became a national trend. Everyone equated possession of material things with quality of life. In fact, the opposite began to be true: somewhere along the way, the quality of life began to part ways with the standard of living. There came a time when, for most people, raising their standard of living invariably caused the lowering of their quality of life.

How did this happen? Well, the standard of living has to do with money: money for a house, cars, gadgets, vacations, etc. The quality of life has to do with time: time for fun, relaxation, hobbies, family, etc. To make more money to buy all the things we feel we must have, we have to borrow the time that was once designated for the family. We have to work longer hours, take a second or third job, and sometimes even resort to fraud. The result is that fewer breadwinners have time for their families.

As the preoccupation with raising our standard of living increased, more women joined the workforce so their families could continue to afford things that were not essential, but were thought necessary to improve the quality of life. When both parents work, children have to be left with strangers to care for them. Millions of children have grown up, and are growing up today, without much-needed parental nurturing and care. Millions have been subjected to emotional, physical and sexual abuse by wicked babysitters and other trusted caretakers. As a result of these traumas, many of these children end up with psychiatric problems later in life.

When both parents work, they often work different shifts. Parents are too busy to spend time together, renew the bonds between them and make joint decisions regarding household issues and children. Millions of parents have grown apart, separated and divorced, resulting in personal trauma for them and their children. These traumatized children grow up into adults who repeat in their own lives what they have learned from their parents. This cycle has snowballed and continued unabated. To find a balance between one's standard of living and quality of life, one has to balance managing money and managing time.

B. Manage your money.

1. Live within your means. This is the most important single rule one must follow in managing money. Be content with what you have. Don't be envious of others; envy causes stress. Don't buy things to impress friends or relatives. Don't try to shore yourself up against your insecurities by buying big items. Do not get into the trap of comparing your wealth with that of others and competing with them. Buy only the things that are necessary. Don't buy something just because you want it, or because it's on sale, or because you have credit cards. Habitual buying has become a national epidemic, and every year more people are filing for bankruptcy. Remember, over sixty-five percent of people live from paycheck to paycheck.

2. Save money regularly. Saving money gives you a cushion during hard times. It also gives you the ability to walk away from your job without feeling trapped in it, and the means to solve difficult life problems. Money in the bank gives you peace of mind and self-confidence. Having adequate savings is one of the best medicines against stress.

3. Buy a house within your budget. Buy a house that's just the right size so that you don't have to make big mortgage payments. Don't buy a house that costs more than one hundred fifty percent of your estimated annual income. If you do, you will find yourself strapped for cash all the time—and that is stress. The most common mistake people make is to buy a big house that leaves little spare money for anything else. Remember, in addition to the mortgage, you will have to pay real estate taxes and pay for repairs and maintenance, heating and cooling, etc. Let the house be near your workplace, so you don't waste time and gas driving back and forth from work. Besides saving money on gas, you can spend that precious time with your family. Have a small yard so you don't spend a lot of time taking care of it. Before you plant trees and shrubs, read the instructions carefully so that you don't have to do the planting twice. People who buy a house in the country, far away from their jobs, often have little time to spend in their homes, as they are busy working day in and day out just to make payments on the house, and also to pay for gas, since they're on the road a lot.

4. Buy a car within your budget, and maintain it well. Buy a small or mid-sized car that has a track record for reliability. An unreliable car is a big source of financial headaches for millions of families. If you buy a car because of your blind loyalty to a brand or dealership, be prepared to waste a lot of money over the years. People who buy cars for patriotic reasons are, in fact, hurting the country in the long run, for obvious reasons. The most common reason that a car breaks down is poor maintenance. Have it serviced every three thousand miles. That small amount you spend on oil changes could save you a lot of unnecessary expense and stress. If it ain't broke, service it regularly. Avoid buying a luxury car just to impress people or to enhance your prestige. If you need a car to enhance your prestige, you probably don't have much prestige, anyway! Five things we must look for in a good car are its track record for reliability, high mileage per gallon, interior space, inexpensive maintenance and a local dealership. I have personally found Toyota cars to be ideal for anyone who wants to minimize his car-related stress.

5. Avoid going into heavy debt except, perhaps, to buy a house and car. Have no more than one credit card. Pay the bills at the earliest possible time. Before you buy anything on credit, except your house and car, you must have enough savings in the bank to pay the bill at the end of the month. People who pile up unpaid credit card bills will soon feel stressed out. Do not deal with the so-called "payday" check-cashing outlets. If you do, be prepared to be mugged!

6. Do not get into a business that you have no business getting into. Before you start a business, be aware of your limitations, and curb your enthusiasm and ambition accordingly. Remember, nine out of ten new businesses don't last beyond the first year. This is because enthusiasm, like greed, has a way of blocking the mind's access to wisdom. Do thorough research before starting a new business. You must know the inside story about the business you intend to start. Talk to people who have owned or run the business previously, to learn more about it. Do not assume that you can do better than they did. When my clients express a wish to open a new restaurant, I tell them to work in a restaurant for one year and learn the ropes. All successful businesses rest on three pillars: honesty, skill and reliability. All unsuccessful businesses are missing at least one of these.

7. Prioritize your spending. This means that you should buy things according to their importance to you. I have lost count of the stressed-out people who have money for luxury items but not for essentials. You have only so much money, and your wants and needs are almost infinite. The solution is to prioritize. Different people have different priorities. For example, some people might think that owning an expensive boat is more important than paying for their children's college educations. Others might think that spending money on flashy clothes is more important than paying their electricity bills. Most stressed-out people who have financial problems have their priorities upside down.

C. Better management of time improves your quality of life.

1. Prioritize your time. You have only twenty-four hours in a day. The question is how you slice it up so that you have enough time for the important aspects of your life. The more time you spend on unnecessary things, the less you have for important things. For example, if you spend two hours a day commuting to and from work, you have lost that much time that you could have spent with your family. You need at least ten hours a day for sleep, cleaning up, eating and meeting basic bodily needs. You are at work for at least eight hours. That leaves six hours a day. You need to distribute this time to meet all your other needs: having fun, entertaining guests, watching television or movies, reading and other hobbies and being with your children, spouse and what have you. Most stressed people have problems prioritizing their time. I have lost count of the people who have canceled their doctors' appointments, claiming they had other important things to take care of. When pinned down, they revealed the more important things: "I had to keep my appointment with my hairstylist," "My housekeeper said she was coming at that time," "I had to go to the post office to pick up a parcel," and some such frivolous thing.

2. Don't overwork. Your brain can tolerate only so much work. If you overwork, you will stop enjoying what you do and find yourself being cranky with your family and friends. People will avoid you. Don't get burnt out! Avoid working a swing shift, because it is guaranteed to cause marital, family and health problems in the long run. Your bonds with your spouse will break down, especially if he or she also works. Your kids will grow up not knowing you. You will have few friends. Your social life will dwindle. Your sleep debt will rise, and you might get into auto accidents. You will soon find yourself having little energy, patience or ability to focus.

3. Avoid sending your wife to work, especially when the kids are of school age. When parents don't spend enough time with their little children, the children do poorly in life. By exposing your kids to babysitters, you are risking traumatizing them emotionally and physically. You must find time to have dinner with your family every day.

4. Find time to have fun with your family. Weekend outings, picnics, vacations, hiking, boating, etc. are activities that help families bond closely.

5. Don't complicate your life with gadgets. If you want to buy modern conveniences (fax machines, cellular telephones, computers, beepers, etc.) do so only if they will save you time and money in the long run. Don't buy them to complicate your life further. You can turn on a cellular telephone only when you want to make a call, or you can keep it on all the time and take calls all day long. The choice is yours.

Bob Kamath, M.D.

3. Reduce conflict with others by not imposing your views on them.

The most common cause of conflict between two people is when one tries to impose his views, beliefs, opinions and ideas on the other. This problem can also show up as one party wanting what the other has or breaking a mutually agreed-upon contract. Here are a few simple principles for minimizing stress in our relationships with those we love.

A. Do not be a control freak. In your relationships with family members and friends, avoid telling them what to do unless they ask for your opinion. If they choose not to follow your advice, you have the option to ignore their decision or respect it and not give them any more advice. Unsolicited advice rarely works. If someone indulges in really outrageous behavior, just register your true feelings and refuse to be a party to it. Let people make their own mistakes and learn from them. Remember, all love is conditional. Only dogs are capable of unconditional love. And these days, even that is doubtful!

B. Give up abusive relationships, regardless of whom they are with. Let go of relationships that you consider detrimental to your mental, physical or financial health. Remember that all relationships end sooner or later—because of death, breakup or a move. As you have read in a previous chapter, if a relationship gives you more heartache than pleasure, cut it loose and move on. This applies to all relationships.

C. Let go and let God. When it comes to your relationship with your children, there are only four good things you can give them: good food for the body, good education for the mind, good values for the soul, and goodbye! for their happiness. Once they turn eighteen, put them in the hands of God and ask Him to take good care of them. If they ask for your help, tell them, "I will help if I can. I won't help if I can't."

D. Develop an attitude of equality and equanimity in your relationships. We are all equals. If you want to be my friend, fine; if you don't want to be my friend, that's fine, too. If you like me, fine; if you don't like me, that's fine, too. If you invite me for a party, fine; if you don't invite me, that's fine, too. And so on and so forth.

E. Learn to say no. Don't get involved in an activity just because someone you know urges or forces you to. You must have your priorities clear: your family comes first, your job is next and then come other activities. It is not hard to say, "I'm sorry, I have other commitments. Maybe some other time"; or "I'm sorry, I cannot contribute to this cause this year. Maybe some time in the future." If they still hassle you, you should not hesitate to say, "Thanks for the call. I must let you go now. Bye!"

F. Be assertive but not aggressive. Don't let anyone abuse you, whether at work or in social circles. If anyone attacks you personally, say, "Why don't you just tell me what your problem is, so I can work on it, instead of indulging in personal attacks against me?" Most people who indulge in personal attacks against others are bullies who are insecure within themselves. Their way of shoring themselves up against their insecurity is to cut others down. If you call their bluff, they back off.

G. Build a social support system. Have at least one person in your life in whom you can confide. Ideally, your spouse should be that person. If possible, go for long walks with that person two or three times a week, and talk out your concerns and feelings. Have a circle of friends and relatives to socialize with. They will form the core of your support system. Your co-workers, neighbors, doctors, pharmacist, dentist, accountant, etc. are also part of your support system.

H. Forgive and move on. In our relationships with others, we are often hurt by their actions. We must cultivate an attitude of forgiveness for their indiscretions, even if they do not ask for it, so that we can move on with our lives. Instead, a lot of people stay angry, bitter, hateful and vengeful. These toxic emotions will slowly kill them from within.

4. Overcome personality weaknesses with a set of codes.

A. Personality weaknesses can cause serious havoc. We have read that at the root of behaviors that bring on stress are seven common personality weaknesses: lust, hate, arrogance, possessiveness, jealousy, greed and insecurity. These are remnants of the primitive man within us. They can be activated under two circumstances.

1) When we are strongly attracted to some sense object; for example, when a married man is attracted to another woman.

2) When the conscious mind becomes disconnected from the wisdom in the hidden mind because of buried, painful emotions. A stressed-out person who robs a bank for reasons not clear to him is an example.

When the mind's actions are under the influence of these weaknesses, there will inevitably be consequences. Here are some of the consequences of these personality traits.

1. Lust, in men and women, leads to infidelity, extramarital affairs and promiscuity, the sexual molestation of children and an addiction to sex. Lust for money leads to money disorder, a condition in which a person becomes obsessed with money. All his or her actions are geared toward making money, by hook or by crook. In extreme cases, such people can commit murder for the sake of money. People who kill their spouses for the insurance money are examples of this disorder. Their obsession with money disconnects their minds from wisdom, and connects them with evil.

2. Greed often leads to fraudulent behaviors. Sometimes greed makes a person fall prey to other people's fraud. Greedy people's judgment becomes impaired and they make many mistakes in simple financial matters, such as paying their taxes. Almost all greedy people get into serious trouble sooner or later, as they make stupid mistakes because of the lapse of judgment that invariably happens when the mind links up with greed.

3. Jealousy causes a person to constantly compare and compete with others. This is known as comparing and competing disorder. Such people simply make themselves miserable by perpetual competition with everyone around them. They can get into serious financial problems.

4. Possessiveness leads to controlling behavior toward children, employees, friends and others that we deal with. Possessiveness of material things makes us worry constantly about losing them. Possessive people simply can't let go or walk away. Almost all possessive people end up with serious psychiatric disorders.

5. Insecurity causes people to show off, trying to make others believe that they are secure. This can lead to their buying a big house, luxurious cars and expensive gadgets. These people soon end up with huge debts. Bankruptcy and divorce are common.

6. Arrogance, or hubris, leads one to make enemies unnecessarily. An arrogant person often does not ask for wise people's advice. He thinks he can pull off anything he wants. He does not learn from his mistakes. His way of coping with his failures is to blame someone else. When we think we are always right, we learn nothing from our mistakes.

7. Hate is an extremely toxic emotion. It destroys the person who harbors it in his heart. A hateful person often indulges in hateful acts against others, including those he loves and cares for. Hate shows up in the form of violence against one's spouse, children, animals and people of other races and religions. Most hateful people end up in prison sooner or later, as their ability to control their unbridled hate is puny.

B. Codes of conduct are needed to put these weaknesses on a leash. These traits are deeply embedded and difficult to root out. All we can hope for is to curb their influence on our conduct by following a set of codes of conduct. For example, we can give up greed and cultivate generosity and altruism; give up insecurity and develop self-esteem; give up jealousy and be happy for others' success; give up hate and cultivate love; give up arrogance and cultivate humility; give up possessiveness and cultivate non-possessive love; and finally, give up lust and cultivate selflessness.

Curbing our personality weaknesses connects our minds with wisdom. This results in the emergence of our God-given strengths. Here are some examples of codes we can follow to curb our personality weaknesses.

"I do not want anything that is not rightfully mine." This code counters greed and translates into paying our taxes on time, not stealing money from our customers, not overcharging our clients and not ripping off people who are at our mercy.

"I will be content with what I have, and I will be happy for the success of others." This counters jealousy and envy. It can stop us from unnecessarily comparing and competing with others.

"I will always admit my mistakes and apologize to those I have hurt." This code can overcome haughtiness and help us to be a little more humble.

"I will not desire any person other than my legitimate

spouse. I will be content with whatever money I make legitimately." This can counter lust.

"I will love everyone enough to let them go. I will not hang onto people and objects." This counters possessiveness.

"I will forgive everyone who has hurt me in any way." This counters hate and anger we might harbor against people who have hurt us.

"I will always feel secure about myself, as God created me." This gives one the ability to overcome his insecurity.

C. Why the lust for sex and money is insatiable.

It is a known fact that the more one has, the more he wants. The common explanation for this is that the person who goes after sex and money is obsessively pursuing pleasure; in other words, he is addicted to sex and money. The reality is, more likely, quite the opposite: a lustful mind that is addicted to sex or money becomes disconnected from the "Pleasure" file in the hidden mind. This means that the person is not able to experience either satiation or contentment from sex or money. Thus dissatisfied, he redoubles his efforts to find satisfaction at any cost. So the sexual addict has sex with more partners, more often; the money addict tries to make more money by hook or by crook. With each success, such a person's mind becomes more disconnected from his pleasure center. That is why a sex addict constantly worries about finding the next partner, and a billionaire appears to be constantly worried about how to make his next billion—even though he does not know what to do with the money he already has. Most billionaires do not feel secure enough to part with their money even for obviously worthy causes, because the more money they have, the more insecure they feel. The only solution for this problem is to cultivate generosity. This immediately reconnects one's mind with his "Wisdom" and "Pleasure" files.

D. Entanglement with people and money can make a monkey out of a wise person. It is a well-known fact that once one's mind becomes strongly attached to sense objects, such as people, money, power, etc., it loses touch with judgment, reasoning and insight. I see parents who are overly attached to their grown-up children, and who think there is nothing wrong in making decisions for them. They are crushed when their children rebuff them. We see this type of lack of judgment in many stressed people who are entangled with sense objects. This reminds me of the tactic that monkey-catchers in India use. Monkeys in India are very clever. They have figured out ways to intimidate people and snatch food from them. Once they get hold of the food, they never let go. Some smart people use this knowledge to catch monkeys. They put some peanuts in a metallic jar with a small mouth. A monkey can put his hand into the jar and take it out as long as he does not make a fist. But once the monkey puts his hand into the jar and grabs a peanut, he is unwilling to let it go, and so he is trapped. If only he let go of the peanut, he could free himself from the trap. Obviously, the attachment to peanuts obliterates the judgment of even the wise monkey. The lesson is that entanglement with sense objects can make a monkey out of even a wise person. In my practice, I see many people who have been made tight-fisted monkeys by their entanglement with sense objects.

5. Be flexible with your beliefs, opinions, views and ideas.

Elsewhere we have read about how inflexible beliefs, opinions, views and ideas can cause stress by interfering with one's ability to adjust to the realities of life. Therefore, tone down these aspects of your personality. A woman who is staunchly anti-gay can be devastated by discovering that her only son is gay. A bigot who hates people of other races can go plum crazy if he discovers that his Caucasian daughter is pregnant by a black man. The point is that there is always a price to pay for strong opinions.

A case study: A twenty-eight-year-old man, a staunch Catholic, met a beautiful twenty-five-year-old non-Catholic woman and fell madly in love with her. After a brief courtship, they moved in together. Even though the young man was head-over-heels in love with the young woman, he refused to have a sexual relationship with her on account of his religious beliefs. He could not marry her for financial reasons. After a while, the situation became unacceptable to his girlfriend. When push came to shove, she left him, saying she could not live like a virgin while appearing to be a common-law spouse. The young man was overwhelmed with grief, and it took him months to recover from the shock. It was hard for him to believe that his girlfriend would not accept his celibacy, rooted in his inflexible religious conviction.

6. Build your self-esteem.

By doing our best at what we do and being productive and creative, we can enhance our self-esteem. When people compliment you for being a good person and for doing a great job, say "Thank you," and accept the compliment. Gradually, this will become an integral part of your identity. People who received little praise and a lot of criticism when growing up can use all the compliments they can get in order to cancel out the damage done by their childhood experiences. When someone compliments you, for whatever reason, do not feel embarrassed and say, "You flatter me. I don't deserve any of this lavish praise." Say "Thank you. I will try to do even better next time." Cultivate noble virtues: forgiveness, mercy, generosity, kindness, humility, goodness of heart, broadmindedness, empathy, nonviolence, truthfulness, fairness, justice, honesty, integrity and all the other good stuff.

Bob Kamath, M.D.

7. A spiritual path: From entanglement to enlightenment!

Religion and spirituality parted ways a long time ago. Religion has degenerated into mindless rituals without much relevance to our daily life. I have encountered many highly religious people who routinely indulge in deceitful business practices. Many degenerates, perverts and terrorists without a grain of goodness call themselves staunchly religious people. In our everyday life, we meet people without any humanity in them who claim to be Christians, Moslems, Jews, Buddhists and Hindus.

A. The basic goal of spirituality is to cultivate goodness in thought, emotion and action. This requires us to take the following steps:

1. Progressively reduce our desire for and entanglement with people, power, money, title, praise and other sense objects.

2. Curb the seven personality weaknesses (lust, greed, jealousy, hate, possessiveness, arrogance and insecurity), which enhance our desire for sense objects and thus create stress.

3. Connect the mind with the seven elements of wisdom (memory of lessons learned, knowledge, judgment, reasoning, insight, moral values and noble virtues). This results in all our actions being guided by wisdom. This simply boils down to "doing the right thing."

B. The spiritual person's love for sense objects is non-possessive in nature. A spiritual person is not expected to live like a monk or hermit. He can live a full life, make as much money as he wants and enjoy all the sense objects in accordance with established moral values and virtues. His attitude toward sense objects is, "If I have it, I will enjoy it. If I don't have it, I won't lament over it." Over a period of time, he trains himself to disentangle from sense objects while being attached to them. A spiritually enlightened person does not feel the necessity to grieve when he loses someone or something, as he has fully understood the impermanence of all sense objects and has

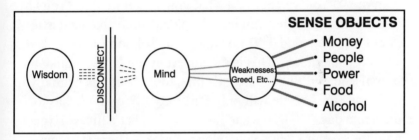

Picture 45: The entangled mind becomes disconnected from its wisdom.

reduced his bonds with them. All his actions are driven by purity of heart and indifference to gain and loss. His selflessness shines through all his actions. A mind thus driven attains supreme peace and tranquility. It knows no stress.

The story of the wise ant: A spiritually enlightened person is like a wise ant, which drinks honey to its heart's content from a honey pot without drowning in it. This ant says, "Ah! How sweet this honey is! I will enjoy it for now. If I feel like having more, I will come back later. I will tell all the other ants about it. Let them also enjoy this delicious gift of nature." An entangled person is like a discontented ant, which drowns in the honey by swimming in it. This ant says, "Wow! I discovered this honey pot. It is all mine! I can do whatever I want with it. I will show everyone that I am the lord of all this honey, and no one else is. I can even swim in it if I want to!" End of story.

Bob Kamath, M.D.

C. Certain philosophical attitudes, rooted in spirituality, help a great deal in coping with life's ups and downs. "You win some, you lose some." "You can't win them all." "This comes with the territory." "That is the nature of the beast." "Nothing is permanent in life." "Money comes, money goes." "I did not bring money with me, and I will not take it with me." "You've got to do what you've got to do." "You have to make do with what you have." "You cannot change destiny." "Let go and let God." "If I have it, fine; if I don't have it, I will do without it." "This is me, like it or not." "If you like me, fine; if you don't like me, that's fine, too." "Put this behind you and move on." "Hate will only hurt me." "Everybody has to die some day." "Forgive and move on." "That's life." "Expect nothing in return when you help someone." There are many more helpful phrases like these.

The true goal of all great sacred spiritual texts, such as the Bible, the Bhagavad Gita and the Koran, is to impart spiritual wisdom to the readers so that they can live a good life, in peace and tranquility. Understood properly, these texts are great treasures of wisdom and guides for life management.

8. Limiting stress that comes from health problems.

A. Managing one's physical health requires moderation in everything. As we get older, our bodies begin to show signs of wear and tear. Aches and pains become common. Health problems begin to crop up, one by one. Most of our health problems come from two sources.

1. Indulging in excess. We have read about how stressed people use certain activities to cope with stress: overeating, smoking, excessive drinking, drug abuse and reckless sexual activity. Most people who indulge in these excesses come down with numerous physical illnesses as they get older. Many become disabled on account of heart disease, lung disease, liver and stomach disease, bone and joint disease, diabetes, and the like. These health problems take away one's peace of mind, enjoyment and financial security.

2. Not meeting the basic needs of the body. These basic needs are adequate rest, proper food and liquids, timely meals, vitamins and minerals, regularity in bowel movements and urination, adequate exercise, daily showers or baths, and the like. Often, people are too stressed or too busy making money to meet these basic requirements of the body.

B. Here are some well-known health tips.
1. Keep your weight under control. Eat in moderation. Eat on time. Don't eat or drink anything between meals except water. Find time to eat your food in peace. Don't have your breakfast or lunch while driving. Learn to listen to your stomach. When your stomach is filled with just the right amount of food, it usually sends a signal: "I'm full. Stop eating!" If you ignore the signal, you will soon gain weight. Let your stomach shrink gradually, so that it will fill up with smaller amounts of food.

2. Get adequate sleep to recharge your system. Get at least seven hours of sleep a night. Go to bed on time and get up in the morning on time. If perchance you lose some sleep, catch up on it as soon as possible to avoid sleep debt. Sleep debt often causes people to fall asleep while driving or performing delicate tasks. Avoid working a swing shift. Avoid sleeping aids. If you are usually a good sleeper and you suddenly find yourself unable to sleep, ask yourself honestly, "What am I worried about?" Then come up with a plan to tackle the problem. If you cannot put your finger on it, start playing your favorite movie on the screen of your mind, focus on it intensely, and you will be asleep before you know it.

3. Pay attention to hygiene. Move your bowels every day, preferably in the morning. Take enough fiber in your daily diet to assist with bowel movement. Find time to empty your bladder at least thrice during the daytime. Take a hot shower daily, before you start your day. Use deodorizers to keep body odor to a minimum. Put on nice clothes before you go to work. Good clothes make people feel better about themselves.

4. Keep your body in good shape. Exercise in moderation at least three times a week. Go for a brisk walk with someone you are close to. Or just do some sit-ups or push-ups when you have time between routine daily tasks.

5. Take vitamins and minerals. If you believe that you might not be getting enough vitamins and minerals in your diet, take a multivitamin tablet daily. If you are over the age of fifty, consider taking a daily tablet of aspirin with your doctor's permission. Keep your cholesterol within normal range.

6. Give up bad habits. If you are a smoker, quit smoking. Smoking is the worst thing you can do to your body and your relationships with others. Drink alcohol in moderation. A glass of red wine before meals might even be good for your heart if you are not taking other drugs.

7. Regulate your life by having predictable habit patterns. You can greatly enhance your productivity by having set times for going to bed, getting up, eating breakfast, lunch and dinner, moving your bowels, etc. Most successful and happy people have well-regulated lives.

8. Do not lose sight of the seven simple pleasure of life: a good night's sleep, a good bowel movement, a good hot bath or shower, a good breakfast, lunch and dinner, good music, good friends and a good sex life.

Made in the USA